Essential Oracle7™

Tom Luers

SAMS
PUBLISHING

201 West 103rd Street
Indianapolis, IN 46290

To my wife and family…thanks!

Copyright © 1995 by Sams Publishing

FIRST EDITION

International Standard Book Number: 0-672-30873-8

Library of Congress Catalog Card Number: 95-74772

98 97 96 95   4   3   2   1

Interpretation of the printing code: the rightmost double-digit number is the year of the book's printing; the rightmost single-digit, the number of the book's printing. For example, a printing code of 95-1 shows that the first printing of the book occurred in 1995.

Composed in AGaramond and MCPdigital by Macmillan Computer Publishing

Printed in the United States of America

Trademarks

Publisher	*Richard K. Swadley*
Acquisitions Manager	*Greg Weigand*
Development Manager	*Dean Miller*
Managing Editor	*Cindy Morrow*
Marketing Manager	*Gregg Bushyeager*
Assistant Marketing Manager	*Michelle Milner*

Acquisitions Editor
Rosemarie Graham

Development Editor
Todd Bumbalough

Production Editor
James Grass

Copy Editor
Angie Trzepacz

Technical Reviewer
David W. Kennedy

Editorial Coordinator
Bill Whitmer

Technical Edit Coordinator
Lynette Quinn

Formatter
Frank Sinclair

Editorial Assistant
Sharon Cox

Cover Designer
Jay Corpus

Book Designer
Alyssa Yesh

Production Team Supervisor
Brad Chinn

Production
Mary Ann Abramson
Angela D. Bannan
Georgiana Briggs, Mona Brown
Michael Brumitt, Terrie Deemer
Mike Dietsch, Judy Everly
Ayanna Lacey, Kevin Laseau
Paula Lowell, Donna Martin
Steph Mineart, Casey Price
Nancy Price, Brian-Kent Proffitt
Bobbi Satterfield, SA Springer
Tina Trettin, Susan Van Ness
Mark Walchle

Indexer
Cheryl Dietsch

Overview

Contents

Acknowledgments

I wish to thank my wonderful family: Cathy, Jonathan, Sarah, and Matthew for their patience and commitment to this project. Without their support this project would not have been possible. Also, I want to thank the Madison Avenue Little League Girl's Softball and Boy's Minor League for providing many hours of excitement and fun. These games were a welcome distraction to the many hours that went into this book. Thank you!

Thanks to the many great people at Sams Publishing for their encouragement, guidance, and patience with me during this project. Specifically, I wish to thank Rosemarie Graham, Acquisitions Editor; Todd Bumbalough, Development Editor; and James Grass, Production Editor.

About the Author

Tom Luers is a head consultant with a leading international information technology consulting firm. Assignments during the last 10 years have taken him to clients in Europe, New Mexico, Indiana, and Ohio. Included in these assignments were the development of client/server applications that were based on Oracle and other relational ANSI-compliant databases. These projects utilized many of the Oracle development tools, such as SQL*Forms and SQL*Reports.

Introduction

Essential Oracle7 is a book that provides the novice and intermediate user a comprehensive and concise repository of "how-to" information on using the Oracle Relational Database Management System. This book starts with an introduction of relational databases and the components of Oracle's database. *Essential Oracle7* then continues into many of the critical features of the Oracle database such as database objects, the structured query language, data access, data integrity, Oracle constructs, security, and server messages and codes. With *Essential Oracle7*, you will find the direct path to guaranteed productivity.

What

This book provides the necessary information for you to learn the Oracle relational database and its many utilities. *Essential Oracle7* is a concise, practical guide which introduces you to the most essential components of the Oracle database and also provides many examples to reinforce your learning. This book will provide only the necessary bare-bones information so that you get exactly the information you need without the distractions of endless stories or useless narratives.

Why

This book is an all-in-one guide that teaches you how to use the most commonly used features of the Oracle database system. Through the use of text and descriptions, which are reinforced by examples, you will learn how to use the Oracle RDBMS. This book is intended to serve as a reference book as well as an initial learning aid.

How

PART I

Overview of the Oracle DBMS

Introduction to the Oracle Relational Database

What Is Oracle?

What Oracle is the most widely used Relational Database Management System (RDBMS) in the world. Oracle Corporation offers this RDBMS as its core product in its product line, which also includes a fourth-generation application development tool set, reporting tools, and utilities. This book presents information that you need to use the Oracle RDBMS, which is also known as the Oracle Server.

The powerful relational model has evolved from the hierarchical and network data models. The most widely accepted and used data model is the relational model. The term *relational* was coined in 1969 by an IBM researcher, Dr. E.F. Codd. A relational model has three major aspects to it:

- Structures—Defined objects that contain data and are accessible to the users
- Operations—Defined actions that manipulate data or schema objects
- Rules—Laws that govern how data can be manipulated and by whom

A relational database is simply defined as a data model that is strictly viewed by its users as tables. A table is a two-dimensional matrix composed of rows and columns. Figure 1.1 illustrates a table. Any time the data is changed in an Oracle database, it is the table or the data therein that is changed. Finally, in the relational database, any data that is the result of a query is presented to the user in the column/row format.

Figure 1.1.
A relational database table.

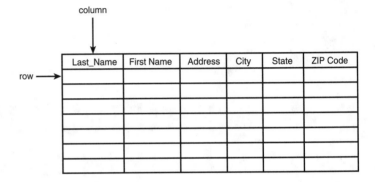

Dr. Codd states that by definition the relation model can answer any question you ask and can execute any command you formulate.

The relational data model uses the word *relational* for a purpose. Relational is used because relationships are easily built between multiple tables. Figure 1.2 shows two tables, EMP and DEPT, and shows their relationship to each other. This relationship is created naturally because they both have a column with a common type of information. In this case, it is the deptno column that the two tables have in common.

Two concepts need to be defined for you to better understand the remainder of this book: database and instance.

A *database* is a collection of data. Oracle stores this data using the relational model. This database refers to both the physical data and the logical memory structures and background processes.

Instance refers to the part of memory that Oracle has allocated for the database, as well as the background processes needed to support the database.

Figure 1.2.
A relationship between EMP and DEPT tables.

table: emp

empno	f_name	l_name	deptno
1	Cathy	Wilson	12
2	Jon	White	14
3	Matt	Baker	12

table: dept

deptno	dept_des	dept_mgr
12	Accts Pay	Adams
13	Admin	Smith
14	Shipping	Jones

Why Use Oracle?

The Oracle database was designed using the relational data model and uses Structured Query Language (SQL) as its query language. Using the Oracle database provides these major advantages:

- Oracle is an "open" system and adheres to the industry-accepted standards for data access languages (SQL).
- Oracle supports databases of all sizes, from several bytes to gigabytes in size.
- Oracle supports a large number of concurrent users. It minimizes data contentions and guarantees data concurrence.
- Oracle supports a true client/server environment. It enables processing to be split between the database server and the client application programs.
- Oracle provides fail-safe security features to limit and monitor data access and usage.
- Oracle behaves the same on all platforms (Windows, UNIX, Macintosh, and mainframes). This is because more than 80 percent of the internal code of Oracle is the same across all platforms and operating systems.

The relational data model offers the following advantages over other traditional data models:

- A data model that is easily understood and visualized
- Integrity laws that are easy to develop and understand to protect data and data structures
- Reduced data storage and redundancy
- Independence of physical data storage and logical database structure

How to Use the Oracle RDBMS

The Oracle RDBMS can reside on a variety of hardware platforms and operating systems, including personal computers. This section of the book gives an overview of the Oracle server architecture and basic concepts for operating and using the Oracle database server. The information provided is based on the assumption that you have the Oracle database installed on your system.

Oracle System Architecture

Oracle processing capability comes from its memory structures and processes. All memory structures reside in the main memory of the computer. The processes are Oracle and user tasks and jobs that work in the memory of these computers.

Oracle uses two main memory structures in its operation. The System Global Area (SGA) is a memory structure that contains data and control information for one Oracle instance. The SGA and the server background process constitute an Oracle instance. The second main memory structure is the Program Global Area (PGA). The PGA contains data and control information for a server process. The PGA is created when a server process is started.

Operating the Oracle Database

An Oracle database is not necessarily always available to all users. When the database is open, users can access the database information. When the database is closed, only the database administrator has access to the database. The database administrator—or users with the DBA privilege—are the only ones who can start up and shut down the database.

There are three steps to starting up the database and making it available for system-wide use:

1. Start an instance
2. Mount the database
3. Open the database

Starting the instance is synonymous with starting the database. When this occurs, Oracle allocates a portion of shared memory and background processes. This allocated shared memory is known as System Global Area. If an instance has just been started, no database is associated with this memory structure. Hence, no user can access the database information.

Mounting the database is the process of associating a database with a previously started instance. After a database is mounted, it is closed to all users until the database administrator opens the database.

Opening the database is the process of making the database available to users for normal database operations. Any authorized database user can connect to an open Oracle database and access its information.

Shutting Down the Oracle Server

There are three steps to shutting down the Oracle database:

1. Close the database
2. Dismount the database
3. Shut down the database

Closing the database causes all database data to be written to the data files. Dismounting the database is disassociating the database from the instance. Finally, shutting down the database causes all server processes to terminate, and the SGA is removed from memory.

Oracle Database Access

An Oracle instance that is started and has an open database can be accessed by users. An Oracle user is anyone who has a user account established in the Oracle server and has been granted the appropriate privileges for data access. The methods of database access can be through the following applications:

- User application in a client/server environment via SQL*NET
- SQL*Plus, one of the most popular access methods
- Oracle tools, such as Developer 2000
- An OCI call or other low-level programming call, such as in C or COBOL, that has embedded SQL in it

The following list illustrates an Oracle RDBMS being accessed by a user in a client/server environment. This illustration describes only the most basic level of operation that Oracle performs.

1. An Oracle server has an instance that is started, and a database that is mounted and open to users.
2. The user application attempts to establish a connection to the Oracle server.
3. The server recognizes the client's request for connection and creates a process on behalf of the user.
4. The user's application receives an acknowledgment of a successful connection and sends SQL statements to access and update the database.
5. The server's process receives the SQL statements and checks the user's access privileges.
6. If the SQL transaction is successful, the server process sends a message to the client application. If it is not successful, the server sends the appropriate error message to the client.
7. During this transaction, the server prevents data contention with other transactions requesting the same data. The server also manages other transactions and watches out for conditions that require intervention.

Golden Rules That Define a Relational Database

When Dr. Codd defined the relational model as a collection of tables, he left some people uneasy with this simplistic definition. In 1985, he created 13 rules that define specifically what a relational database is.

1. All information in the Oracle database is explicitly represented as values in a table.

2. All data items in a table are always accessible by giving the table name, column, and row.

3. Null values are valid datatypes in the relational database. They represent missing information.

4. The relational database represents the database descriptions in the same simplistic logical format as that of tables.

5. Several languages can be supported by the relational model, but SQL is its primary interface language.

6. All views are updatable, if the view is on one table.

7. The relational model treats all base relations and derived relations as a single operand for the update, insert, and delete operations on data as well as on retrieved data.

8. Logical aspects of the database are completely separated from the physical aspects of the database.

9. Data is preserved when logical non-impairment changes to the database are made.

10. Integrity constraints for a relational database are made in the database sublanguage (SQL) and stored in the database catalogue and not in any application.

11. Data distribution can occur without interruption to the application programs. Data distribution is the process of copying data to a remote database.

12. Integrity rules and constraints cannot be bypassed by any access language.

13. A relational DBMS must be able to manage databases entirely through its relational capabilities.

Oracle Data Dictionary

Central to the Oracle database is the data dictionary. This read-only tool provides all users of the database information about its associated database. The data dictionary is automatically created when the database is created. Oracle updates the data dictionary in response to every Data Dictionary Language (DDL) command issued. Please refer to Chapter 11, "SQL Operators and Conditions," for information on the DDL commands.

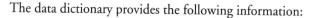

The data dictionary provides the following information:

- Names of all database objects including tables, views, snapshots, indexes, synonyms, procedures, functions, and so forth
- Names of the Oracle database users
- Privileges and roles that each user has been granted
- Integrity constraint specifics
- Default values for columns
- Space consumption and allocations
- Auditing information

The Oracle relational database's data dictionary is comprised of two essential components:

- Base tables—These tables are the foundation of the dictionary which stores information about the database. These tables are accessed directly by Oracle itself and rarely accessed by any of the Oracle users. The data stored in these tables is stored in Oracle's own internal format which the end user would not be able to read.
- User accessible views—These views summarize and present the information that reside in the base tables of the data dictionary. These views decode the cryptic base table information for the user. Most users have access to these views rather than having access to the base tables.

The data dictionary is owned by the Oracle user Sys and therefore no user has the privileges to alter the data dictionary directly. Public synonyms are usually created on many of the database views so they are easily accessible by the end users. The database administrator has the responsibility to create these synonyms.

Access to the data dictionary is always available when the database is open. If the database is closed, then all corresponding data dictionary views become inaccessible.

The data dictionary is logically a set of tables and views. These may be accessed by user queries to obtain information about the data base. The data dictionary consists of a set of views that are accessed through the SQL language. Certain views are accessible by all users while others are intended for the database administrators only.

The following is a brief list of some of the views that are available to all users that have the create session system privilege. For a complete list of the views available, see your database administrators.

- `all_col_comments`—Comments on columns of accessible tables and views.
- `all_constraints`—Constraint definitions on accessible tables.
- `all_db_links`—Database links accessible to the user.
- `all_errors`—Current errors on all objects accessible to the user.

- `all_indexes`—Description of indexes on tables accessible to the user.
- `all_objects`—Objects accessible to the user.
- `all_sequences`—Description of sequences accessible to the user.
- `all_snapshots`—All snapshots accessible to the user.
- `all_synonyms`—All synonyms accessible to the user.
- `all_tables`—Description of tables accessible to the user.
- `all_triggers`—Information about triggers accessible to the user.
- `all_users`—Information about all users of the database.
- `all_views`—Text of views accessible to the user.

Essential Summary

What
This chapter introduced you to Oracle's relational database system. The Oracle database is the world's most popular relational database. The relational data model is defined as a two-dimensional matrix composed of rows and columns. Access to data in the database is achieved by knowing its table name, column, and row.

Why
The Oracle relational database provides a database that is easy to understand, easy to use, and flexible enough to meet all your database needs. This database is an open system and adheres to industry standards for data access language (SQL).

How
This chapter presented the steps necessary to start and stop an Oracle database. Also, you learned that the word *relational* means a collection of tables that are associated with each other by a common column.

Logical Database Storage Structures

Oracle logical storage structures dictate how the physical space of a database is used. You can manipulate these logical storage structures to fine-tune disk space usage.

What Is a Logical Storage Structure?

A logical storage structure is an allocated unit of storage space. Its primary purpose is to define how the physical storage space of the database will be used. It is used to create the relational data model out of the physical structure of the database.

Logical storage structures include tablespaces, segments, extents, blocks, and data files. Oracle allocates database space for all the data in a database. The units of storage are data blocks, extents, and segments. These structures can be manipulated by database operations.

Why Use Logical Storage Structures?

Why

Logical storage structures dictate how the physical space of the database will be used. The schema objects and the relationships among them form the relational design of the database. This logical configuration of the database has a tremendous impact on database performance. Therefore, it is important to understand what the logical structures are and how they relate to each other.

An Oracle database has both a physical and a logical structure. The physical structure contains the actual data files, control files, and log files. By separating the two types of structures, each can be managed independently of the other without affecting access to each other.

When logical storage structures are created, space is allocated in the database according to predefined criteria. The database administrator has the ability to override or reconfigure the database criteria to fine-tune disk space usage. To know how to allocate space efficiently and effectively, you need to understand how space is used in the database.

How to Use Logical Storage Structures

How

An Oracle database logical structure is defined by the following features:

- Tablespaces
- Segments
- Extents
- Data blocks

Figure 2.1 shows the relationship between the logical storage structures.

Figure 2.1.
The hierarchy of the logical storage structures.

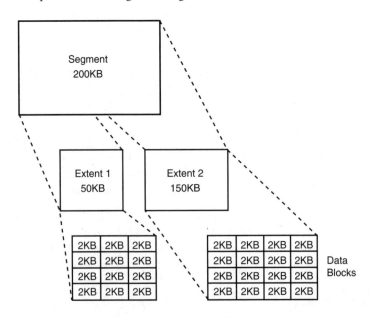

Tablespaces

When an Oracle database is created by the database administrator, it is divided into multiple logical units called *tablespaces*. The data portion of the database is logically stored in the tablespace and physically stored in the data files that are associated with the tablespace.

In addition to logically storing data, the database administrator can use tablespaces to perform the following functions:

- Control physical disk space consumption by the database
- Allocate specific disk quotas to individual users
- Allocate data storage across multiple physical storage devices

When a tablespace is created, the System tablespace and data files are automatically created. The System tablespace contains the entire data dictionary for the database. It is strongly recommended that at least one additional tablespace be created to keep the system dictionary information separate from the data.

Using multiple tablespaces provides flexibility in executing database operations. Some benefits obtained when using multiple tablespaces include:

- Separation of system data from the user's data
- Enables one application to be separated from another application
- Provides the opportunity to take individual tablespaces offline while keeping others online
- Ability to store different tablespaces on separate disk drives to improve performance and reduce data contention

You should only create enough tablespaces to meet your needs. Fewer tablespaces is better than many tablespaces. Within each tablespace, create as few as possible data files. These data files should be as large as possible. If you need to increase the size of a tablespace, add one or two large data files rather than several smaller ones. The main reason for this fewer-is-better concept is that most operating systems have a maximum limit on how many open files it can have at one time. These limits directly affect the number of tablespaces that can be online concurrently.

The System tablespace also contains rollback segments and PL/SQL program units such as procedure functions, triggers, and packages. If any of these PL/SQL units are created for a particular database, the database administrator must take into consideration the space requirements for such objects. As such, the administrator will allocate more space for the database.

The System tablespace must always be kept online because Oracle always needs access to the data dictionary.

An Oracle tablespace is usually kept online so that the data contained therein is available to the database users. The database administrator might need to take the tablespace offline for any of the following reasons:

- To perform maintenance or backup operations on the database
- To make a group of tables unavailable during the upgrade or modification to an application
- To make a portion of a database unavailable while the remainder of the database is on-line

Oracle prevents execution of SQL statements that reference the offline tablespace. Any active SQL transactions that reference the offline tablespace will complete normally. Data integrity is maintained in the rollback segments for these active SQL segments.

A tablespace cannot be taken offline if there is an active rollback segment that refers to it. The rollback segment must be resolved before the tablespace can be moved to offline status.

An offline tablespace cannot be read or manipulated by any application or utility other than Oracle.

Tablespaces and Datafiles

Every tablespace contains at least one physical data file. The data file that is associated with a tablespace contains the data for that tablespace. Data files are associated with only one tablespace and one database.

The inital data file for every database is to hold the System tablespace. This file is required to hold the data dictionary and rollback segment and must be initially a minimum 2KB in size. You may add additional data files to the tablespace as the database grows in size. Usually, it is best to add a few large data files rather than several smaller data files.

The tablespace and its data file are empty when initially created. However, they have space allocated to them to hold future database data. Data segments are created in the tablespace to hold this data. As a segment is created and grows in a tablespace, Oracle uses the free space in the associated data files to allocate extents for the segment. Note that a logical storage object does not correspond with a specific data file. Rather, a data file is a repository for the data of any object within a specific tablespace.

Creating New Tablespaces and Datafiles

To create a new tablespace you need the create tablespace system privilege. Simply issue the create tablespace command or use the create tablespace dialog box in SQL*DBA to create the new tablespace. The following statement creates a tablespace named dbt_user_01. Once created, this tablespace is left offline:

```
create tablespace dbt_user_01
datafile '<directory>/datafile_01' size 10m
default storage (
initial 50k
next 40k
minextents 10
maxextents 50
pctincrease 0)
offline;
```

To add a new datafile to an existing tablespace, issue the alter tablespace command or use the SQL*DBA add data file to tablespace dialogue box. You do need the alter tablespace system privilege to perform these actions.

The following example will add a new datafile to the existing tablespace named dbt_user_01:

```
alter tablespace dbt_user_01
add datafile '<directory>/new_file_name_2' size 5m
```

Viewing Tablespace and Data file Information

Oracle provides several predefined views that enable you to obtain information about tablespaces and data files. These views are named:

- dba_tablespaces
- user_tablespaces
- dba_data_files
- user_extents
- dba_extents
- user_segments
- dba_extents

These views provide a wealth of information regarding the logical structures and size of the tablespaces and data files.

The following example uses the dba_tablespace view to obtain the default storage information for the tablespace dbt_user_01:

```
select tablespace_name "Tablespace",
initial_extent "Init_Ext",
next_extent "Next_Ext",
max_extents "Max_Ext",
pct_increase "PCT_Incr"
from sys.dba_tablespaces;
```

sample output:

Tablespace	Init_Ext	Next_Ext	Max_Ext	PCT_Incr
system	10240000	10240000	99	50
DBT_USER_01	51200	40960	50	0

You should take the time and look at all these views to get a comprehensive understanding of your current tablespaces and data files.

Segments

Segments are the physical counterparts of the database objects that store data. A segment is composed of extents. The space that is allocated for segments is not released until the segment is dropped or truncated.

Oracle defines four types of segments:

- Table
- Index
- Rollback
- Temporary

Table Segment

The table segment, also known as the data segment, stores the data from tables, clusters, and snapshots. This type of segment is created indirectly via the `create table` /`cluster` /`snapshot` commands.

The table segment is usually very active because this is where the data is kept. A large number of SQL transactions manipulate the data. For proper performance, it is important that the database administrator allocate the correct amount of storage to the segment. If the segment consistently acquires extents, the data becomes fragmented, and performance suffers. The database cannot guarantee contiguous allocation of extents.

The `pctfree` command can be used to monitor the amount of free space a segment has. Free space can then be used internally for the tablespace or freed back to the database.

Index Segment

The index segment is created to hold the data of an index to a database. This segment is created indirectly via the `create index` command. This command enables you to define parameters for the extents of the index segment and the tablespace in which to create the index. Please refer to Chapter 7, "Indexes and Sequences," for additional information about indexes.

Rollback Segment

A rollback segment is a portion of the database that records the actions of a SQL transaction that should be rolled back if desired. A rollback sets the database data back to the way it was at the last save point or commit.

Every transaction has an associated rollback segment. This segment is usually assigned automatically by the database. However, you can explicitly assign a transaction to an appropriate rollback segment.

The rollback segment contains several pieces of information. Included in this information are the filename and block ID for the data that was changed and the data as it existed prior to the last transaction.

These rollback segments can be read and written only by Oracle.

Temporary Segment

A temporary segment is a work space for temporary work within a tablespace that is used to hold intermediate results of a SQL transaction. For example, a temporary segment would be created as a working area for a sorting operation. The following SQL commands might require a temporary segment:

- `Create index`
- `Select...order by`
- `Select...distinct`
- `Select...minus`
- `Select...intersect`

Extents

An extent is a logical storage structure made up of a contiguous number of blocks. Each type of segment is made up of one or more extents. As a segment runs out of storage space, Oracle allocates a new extent for the segment.

Every segment is created with at least one initial extent. The following steps are performed to allocate a new extent for a segment:

1. Oracle searches through the tablespace looking for the first free contiguous set of data blocks that add up to an incremental extent's size.
2. Once Oracle finds the necessary free space, a portion of that free space equivalent to the incremental size of an extent is allocated for that extent.
3. The data dictionary is updated to show that a new extent has been allocated and that the allocated space is no longer free.

Extents of segments can be deallocated when they are no longer needed. Typically, extents are not returned to the tablespace as free space until the segment is returned as a complete unit. An example of this is when a table is dropped and the segments and extents are freed up.

When extents are freed up, the data dictionary is updated to reflect the recaptured extents as available space. All data in the blocks of the freed extents is no longer accessible.

Data Blocks

The data block is the smallest storage unit that Oracle uses to store data. A data block corresponds to a block of physical bytes on a disk. The storage space within data files is in data blocks.

The Oracle data block format is similar regardless of whether the data block contains a table, index, or clustered data.

The data block includes the following components:

- Header—Contains general block information such as block address and segment type.
- Table Directory—Contains information about the tables having rows in this block.
- Row Directory—Contains row information about the rows in the block.
- Row Data—Contains table or index data. Oracle allows rows of data to span several blocks. Row data space is not reclaimed by the server when rows are deleted. This space is reused only when new rows are inserted into the block.
- Free Space—Used to insert new rows and for updates to rows that require additional space.

Figure 2.2 shows the components of a data block.

Figure 2.2.
Components of a data block.

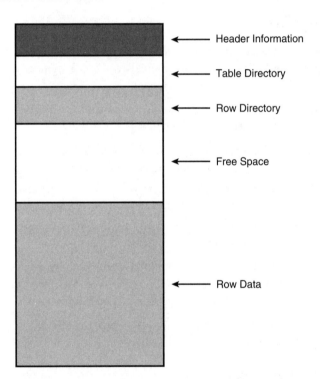

Two space management parameters, pctfree and pctused, are available to the developer to control the use of data block free space. Both of these parameters can be specified only when creating or altering tables and clusters.

The pctfree parameter is used to define the percentage of a data block to be kept free for possible updates to rows that already exist in that data block. The following example, when used with the create table command, will reserve 35 percent of the data block used for the table as free space for possible future updates:

```
pctfree 35
```

The `pctused` parameter is used to define the percentage of space in the data block that Oracle will attempt to fill before it allocates another extent. The following example, when used with the `create table` command, instructs Oracle not to insert any more rows into the data block until there is at least 40 percent of the block free:

```
pctused 40
```

`pctfree` and `pctused` work together to optimize space utilization in the data blocks and extents within a data segment.

Essential Summary

Logical storage structures create the relational data model in the physical database. These structures define how the physical database will be utilized.

What

Logical storage structures are necessary for the database administrator and developer to maximize efficiency of the database. You use these structures also to improve disk space utilization by reducing data redundancy.

Why

The Oracle database is logically divided into units called tablespaces. The data portion of the database is stored in data files. A tablespace has at least one segment to store the database data. Each segment is composed of extents. An extent is made up of contiguous units of storage space called data blocks.

How

Database Design

What Is Database Design?

What Database design is the process you go through to prepare for the physical creation of an Oracle database. The steps include the discovery of the business processes the database supports, as well as the creation of the physical design of the database. This chapter reviews the steps necessary to design a database.

Why Use Database Design?

Why Proper database design is absolutely vital to the success of the database and any application using the database. Without designing a database correctly, the following problems can be introduced into the database:

- Data integrity is compromised because integrity constraints cannot be designed or implemented correctly
- Data becomes redundant and a larger burden is placed on the individual applications to keep the data in sync
- Performance is affected because additional queries might be necessary to complete a `select` statement

How to Perform Database Design

How

The following steps are necessary to create an Oracle database:

1. Create a business model and definition
2. Create a data entity model
3. Create a database design
4. Create a table definition
5. Create a relational table

Creating a Business Model and Definition

This first step involves learning about the business and the business processes the Oracle database will support. Your goal is to determine whether there is a problem with the current business processes or an opportunity for process improvement and enhancement. To develop an understanding of the business and its processes, you perform the following activities:

- Conduct interviews of the following people:
    a. Managers and supervisors of the business processes.
    b. Potential end users.
    c. Potential end beneficiaries. These are people who might not directly use the new database but will receive information or benefit from the database.
- Discover the mission statement of the business. It is always good to know the goals of a business so your application and database goals are consistent.
- Work with the users and supervisors to define the application's mission statement. You want to define what the business wants the database and application to do.
- Analyze the current system specifications.
- Discover through the business the future system specifications for the database.

At this point, you'll have large volumes of data which may include forms, manuals, reports, notes, and many other forms of information. You need to understand all this information, and organize it before proceeding on to the next step.

Creating a Data Entity Model

Once you have collected the preceding information, you need to build a model or a graphical representation of the business needs and rules. For example, let's say you learned the following information from the business during the preceding interviews:

- The business needs to track which salespeople are assisting which customers
- They need to know the name and phone number of the customer
- They want the ability to quickly find a specific customer's information

One proven modeling technique to graphically represent the business processes is the Entity Relationship Diagram (ERD) model. This model is composed of three components:

- Entity—An item of significance about which information needs to be known
- Attribute—Something that describes or qualifies an entity
- Relationship—An association between two entities

Only something that is of significance to the business becomes an entity. Any descriptions about an entity become your attributes. The business information you have obtained should describe relationships between entities.

Taking this example a little further, let's create a simple ERD for the example. See Figure 3.1 for an example of an Entity Relationship Diagram.

Figure 3.1.
A simple Entity Relationship Diagram.

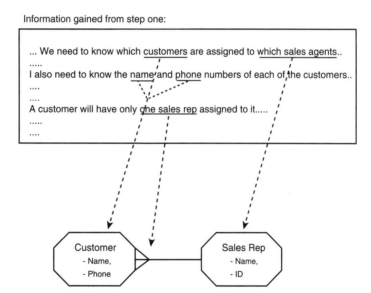

Information gained from step one:

... We need to know which <u>customers</u> are assigned to <u>which sales agents</u>..
.....
I also need to know the <u>name</u> and <u>phone</u> numbers of each of the customers..
....
....
A customer will have only <u>one sales rep</u> assigned to it.....
.....
....

Customer
- Name,
- Phone

Sales Rep
- Name,
- ID

Once you have created the initial ERD, review it with the business areas to make sure it is correct and to refine it as necessary.

Benefits obtained by the use of ERDs include the following:

- The ERD diagram documents the information requirements for the organization in a clear, precise format
- This pictorial approach to modeling makes it easy to understand
- The simplicity of the model makes it easy to work with

Creating a Database Design

Now that the ERD is complete, this model, along with the business information collected in Step 1, can be used to directly create a database design. Figure 3.2 shows how you map the ERD to a standard database instance chart.

Figure 3.2.
Mapping the ERD to the
instance chart.

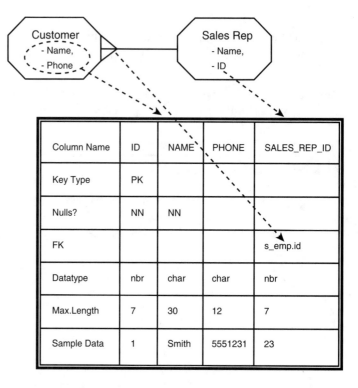

Column Name	ID	NAME	PHONE	SALES_REP_ID
Key Type	PK			
Nulls?	NN	NN		
FK				s_emp.id
Datatype	nbr	char	char	nbr
Max.Length	7	30	12	7
Sample Data	1	Smith	5551231	23

The instance chart is composed of rows that define the critical characteristics of a database. The entities from the ERD become tables; the attributes become the columns of the tables; and the relationships become the foreign keys.

Once this chart is completed, review it again with your business areas to check for completeness and accuracy.

Creating a Table Definition

In Oracle, the SQL statement create table is used to create the physical tables in Oracle. The collection of these tables, along with security considerations, makes up the basis of the relational database.

Figure 3.3 shows how easy it is for the create statement to be modeled after the table instance chart.

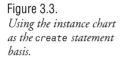

Figure 3.3.
Using the instance chart as the create statement *basis.*

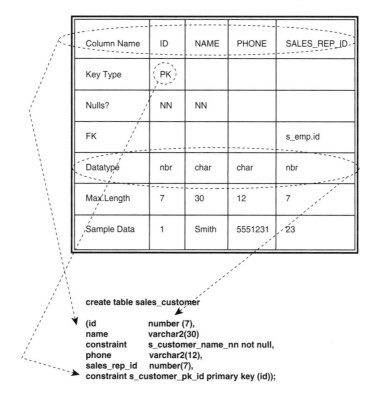

Chapter 5, "Tables," provides more information about the creation of tables.

Creating a Relational Table

Now it is time to create the table. You create a table by defining the table name and the table columns and their descriptions using a SQL statement. The following statement creates the table used in the figures:

```
create table sales_customer
(id number (7),
name varchar2(30)
constraint s_customer_name_nn not null,
phone varchar2(12),
sales_rep_id number(7),
constraint s_customer_pk_id primary key (id));
```

Once this statement is issued through SQL*PLUS or SQL*DBA, the table physically exists in the Oracle relational database.

Additional ERD Concepts

A relationship is a two-directional association between two entities. The previous examples have discussed relationships that are simple in nature. In the real world, relationships tend to be a little more complex.

The following types of relationships can exist between objects:

one-to-one	This relationship is the most simplistic of relationships. For every one occurrence of an entity, there is a corresponding single entity. An example of this is where a person has one and only one unique employee number.
one-to-many	In this relationship, for every single entity there are many corresponding entities. An example of this is where a single company has many employees belonging to it.
many-to-one	This is when many entities all have a corresponding single entity. An example of this is where you have many employees belonging to a single company.
many-to-many	This is where many entities associate with many other entities. An example of this would be the relationship between employees and skills. An employee can have many skills, and a skill can have many employees capable of performing it.
or zero	This is a qualifier that can be applied to any of the preceding relationships. If applied to the one-to-many relationship, it would be read as one-to-zero-or-many. This means that an employee can have many skills or can have no skills at all.

Figure 3.4 provides examples of how to create these various relationships in the ERD.

Figure 3.4.
*Ways to represent
relationships in your
ERD.*

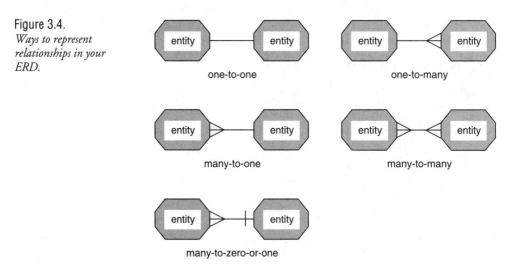

Data Normalization

Normalization is a process in which you eliminate the problems of data redundancy in the database design and build a data model that supports different functional requirements and alternate database designs.

Normalization is a successive process where you apply the following three rules to the data:

- All attributes must be single-valued. This is called first normal form. This means that the attribute data is not repeated. For example, what if you had a customer entity defined as the following?

```
customer
id
first date of contact
first contact location
first contact result
second date of contact
second contact location
second contact result
third date of contact
third contact location
third contact result
```

    The date, location, and result attributes are repeated and therefore are not considered to be single-valued. To normalize this table, convert the entity by creating an additional entity called contact, with a many-to-one relationship to customer. Have the date, location, and result attributes in the contact entity and the ID in the customer entity. This process eliminates the repeated values.

- An attribute must depend upon its entity's entire unique ID. This is called second normal form. Move the attributes to a table where they depend upon the primary key. Do not have a table that has attributes that do not solely depend upon the key.

- Non-unique ID attributes can be dependent upon another non-unique ID attribute. This is referred to as normalized or third normal form data.

When normalization is complete, each table must have exactly one primary key, and the data in the table is dependent solely upon the table's primary key.

Essential Summary

Database design involves going through several steps to collect, analyze, and model business information data. This chapter presented the steps necessary to analyze and model data. **What**

Good database design is necessary because without it, performance would suffer, data integrity would be jeopardized, and your database would become rather large because duplicate data would be collected. **Why**

Achieving good database design takes practice and experience. However, you can follow the steps presented here to make a solid and well-designed database. **How**

PART II

Database Objects

Datatypes

All data elements, variables, and constants that are stored in the Oracle database are characterized by their type and length. This characterization is defined as the object's datatype.

What Are Datatypes?

What Tables are the storage vehicles within a relational database. The columns of the table define the characteristics of the data as well as giving the data a name.

The characteristics of the column, as well as variables and constants, are made up of a datatype and length. This datatype is a static set of properties with a predefined value. These properties cause the Oracle server to treat one datatype differently from another datatype.

Oracle recognizes internal and external datatypes. An internal datatype is one that describes columns of tables, clusters, and procedure arguments. The Oracle precompilers recognize other datatypes that are in embedded SQL programs. These datatypes are called external datatypes and are associated with host variables. This chapter is focused on the Oracle internal datatypes.

The Oracle internal datatypes are:

- `char`
- `varchar2`
- `varchar`
- `number`
- `date`
- `raw`
- `long raw`
- `rowid`
- `long`
- `mlslabel`

This chapter discusses each of these datatypes.

Why Use Datatypes?

Using datatypes within the relational database gives you the following benefits:

- They restrict the range of values that data items can contain. For example, a datatype of `date` cannot take on a value of `JIM`.
- They enable you to conserve storage space by tailoring the datatype to the data being stored.
- They enable data conversion automatically under certain conditions.

How to Use Datatypes

The following sections describe each of the Oracle server datatypes that can be used for column, variable, and constant definitions.

char Datatypes

The `char` datatype is used to define a column that contains fixed-length character strings. The length of these strings ranges from 1 to 255. This datatype stores alphanumeric data. When using the `char` datatype, Oracle ensures the following:

- When a column is defined, or a value is inserted into a column, the data value is fixed in length.
- If the data value is shorter in length than the length defined for the column, blank spaces will be added to the value.
- If the data value is longer than the length defined for the column, Oracle returns an error code.

- If the longer data value has trailing blanks, the blanks are trimmed from the data to the fixed length.

The following is an example of a char data item definition:

```
Part_Number    char(15)
Data example: "TY33693X1      "
```

varchar2 Datatype

The varchar2 datatype is used to define a column that contains variable-length character strings. The length of these strings can range from 1 to 2,000 bytes. For a column that is defined as varchar2, each datatype is stored as variable-length.

When using the varchar2 datatype, Oracle ensures the following:

- When a column is defined, or a value is inserted into a column, the data value is variable in length.
- If the data value is shorter in length than the length defined for the column, no blank spaces will be added to the value. It is a non-padded data value.
- If the data value is longer than the length defined for the column, Oracle returns an error code.
- If the longer data value has trailing blanks, the blanks are trimmed from the data to the maximum length.

The following is an example of a varchar2 data item, Part_Number, that is defined with a maximum length of 15 bytes:

```
Part_Number    varchar2(15)
Data example: "TY33693X1"
```

varchar Datatype

In the current release of Oracle 7.1, the varchar datatype is synonymous with the varchar2 datatype. In future releases of the Oracle RDBMS, the varchar datatype might store variable-length character strings compared with different comparison semantics. Therefore, you should always use the varchar2 datatype rather than the varchar datatype.

The following is an example of a varchar data item definition:

```
Part_Number    varchar(15)
Data example: 'TY33693X1'
```

number Datatype

The number datatype stores fixed and floating point numbers.

A number of virtually any magnitude can be stored. The number datatype can be defined with a precision and a scale. Precision is equal to the total number of digits in the number; scale refers to the number of digits to the right of the decimal point. These numbers can be stored with up to 38 digits of precision and a scale ranging from –84 to 127.

The following is an example of a `number` data item definition:

```
Part_Price     number
Data example: '336100'
```

or

```
Part_Price     number(6,2)
Data example: '3361.00'
```

In this example, `(6,2)` represents the following:

- 6 is the precision. Precision is synonymous with the total number of digits allowed. This includes the total number of digits on both sides of the decimal point.

- 2 is the scale, or the number of digits to the right of the decimal point.

It is always a good idea to specify the precision and scale of the data item. This provides data integrity checking while inputting data.

date Datatype

The `date` datatype stores the date and time in columns of a table and has a precision of one second. This datatype stores the four-digit year, month, day, the hours, the minutes, and the seconds since midnight.

For input and output of dates, the default date format is DD-MON-YY. Time is stored as HH:MM:SS. You cannot specify a date literal. If you don't specify a time component in a date value, the default time is 12:00:00 a.m. Likewise, if you omit the date component of a date value, the default date is the first day of the current month. The valid range for dates is January 1, 4712 B.C. to January 1, 4712 A.D.

Date Formats

Oracle provides several character literals that may be used as format codes that:

- Translate a date value that is in a non-default date format. This is usually used in functions such as the `to_char` function.

- Translate a character value that is a format that is in a format other than the default date format. This is usually used in the `to_date` function.

These format characters do not change the internal representation of the data; it only changes the way the data is presented to the user. The following is a list of the Oracle format codes that may be used with the `to_date` and `to_char` functions:

- MM—Number of month.
- MON—Three-letter abbreviation of month all capitalized.
- Mon—Three letter abbreviation of month with first letter capitalized.
- mon—Three letter abbreviation of month with all letters in lower case.
- RM—Roman numeral month.

- J—Julian date. This equates to the number of days since January 1, 4712 B.C.
- DDD—Number of days since this year's January 1st.
- DD—Number of the day in the month.
- D—Number of the day in the week.
- DY—Three-letter abbreviation of day.
- Dy—Three-letter abbreviation of day with inital letter capitalized.
- DAY—Day of week spelled out fully in all capitalized letters.
- Day—Day of week spelled out fully with initial letter capitalized.
- day—Day of week spelled out fully in lowercase letters.
- CC—Century.
- SCC—BC century prefixed with a "-".
- YYYY—Full four-digit year.
- SYYY—Signed four-digit year. If B.C., then prefix year with "-".
- IYYY—ISO four-digit year.
- YYY—Last three digits of the year.
- IYY—Last three digits of the ISO year.
- YY—Last two digits of the year.
- IY—Last two digits of the ISO year.
- RR—Similar to the YY date format, but this is used for years in other centuries. See following additional RR explanation later in this chapter.
- Y—Last digit of year.
- I—Last digit of year.
- YEAR—The year spelled out.
- Q—Quarter of the year.
- WW—Number of week in the current year.
- W—Number of week in the month.
- IW—Number of week in the ISO year.
- HH—Hour of the day using 12-hour clock.
- HH24—Hour of day using 24-hour clock.
- MI—Minute in the hour.
- SS—Second of the minute.
- SSSSS—Seconds since midnight.
- A.M.—Displays a.m. depending on time of day.
- P.M.—Displays p.m. depending on time of day.
- BC—Displays either B.C. or A.D. depending on the year.

The following examples will use the to_date and to_char functions for illustrative purposes. These functions read in a string in a given format and converts into the default Oracle date format or user-specified format.

Converts MM/DD/YY formatted date to standard default format:

```
select to_date('04-21-95','MM/DD/YY') "Formatted" from dual;
```

Sample output:

```
Formatted
---------
04-APR-95
```

Converts the employee's starting date to Julian format:

```
select to_char (hiredate, 'J') "Julian" from emp;
```

Sample output:

```
Julian
------
2444591
2444656
2444658
2444697
2444876
2444726
2444765
2445313
2444926
2444856
2445347
2444942
2444942
2444993

14 rows selected.
```

Converts the input to 29-Sept-86:

```
update emp
set hiredate = to_date('86 09 29','yy mm dd');
```

RR Date Format

The RR date format is similar to the YY date format. The century returned by the to_date function with the YY date format is always the current year. The RR date format enables you to store dates in different centuries. Oracle determines the century of the date string that uses the RR format by evaluating the last two digits of the current year and the specified two-year digit. Figure 4.1 summarizes the behavior of the RR date format element.

The following example uses the RR format.

Figure 4.1
The RR Date Format Element behavior.

Specified Two-Year Digit

		0 - 49	50 - 99
Current Year (Last Two Digits)	0 - 49	Use current century	Use last century
	50 - 99	Use next century	Use current century

```
select to_char(to_date('03-OCT-21','DD-MON-RR'),'YYYY')
"RR Formated Year" from dual;
```

Sample output:

```
RR Formated Year
----------------
2021
```

Format Modifiers

The to_char function may accept two format modifiers when processing dates. They are:

- fm—Suppresses leading blanks in the return values of the to_char function
- fx—Specifies exact matching for the character argument and date format model to the to_date function.

In this first example, no format modifiers will be used to format the output. In the second example, the same query will be issued, but the output is formatted with the fm format modifier.

```
select hiredate, to_char(hiredate,'Month, dd, YYYY')
"UN- Formatted Date" from emp;
```

Sample output with no format modifier being used:

```
HIREDATE      UN-Formatted Date
--------      -----------------
17-DEC-80     December, 17, 1980
20-FEB-81     February, 20, 1981
22-FEB-81     February, 22, 1981
02-APR-81     April   , 02, 1981
```

By default, Oracle lines up the fields in the results. This example will now use the format modifiers to truncate the leading spaces from the results fields:

```
select hiredate, to_char(hiredate,'fmMonth, dd, YYYY')
"Formatted Date" from emp;
```

Sample output using the fm format modifier:

```
HIREDATE      Formatted Date
--------      --------------
17-DEC-80     December, 17, 1980
20-FEB-81     February, 20, 1981
22-FEB-81     February, 22, 1981
02-APR-81     April,   02, 1981
```

Date Format Suffixes

Oracle enables you to add any of the following suffixes to a date format element. When using a suffix, the returned date is always in English.

- TH—Adds the letter TH to the date. For example, you may specify a date format of DDTH to obtain the return value of 4TH.
- SP—This suffix is for the date to be spelled out. For example, add the SP suffix to the DD date format element to obtain the return value of FOUR.
- SPTH—This will spell out the ordinal value. For example, if the date format element is DDSPTH, the result would be FOURTH.

This example will use the th format suffix along with the fm date format modifier to create an attractive output result:

```
select hiredate, to_char(hiredate,'fmMonth, ddth, YYYY')
"Formatted Date" from emp;
```

Sample output using the th suffix and the fm modifier:

```
HIREDATE       Formatted Date
--------       --------------
17-DEC-80      December, 17th, 1980
20-FEB-81      February, 20th, 1981
22-FEB-81      February, 22nd, 1981
02-APR-81      April, 2nd, 1981
```

Date Arithmetic

Oracle permits data arithmetic—that is, the adding or subtracting of one date from another date. This arithmetic takes into account and adjusts for historical calendar anomalies. For example, the year 0 does not exist. Also, leap years are accounted for.

Oracle interprets any number constant in a date arithmetic statement as number of days. For example, the following expression is equal to tomorrow or the current day plus one day.

```
select sysdate, sysdate+1, sysdate-1 from dual;
```

Sample output:

```
SYSDATE     SYSDATE+1     SYSDATE-1
-------     ---------     ---------
15-JUN-95   16-JUN-95     14-JUN-95
```

Many date operations have a result that includes a fraction or a remainder. This is due to the fact that the date contains a time component as well. Hence, the fraction in the result is usually a portion of a day.

long Datatype

long datatypes store variable-length character data containing up to two gigabytes of information. Although long datatypes can serve many useful purposes, they have the following restrictions:

- Only one long column is allowed per table
- long columns cannot be indexed
- long columns cannot appear in integrity constraints
- long columns cannot be referenced by SQL functions, such as substr, length, and so on
- long columns cannot be used in where, group by, order by, or connect by clauses
- long variables or arguments cannot appear in a PL/SQL program unit

raw and long raw

These datatypes are intended for binary data. They should not be used when data will be interpreted by Oracle. These datatypes are ideal to store multimedia data or other binary files.

raw is similar to the varchar2 datatype, and long raw is similar to the long datatype. The only exception to this comparison is that no character set conversions are performed for the raw datatypes. raw datatypes can be indexed, but long raw datatypes cannot be indexed.

rowid Datatype

The rowid datatype corresponds to the physical address of a row in a nonclustered Oracle table. It is a unique identifier of a row. A rowid uses a binary representation of the physical address. When queried using SQL*Plus or another Oracle tool, the binary representation is converted to a hexidecimal representation.

Each table in an Oracle database has this rowid column, but you will not see it listed when you perform a select * from statement or a describe statement. However, each row address can be retrieved with a SQL query using the reserved word rowid as a column name. The following illustrates a SQL statement that uses the rowid datatype as well as its output:

```
SELECT rowid, ename FROM emp;
```

Sample output:

```
rowid               EMP_NAME
--------------------------
000C0B7.0000.0001   'WHITE'
```

The rowid translates as follows:

000C0B7	This is the data block that contains the row. Block numbers are relative to their data file and not the tablespace.
0000	This is the row sequence number in the block. The first row is always 0.
0001	This is the data file number that contains the row.

rowid datatypes provide Oracle with the following benefits:

- They are the fastest means of accessing rows.
- They can be used to see how a table is organized.
- They are unique identifiers for rows in a given table. rowids are used in the construction of indexes.

rowids can be selected or used in a where clause, but they cannot be changed by insert, update, or delete operations. However, rowids can change if the table is exported and imported.

mlslabel Datatype

Trusted Oracle 7.*x* provides one new datatype: the mlslabel datatype. Trusted Oracle is Oracle Corporation's multilevel secure database management system product. It is designed to provide the high level of secure data management capabilities required by organizations processing sensitive or classified information. You can declare columns of the mlslabel datatype in standard Oracle, as well as in Trusted Oracle, for compatibility with Trusted Oracle applications.

The mlslabel datatype is used to store the binary format of an operating system label. The maximum width for this datatype is 255 bytes. mlslabel is stored as a variable length tag that maps to a binary label in the data dictionary. The reason that mlslabel data is stored as a representative tag instead of the binary label itself is that binary operating system labels can be very long. Because a label is stored for every row in the database, storing a large number of labels can consume a lot of storage space.

Datatype Conversions

Oracle automatically converts data from one datatype to another under certain circumstances. You can also use Oracle functions to explicitly convert data using one of the following functions:

- to_char()
- to_date()
- to_number()
- to_label()
- chartorowid()
- rowidtochar()

For assignments, Oracle implicitly performs datatype conversions for the following:

- varchar2 or char to number
- number to varchar2
- varchar2 or char to date

- date to varchar2
- varchar2 or char to rowid
- rowid to varchar2

The assignment conversion succeeds if Oracle can convert the datatype of the value used in the assignment to that of the assignment's target.

For expression evaluation, Oracle implicitly performs datatype conversions for the following:

- varchar2 or char to number
- varchar2 or char to date

char to number conversions succeed only if the character string result represents a valid number. char to date conversions succeed only if the character string result has the default date format DD-MON-YY.

null

null is not an Oracle datatype, but it is an important concept to cover at this time. null appears in table columns and SQL expressions.

null is defined as a value that is unknown, meaningless, or irrelevant. Any Oracle datatype can be null. If a row lacks a value for a particular column, that column value is null. nulls can appear in any column as long as it is not restricted with the not null or primary key integrity constraint.

Do not treat the value of zero as null. Zero is a number and has meaning. null in a number datatype column is not the same as zero. A character value with a length of zero is considered null.

To test for nulls, use the comparison operators is null and is not null. Because null represents a lack of data, a null cannot be equal or not equal to any value. The following example shows a select statement that will select any record where the balance is not null:

```
SELECT acct_nbr, acct_name, balance
FROM accts
WHERE overdue bal IS NOT null;
```

Essential Summary

This chapter introduced you to the Oracle datatypes as characteristics of data. These characteristics are a predefined static set of information that define the data item's type and its length. The datatypes cause Oracle to treat one datatype differently from another datatype.

What

Datatypes enable Oracle to conserve storage space by tailoring datatypes to the data being stored. Additionally, datatypes assist you by restricting the range of values that data items can contain, thereby contributing to the integrity of the data.

Why

Part II

How   You learned how to define datatypes in column definitions, variables, and constants. You first determine the type of data the item will have, then you define its length. Oracle converts datatypes to other datatypes either implicitly or explicitly. Oracle allows this conversion to happen only between certain datatypes.

Tables

Tables are the fundamental storage structures of the Oracle relational database. Tables are composed of columns and rows.

What Is a Table?

A table can be visualized as a two-dimensional matrix that has a series of rows and columns. A column represents a single type of data about an entity. An example of a column might be last_name or city. A row is a collection of data for each column in a table. For example, a row from a table that contains city name and state name columns would be "Lexington KY" or "Denver CO."

A table has a fixed number of predefined columns and usually contains multiple rows. The number of rows can range from 0 to almost unlimited. The true constraint on the number of rows is the size of the database.

The Oracle table can be used to hold information about a single entity. Such a table might represent a list of employee names or a list of department numbers for your company. A table can also represent relationships between two entities. This type of table could show you the relationship between an employee and the department number they are assigned to.

Why Use Tables?

Why

The relational database stores data in logical storage units called tables. Tables provide the relational model with its flexibility and strength. Using tables provides the following benefits:

- The database becomes easy to understand due to the simplistic column/row make-up of tables
- Relationships between data in different tables are easily accomplished with tables
- Integrity rules are quickly developed
- Tables reduce storage space requirements and data redundancy
- Oracle enables you to create meaningful names for tables and columns, thereby improving database comprehension

Once you create a table, you can insert rows of data into it using SQL statements. This table information is then available for queries, updates, and deletions.

How to Use Tables

How

The following sections of this chapter explain how to create, modify, and drop tables.

Plan for Tables

The Database Administrator is usually responsible for establishing storage parameters and defining clusters for tables. The DBA must use the information from the application developer on how the application will be used and the types of data expected to complete these tasks.

The following are the general guidelines to follow when planning for a new table.

- Tables are normalized.
- Columns that allow nulls are defined last to conserve on storage space.
- Cluster tables whenever possible.
- Specify the correct pctfree and pctused during table creation.
- Specify the initrans and maxtrans parameters during table creation.
- Define which tablespace the tables are to be located.
- Estimate table size and then set storage parameters. Use these estimates to plan for the necessary hardware and disk usage.

If you see that you will be having very large tables, such as those with millions of rows, require special attention. If the table is going to grow over time to be very large, be sure that its extents are large enough so that the segment does not have too many extents.

Two more considerations for large tables is to plan to have the table in a different tablespace than its indexes. Also, allocate sufficient temporary space for actions such as sorting.

Calculating Table Size

Follow the next six steps to calculate a tables projected size. These steps will provide a reasonable estimate and not a precise number.

1. Determine the space required by the data block header. This is determined by the following formula:

   block header = (fixed header + variable transaction header) + (table directory + row directory)

   fixed header = 57 bytes

   variable trans header = 23*the intrans value

   table directory = 4

   row directory = 2*# of rows in a block

2. Determine the available data space per data block. This is calculated by the following formula:

   available data space = (block size–total block header)–((block size–(fixed header+variable transaction header))*(pctfree/100))

   You can obtain the current block size by issuing the show parameters db_block_size command.

3. Calculate the combined data space by the values of a typical row. This is achieved by evaluating the number of rows in a tables, the column datatypes, and the average value size for variable length columns. Issue the avg function on each row to determine its average size.

4. Calculate total average row size by using the following formula:

   total average rows size = row header + A + B + C

   A = total length of all columns that store 250 bytes or less.

   B = total length of all columns that store more than 250 bytes.

   C = combined data space of all columns (from step 3).

5. Determine the average rows per block with the following formula:

   avg rows/block = available space/average row size

   The available space is calculated from step 2, and the average row size is from step 4.

6. Calculate the number of blocks and bytes with the following equation:

   # of rows and blocks = # rows/avg. rows per block

   The average rows per block was determined in step 5.

Designing Tables

The first step in creating a new Oracle table is to design the table. Here are some good guidelines to follow when designing a table:

- Use meaningful and descriptive names for the table and columns
- Select the proper datatype for each column
- Normalize tables when possible
- Define columns that allow `nulls` last to conserve storage space
- Be sure to document the table's name and purpose with the `comment` command
- Have one table for relationship type data and a separate table for data

Prior to creating a table, you should decide if integrity constraints are required. Integrity constraints can be defined on the columns of a table to enforce certain business rules of your database automatically. For example, if you had a table that contained employee information, you might want to use the `not null` integrity constraint on the emp_name column. This constraint will force the user to insert a value in this column for every row in the table.

Creating Tables

To create a table, create a SQL script using the `create table` command. The general syntax for the command to create a table follows:

```
create table tablename
(column_name   datatype   constraint,
(column_name   datatype   constraint)
```

Table names and column names can be from 1 to 30 characters long. The first character must be alphabetic. The table name cannot be the name of another object owned by the same Oracle server user. A *constraint* is a rule that restricts the data values for one or more columns in a table.

The following is an example of a SQL script that will create an employee table with five columns. The table will contain the employee number, the employee's first and last name, the department number the employee is assigned to, and their hire date.

```
create table emp (
empno          number(15)    primary key,
first_name     varchar2(20)      not null,
last_name      varchar2(40)      not null,
deptno         varchar2(12),
hire_date      date          not null)

pctfree 20
pctused 40
tablespace emp_01
storage ( initial 50k
next 50k
maxextents 15
pctincrease 25);
```

empno is defined as the primary key for the table. The purpose of the primary key is to uniquely identify that particular row in the table. The `not null` constraints on some of the rows indicate that those columns must contain a value for every row.

`pctfree` is a value that represents the percentage of each data block that is reserved as free space for future expansion. In this example, 20 percent of each block is to be set aside for future use.

`pctused` defines the maximum percentage an extent block can fill up before Oracle stops inserting new records into the extent. In the preceding illustration, Oracle allows the extent to reach a maximum of 40 percent full before a new extent is allocated.

Oracle uses this free space in the extent as working space during inserts and updates. Although a low `pctused` value increases unused storage space, it improves the processing efficiency of certain SQL commands. A higher `pctused` value reduces the unused storage space but degrades the performance of the `insert` and `update` executions.

This table will be created in the emp_01 tablespace. Storage is defined using an initial allocation of 50KB, with the next extent being 50KB in size. If the table continues to grow, additional extents will be given to the table to use for growth. These extents will be allocated one at a time until a total of 15 extents are issued. If the table needs additional space, an Oracle error will be issued indicating that the maximum number of extents allocated has been reached. Each of these 15 extents will grow at a rate of 25 percent for each successive extent. That is to say that the fist extent will be 50KB in size. The next (second) extent will be 50KB as well. The third extent will be 62.5KB (50×1.25), and the fourth will be 78.1KB (62.5×1.25), and so on.

Table Comments

To add comments about the table or columns into the data dictionary, use the `comment` command. The following example creates a comment in the data dictionary for the column hire_date in table EMP:

```
comment on column emp.hire_date
IS 'This date represents the date the employee was hired. Column Start_date
represents the date the employee actually began the position';
```

To remove the comment from the previous example, use the following example:

```
comment on column emp.hire_date is''
```

The following example creates a comment in the data dictionary for the DEPT table:

```
comment on table dept is' This is the master list of department numbers and
descriptions for the company'
```

Loading a Table During Table Creation

When you create a new table, you have the option to populate the table at the same time. In your SQL statement you would add the as clause to your `create table` SQL statement. The following example creates the EMP table and loads the contents of the UK_EMP table into it:

```
create table emp (
empno,
first_name,
last_name,
deptno,
```

```
hire_date)

pctfree 20
pctused 40
tablespace emp_01
storage ( initial 50k
next 50k
maxextents 15
pctincrease 25)

as select empid, f_name, l_name, dept, hire_date from uk_emp;
```

When you use the as clause, the column definitions can specify only the column names, default values, and integrity constraints. Datatypes are not permitted with the as clause.

Oracle derives the columns' datatypes and lengths from the subquery. Oracle also automatically defines not null constraints on columns in the new table if they existed on the corresponding columns of the select table.

The create table command cannot contain both the as clause and a referential integrity constraint definition.

Creating Table Clusters

Clusters are an optional method of storing table data. Tables that are frequently accessed together can be physically stored together in the same data blocks. The tables in the cluster are stored together to improve server performance by reducing the number of disk I/Os.

A cluster key is defined as the related columns that the clustered tables have in common. The cluster key value is stored only once in the schema, thereby reducing the storage requirements and overhead processing.

A cluster index must be explicitly created on the cluster key columns. This index is used to locate specific rows of data.

The following example executes the create cluster command to create a cluster named emp_dept. This cluster will hold tables that are clustered by the deptno column:

```
create cluster emp_dept (deptno number(5))
pctused 80
pctfree 5;
```

Tables are added to the cluster by adding the cluster clause in the create table command. For example, the following creates two tables, EMP and DEPT, in the emp_dept cluster:

```
create table emp (
empno          number (15),          primary key,
first_name     varchar2(20)           not null,
last_name      varchar2(40)           not null,
deptno         varchar2(12),
hire_date      date,                  not null)
```

```
pctfree 20
pctused 40
tablespace emp_01
storage ( initial 50k
next 50k
maxextents 15
pctincrease 25);
```

The following SQL statement creates the cluster index needed for the cluster emp_dept:

```
create index i_emp_dept
on cluster emp_dept;
```

To create a cluster in your schema, you must have the create cluster system privileges. To create a cluster in someone else's schema, you must have the create any cluster system privileges.

Dropping Table Clusters

To drop a cluster from the database, you issue the drop cluster command:

```
drop cluster emp_dept;
```

A cluster cannot be dropped if it has tables in it, so you should include the including tables optional clause in your drop cluster command. Furthermore, you should include the cascade constraints optional clause to drop all referential integrity constraints outside the cluster that refer to keys in the clustered tables.

The following script will drop the cluster emp_dept, the clustered tables EMP and DEPT, and any integrity constraints found outside the cluster:

```
drop cluster emp_dept
including tables cascade constraints;
```

You can drop a cluster in your schema. To drop a cluster outside your schema you must have the drop any cluster system privileges. A schema is the collection of tables, views, and privileges that make up your database.

Altering Tables

Oracle enables you to modify any existing table. You might need to alter the table for any of the following reasons:

- To add one or more columns to a table
- To add or drop constraints associated with a table
- To modify the pctused or pctfree parameters
- To modify an existing column definition, such as the datatype or length

When altering the column definition of a table, the table must be empty for you to do the following:

- Decrease the length of a column
- Change the datatype of a column

Increasing the length of a column with datatype char can be very time-consuming. This is because the char datatype causes Oracle to pad with blanks each row of the table for the altered column.

To alter an existing table, use the alter table command. The following code adds a new column to the table DEPT:

```
alter table  dept
add (dept_mgr varchar2(35));
```

The next example modifies table EMP, indicating that the salary field must be entered:

```
alter table  emp
modify (sal not null);
```

This example modifies table EMP by adding a foreign key constraint:

```
alter table  emp
add constraint s_dept_man_id_fk foreign key (deptno) references dept;
```

This final example removes a constraint from table DEPT:

```
change dept to emp
alter table  dept
drop constraint s_dept_man_id_fk;
alter table emp
```

To alter a table, the table must exist in your schema, or you must have either the alter privilege for the table or the alter any table system privilege.

Dropping Tables

You can use the drop table command to remove a table and all its data from the database. For example, the following command drops the table DEPT:

```
drop table dept;
```

To drop a table, the table must exist in your schema or you must have the drop any table system privilege.

Dropping a table has the following effects:

- The table definition is removed from the data dictionary, making the table and its data inaccessible. This effectively deletes the rows of the table.
- All indexes and triggers associated with the table are dropped, whether they were created by you or another user.

- Views and synonyms that refer to the table are not dropped but become invalid.
- All blocks that were allocated for the table are returned to the tablespace as free space and can be used by any other object requiring new extents.

Truncating Tables

An efficient way to delete all rows from a table is to use the `truncate table` command. This command deletes all records from the table and frees up the allocated space that was being used to hold the deleted records.

The `truncate table` command is more efficient and quicker than the `delete from` command. Users usually encounter two problems when they attempt to delete large volumes of records with the `delete from` command. First, they might receive an error stating that their rollback segment is too small. This is a misleading error because the rollback segment is usually sized correctly, but the attempted transaction is too large. Second, the table object retains its allocated space when the `delete from` command is completed. Oracle does not free up the space when the command is completed. Hence, you gain back zero bytes of space.

The `truncate table` command solves both of these issues. It does not use the rollback segment during its execution. Therefore, it is quicker and you don't have the space limitations of the segment. Using `truncate table` frees up the tablespace immediately upon execution.

The `truncate table` command cannot be rolled back. Care must be exercised when using this command in your application. To use the `truncate table` or `truncate cluster` command, the table or cluster must reside in your schema or you must have the `delete any table` system privilege.

The following is an example of the `truncate table` command being used to delete all the records in the DEPT table:

```
truncate table dept;
```

Essential Summary

This chapter introduced you to tables, which are the most fundamental logical storage structures in the Oracle relational database. Tables can be viewed as two-dimensional arrays that contain a predetermined number of columns and multiple rows. **What**

The use of tables is essential to the use of the Oracle relational database. Tables provide a simplistic logical structure that is easily visualized and flexible to meet your database needs. Tables provide a means to reduce data storage space requirements. **Why**

This chapter walked you through the necessary steps to create and alter tables. With the `create table` command, you can fine-tune space storage as well as establish various constraints. **How**

Synonyms

Synonyms are an important feature of the Oracle relational database; they provide a convenient and secure way to access database objects.

What Is a Synonym?

What A synonym is an alias for an Oracle object. The synonym is not an actual Oracle object, but rather it is a direct reference to an object. This object can be a table, view, snapshot, sequence, procedure, function, package, or another synonym. The only restriction regarding the object is that it cannot be contained inside a procedure. Synonyms are created to point (using the exact address) to these objects, so that users need to know only the synonym's name. Users are shielded from having to know the object's owner, name, and server name of the object.

Why Use Synonyms?

Why

Synonyms provide many benefits, including the following:

- Requiring no storage other than their definition on the data dictionary
- Simplifying SQL coding
- Improving database security
- Providing public access to an Oracle object

Synonyms are also very useful in the database environment because they hide the identity of the objects being referenced. This is advantageous because if the underlying object is renamed or moved, only the synonym needs to be redefined. This enables the application using the synonym to continue without modification or recompilation.

Synonyms are used to improve database security by masking the underlying object's actual name, owner, and location. This holds true for distributed databases where an object can be referred to on a remote database.

Private and public synonyms can be created. Private synonyms are available to a specific user. Privileges to the synonym are explicitly granted to the user. Public synonyms are owned by the public user group and are shared by all users in the database.

How to Use Synonyms

How

Use the SQL command `create synonym` to create a synonym. The following example creates a public synonym named emp for the table EMPLY in the schema emp_01:

```
create public synonym emp FOR emp_01.emply;
```

To create a private synonym for table EMPLY in the schema emp_01, your SQL statement would be as follows:

```
create synonym emp for emp_01.emply;
```

The following example creates a synonym part that references the part_number in the table MASTER_PART, which is located in the remote database corp:

```
create synonym part FOR master_part.part_number@corp;
```

You must have `create synonym` system privileges to create a private synonym in your schema, or `create any synonym` system privileges to create a private synonym in another user's schema. To create a public synonym, you must have `create public synonym` system privileges. Synonym names must be unique within the schema. You can give the synonym the same name as the base table that it references.

Referencing Synonyms

You reference a synonym in a SQL statement the same way that you reference the underlying object. The following two code examples illustrate the use of synonyms in SQL code.

Not using synonyms in the SQL statement:

```
select * from emp_01.emply;
```

Using synonyms in the SQL statement:

```
select * from emp;
```

A synonym can be used to stand for its underlying object in any of the following Data Manipulation Language statements:

- `select`
- `insert`
- `update`
- `delete`
- `explain plan`
- `lock table`

Synonyms can also be used in the following Data Dictionary Language statements:

- `grant`
- `comment`
- `revoke`
- `audit`
- `noaudit`

You can use any private synonym that is in your schema or any public synonym for which you have the correct privileges to access the underlying object. This access can be explicitly granted from an enabled role, or from public. You can also reference any private synonym contained in another schema if you have been granted privileges for the synonym. The following code creates the synonym emp and grants `select` privileges on table EMP to USER_01:

```
create public synonym emp for emp_01.emply;
```

```
grant select on emp to USER_01;
```

USER_01 can now perform a `select` on the object by referencing the synonym emp or by using the full table name emp_01.emply.

A private synonym name must be unique from all other objects in its schema. The Oracle server will attempt to resolve references to an object at the schema level before resolving them at the public synonym level. If the synonym's referenced object is not prefaced with the schema name or not followed by a database link, Oracle assumes the synonym to be public. The following examples illustrate the Oracle server resolving synonym references.

In this example, schemas corp and division contain a table named DEPT. A public synonym named dept references corp.dept. If the user division issues the following SQL statement, Oracle returns rows from division.dept:

```
select * from dept;
```

For division to access the corp.dept table, the following SQL statement would need to be issued:

```
select * from corp.dept;
```

Any user whose schema does not contain the object DEPT would take advantage of the public synonym dept with the following SQL:

```
select * from dept;
```

This would return rows from the corp.dept table.

Synonyms for Packages and Procedures

You can create synonyms for stand-alone Oracle packages and procedures to mask the name and owner of the package or procedure as well as to provide location masking for remotely stored packages and procedures.

When a privileged user needs to execute a procedure, an associated synonym can be used. Because the procedures defined within a package are not individual objects, synonyms cannot be created for individual procedures within a package.

Dropping a Synonym

To remove a synonym from the database and its data dictionary, use the drop synonym command. You use the public keyword to drop a public synonym. The following example drops the private synonym emp:

```
drop synonym emp;
```

The following SQL statement drops the public synonym dept:

```
drop public synonym dept;
```

Any reference to a dropped synonym becomes invalid. For example, if a procedure used the dropped synonym dept, the procedure would stop working because it would not understand the word dept. Synonyms that reference tables are not dropped when their associated tables are dropped. Synonyms that reference a dropped table simply become invalid.

Renaming a Synonym

You can rename a private synonym of a table by using the `rename` command. The following example renames the dept synonym to the bus_unit synonym:

```
rename dept TO bus_unit;
```

All grants and indexes belonging to the old synonym are transferred to the new synonym.

Essential Summary

This chapter introduced you to synonyms, which provide an efficient and secure way to reference Oracle objects. Synonyms are aliases to objects like tables, views, snapshots, functions, and packages. **What**

Synonyms are used to simplify SQL coding and improve database security. This is achieved by masking the underlying object's real name, owner, and location from the user. The user needs to know only the synonym's name and none of the specific information about the referenced object. **Why**

This chapter taught you how to create, use, and delete both private and public synonyms. You saw how to create the synonym so that it referenced the correct database object in both your own schema and a remote database. **How**

Indexes and Sequences

Indexes and sequences are two database schema objects that assist you in quickly and uniquely accessing specific data.

What Are Indexes and Sequences?

What The Oracle server uses rowid to find exactly where the row is physically located in the database. An *index* is a database structure that is used by the server to find a row in a table quickly. The index is composed of a key value (the column in a row) and the rowid.

A *sequence* is a sequential list of numbers that is generated by the Oracle server. Oracle provides a sequence number generator that is used for automatically generating unique primary keys for your data.

Why Use Indexes and Sequences?

Why

Indexes are used in Oracle to improve the performance of your queries. Indexes provide a faster access route to table data. Properly used, indexes are the primary means of reducing disk I/O.

To illustrate a practical use of indexes, look at an everyday use of indexes, such as this book. It has an index that assists you in quickly finding the information you are searching for. It gives you the exact location of the information through the use of a page number. Without this index, you might conceivably have to search through each page of the book to find what you are looking for. Clearly, indexing an important column will speed up Oracle's response to a query.

The Oracle Server generates unique sequence numbers that can be used as primary keys. This is beneficial because the sequence numbers are automatically generated and can be used to coordinate keys across multiple tables.

Without the Oracle sequences, sequential numbers would have to be generated in your application. A primary key can be created by selecting the most recently produced sequential value. Additionally, creating sequential primary keys programmatically causes a lock to be placed on the table that contains the sequential numbers. This method requires other database users to wait their turn to obtain the next value of the primary key. Oracle sequences eliminate this locking and improve the concurrence of your application.

How to Use Indexes

Indexes are created on one or more columns of a table. Once created, an index is automatically maintained by the Oracle server. Changes to table data are automatically incorporated into all relevant indexes, with complete transparency to the users.

Indexes are physically and logically independent of the table's data. They can be dropped and created any time with no effect on the tables or other indexes. If an index is dropped, all applications continue to function; however, access to previously indexed data might now be slower.

You can create an unlimited number of indexes on a table. However, you should consider your application requirements and performance considerations in determining which columns should be indexed. The more indexes there are on a table, the more overhead that is incurred every time the table is altered. Specifically, when rows are inserted or deleted, all indexes on the table must be updated as well. Additionally, when a column is updated, all indexes on that column must be updated.

Creating Indexes

It is better to create an index on a table's column after it is populated with data. Loading data into a table is more efficient with no indexes. The only exception to this rule is if you are loading data into a cluster—then your index should be created prior to data loading.

You should keep in mind the following general guidelines when creating an index on a table:

- Index a column only if you frequently want to retrieve less than 15 percent of the rows in a large table. This percentage varies depending on the table-scan speed and how clustered the data is about the index key. Usually, the faster the table-scan, the lower the percentage should be. The more clustered the row data, the higher the percentage.
- Index columns are used in joins to improve the multiple table join.
- Do not index small tables with few rows.
- Primary and unique keys automatically have indexes, but it is usually a good idea to create an index on any foreign keys also.

The data in the columns usually determines if you should create an index on a column or not. If the column data contains many nulls and you frequently search for these nulls, do not create an index on this column. Likewise, if the column contains very similar data, don't create an index on that column. However, if your column contains relatively unique values or a wide range of values, indexing is appropriate for this column.

A table can have an almost unlimited number of indexes. However, the more indexes a table has, the more overhead is incurred as the table is altered. For example, when an insert is executed on a table, all the indexes have to be updated. This degrades server performance.

There is a balance or a trade-off between query access speed and the speed of an update or insert on a table. If a table is usually read-only, having more indexes is helpful, but if a table is heavily updated, having fewer indexes is helpful.

The following example creates a unique index on the phone column in the EMP table:

```
create unique index i_emp_phone_uk on emp(phone);
```

You can also create a composite index for multiple columns. The following example creates a composite index on the city and ZIP code columns in the table EMP:

```
create index i_emp_city_zip
on emp (city, zip);
```

In a composite index you place the most selective column first. You can have up to 16 columns in a composite index; these columns can appear in any order and need not be adjacent in the table.

To create an index, you must own the corresponding table or have the `index object` privilege for it. Additionally, the schema that contains the index must also have a quota for the tablespace intended to contain the index or have the `unlimited tablespace` system privilege.

Indexes can be unique or non-unique. Unique indexes guarantee that no two rows of a table have duplicate values in the columns that define the index. Non-unique indexes do not impose this restriction on the column values. Because uniqueness is purely a logical concept, it should be part of the column's definition. Oracle enforces unique integrity constraints by automatically creating a unique index on the unique key. Oracle also creates a unique index for the primary key column.

When creating an index, you have the option to specify values on the following parameters. If no value is provided in the create index statement, then the default will be assumed for each.

- `tablespace`—Indexes may be created in any `tablespace`. It does not have to be the same `tablespace` as the table it indexes. Using a different `tablespace` for a table and its index produces better performance due to a reduction in disk contention. Using the same `tablespace` makes it more convenient for the maintenance of the two objects. For example, table backups are easier to perform when the two objects are on the same `tablespace`.

- `cluster`—Provides the name of the cluster key that is indexed for a cluster. `Clusters` have their keys indexed for their associated tables to be accessed.

- `pctfree`—When the table index is created, data blocks of the index are filled with the existing values in the table up to the `pctfree` limit. The area reserved by `pctfree` will not be used for indexes. If no more space is available in the appropriate index block, the indexed value is placed in another index block. Therefore, if you plan on inserting many rows into an indexed table, `pctfree` should be set high to accommodate the new index values. If the indexed table is relatively static, a lower `pctfree` value is appropriate so fewer blocks are required to hold the index data.

- `initrans`—This defines how much space can be initially allocated for transaction entries in the data blocks of an indexed segment.

- `maxtrans`—This defines the maximum amount of space ever to be allocated for transaction entries in the data blocks of an indexed segment.

- `storage`—This explicitly sets your storage parameters. It is better to have fewer but larger extents rather than many smaller extents.

Dropping an Index

You might need to drop an index for a variety of reasons, including the following:

- The index is no longer needed
- Applications do not use queries that use the index
- Performance is not improved by the index, so you can remove the overhead by dropping the index
- The index becomes too fragmented, so it must be dropped prior to being rebuilt

The following example drops the index i_emp_city_zip:

```
drop index i_emp_city_zip;
```

When an index is dropped, all extents of the index segment are returned to the containing `tablespace` and become available for other objects in the `tablespace`. Indexes are automatically dropped if the associated table is dropped.

To drop an index, the index must be in your schema or you must have the `drop any index` system privilege.

Clustered Indexes

Once clustered tables are created in your database, a cluster index must be created prior to any inserts executed. The use of clusters does not affect the creation of additional indexes on the clustered tables; they can be created and dropped as usual.

The following statement creates a cluster index for the dept_div cluster:

```
create index dept_div_index
on cluster dept_div
initrans 2
maxtrans 255
tablespace user_01
storage (
initial 50k
next 50k
minextents 5
maxextents 25
pctincrease 20)
pctfree 20;
```

To create a cluster index, one of the following must be true:

- The cluster must be in your schema and you have the create index system privilege
- You have the create any index system privilege

In either case, you must have sufficient space in your tablespace or you have the unlimited tablespace system privilege.

To alter a cluster index, you use the alter index command. The following statement increases the storage parameters for the cluster index dept_div_index:

```
alter index dept_div_index
storage (pctincrease 25)
```

A clustered index may be dropped without affecting the cluster or its clustered tables. However, the clustered tables may not be used without a clustered index. Therefore, you normally would not drop a clustered index unless you planned to rebuild it or you plan to drop the entire cluster.

How to Use Sequences

Sequences are created to simplify programming tasks by creating a sequential list of numbers that programmers can draw upon for generating primary key values. Sequence numbers are Oracle integers of up to 38 digits.

Creating a Sequence

To create a sequence in your own schema, use the create sequence command:

```
create sequence s_empno
increment by 1
```

```
start with 1
nomaxvalue
nocycle
cache 15;
```

The preceding example creates a sequence named s_empno. The sequential list of numbers starts with the value 1 and is incremented by 1 for each successive number. There is no maximum value for this sequence, so the sequence will not cycle over and begin from its initial value. Finally, the Oracle server pregenerates up to 15 sequence values in memory for faster performance.

When the cache parameter is used, the sequences specified by this command are created directly in cache memory. Once these sequences are used from cache, the next set of sequence numbers will be generated in memory. Choosing a high value for the cache enables you to access more sequence numbers with fewer I/O reads from disk.

You can confirm the existence of sequences by selecting from the data dictionary table user sequences. The following example displays the name and description of all sequences that exist in the user's schema:

```
select sequence_name, min_value, max_value
increment_by, last_number
from user_sequences:
```

The output will appear as follows:

sequence_name	min_value	max_value	increment_by	last_number
S_EMPNO	1	999999	1	389
S_DEPTNO	1	999999	1	24

Altering Sequences

You can alter any of the parameters specified in the create sequence command by issuing the alter sequence command:

```
alter sequence s_empno
maxvalue 50000
cache 20
cycle;
```

This example changes the cache value to 20 and now allows the sequence generator to start over when the maxvalue is reached. Whenever you alter a sequence, the changes take effect only for future sequence numbers.

Using Sequences

Once the sequence is defined, it can be used and incremented by many users. Oracle does not wait for a transaction that accesses the sequence number to complete before that sequence can be used by another user.

A sequence is referenced via SQL with the nextval or currval psuedo-columns. The next sequence value is generated with the nextval psuedo-column, whereas the existing value of the sequence is repeated with the currval psuedo-column.

In the following example, the sequence s_empno is used to insert a new row in the EMP table:

```
insert into emp (empno, first_name, last_name)
values (s_empno.nextval, 'thomas','smith');
```

Here is an example to illustrate the use of nextval in an update command:

```
update dept
    set deptno = s_deptno.nextval
    where deptno = 19;
```

Once a new sequence number is generated, it is available only to the session that created it. All other users that use the same sequence will obtain a new and unique sequence value for their own session.

To use the current value of the sequence number in your current session, use the currval psuedo-column. Currval is valid only if nextval has been used in this same session. The following example uses the same sequence value as in the previous example:

```
insert into table dept (deptno,empno)
values (s_deptno.nextval,s_empno.currval);
```

The psuedo-columns nextval and currval can be used in the following situations:

- value clauses on insert statements
- The select list of a select statement
- The set clause of an update command

These psuedo-columns cannot be used in the following situations:

- A select statement that has the distinct clause
- A select statement that has the order by or group by clause
- A select statement that is used in a union, minus, or intersect operator
- A subquery, view query, or snapshot query

To use a sequence, it must exist in your own schema or you must have select object privileges for another sequence.

Dropping a Sequence

To drop a sequence, use the drop sequence SQL command. For example, the following line drops the sequence s_empno:

```
drop  sequence s_empno;
```

You can drop a sequence in your schema or you need the drop any sequence system privilege.

Essential Summary

What

This chapter introduced you to the database objects index and sequence. An index uses the rowid to find the physical row that is queried. A sequence is a sequential list of unique numbers that are used to automatically generate primary key values.

Why

The index and sequence structures are used to simplify programming efforts and to improve database performance. An index provides the fastest route to the physical location of your data. A sequence is generated to provide a primary key value for each row.

How

This chapter illustrated the steps necessary to create an index on a table to improve server performance.

The chapter also provided some guidelines on when to create table indexes. Steps were also given for how to generate and use sequences. Examples were given to show how you can use sequences to keep integrity between multiple tables.

Views

Views are logical tables that provide a window into one or more tables or views.

What Is a View?

What A view appears to be a table containing columns and rows that can be updated, inserted into, or deleted from just like a table. A view is actually a logical table that does not store data. It derives its data from the tables or views on which it is based. All operations performed on a view actually affect the base tables of the view.

A view is defined using a query and can thus be thought of as a virtual table or a stored query. Because views look and act like tables, they can be used in most places like a table.

Views are dynamic and always display current table information. Views are not like Oracle snapshots that present a picture of data from the past. As the base tables of the view are manipulated, these changes are instantly reflected in the view.

Why Use Views?

Views enable you to present data in a different representation than that which is stored in the tables. Views enable you to tailor the presentation of data to different kinds of users who might have different data needs.

Views are often created for the following reasons:

- To provide an additional level of database security by restricting access to a predetermined set of rows and columns of a table. This enables users to see a restricted subset of data.
- To simplify data presentation to the users by hiding underlying joins and table structures.
- To present the data in a different representation than that of the base tables.

Figure 8.1 shows a view that joins two tables to make one virtual table for the user to access.

Figure 8.1.
Creating a view from two tables.

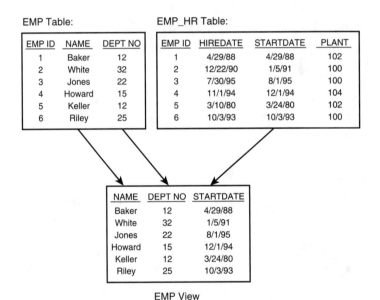

EMP View

Views can also make programming easier by having a virtual table available to query against as opposed to querying each of the underlying tables.

How to Use Views

A view can be thought of as a mirror image of an existing table or another view. Views act very similar to tables. For example, like tables, you can have up to 254 columns in a view. Views can be queried, updated, and inserted into. All operations performed on a view actually affect the underlying, or base, tables of the view. Additionally, views are subject to the integrity constraints and triggers of the base tables.

Creating Views

Use the SQL command create view to create a view. You can define a view with any query that references tables, snapshots, or other views. The definition of the view is stored in the data dictionary.

The following example creates a simple view named emp_view:

```
CREATE VIEW emp_view AS
SELECT empno, f_name, l_name, deptno
FROM emp
WHERE deptno = 12
WITH CHECK OPTION CONSTRAINT emp_cnst;
```

The view emp_view will reference rows only where deptno is 12. with check option creates the view with the constraint that insert and update statements issued against the view are not allowed to create or result in rows that the view cannot select. In the preceding example, only rows with a deptno equal to 12 can be inserted into the view.

The following code creates a more complex view that joins data from multiple tables:

```
CREATE VIEW emp_dept_name as
SELECT f_name, l_name, empno, dept.deptno
FROM emp, dept
WHERE emp.deptno = dept.deptno;
```

The create view command includes the following restrictions:

- with check option is not specified in this example because rows cannot be inserted into or updated in a view defined with a query that contains a join.
- You cannot use the order by or for update clauses.

When a view is created that uses a wildcard value (*) in its top level query, Oracle expands the query to include the actual column names when the view is stored in the data dictionary. For example, the following will create a view emp:

```
CREATE VIEW emp AS SELECT * FROM corp.emp;
```

Oracle stores the defining query in the data dictionary as follows:

```
SELECT "EMPNO","F_NAME","L_NAME","DEPTNO";
FROM CORP.EMP;
```

Quotation marks are placed around the column names to account for the possibility that the base object column names were originally entered with quotes.

Oracle gives you the flexibility to create a view of tables even if the tables don't exist. `create view force` will force Oracle to create the view even if the tables don't exist or the user doesn't have privileges on the table. Oracle will create the view under these circumstances, but the user will not be able to use the view. The view will become valid and accessible by users once the base tables are created, privileges created and the view recompiled. The `create view noforce` will create the view only if the base tables exist and the user has privileges on these tables.

View Privileges

To create a view in your schema, you must have the `create view` system privilege. The `create any view` system privilege is required to create a view in another user's schema. These privileges can be acquired explicitly or via a role.

The owner of the view must be explicitly granted the necessary privileges to access all objects referenced by the view. The owner cannot obtain these privileges through a role. Likewise, you can use the view only in a manner that is consistent with the privileges granted to the owner. For example, if the view owner is granted only the `update` privilege for the EMP table, you can use this view only to update the rows in the EMP table.

Replacing Views

To change the definition of a view, the view must be replaced. Views can be replaced in two ways:

- The view can be dropped and then re-created with the new definition. When the view is dropped, all grants and privileges are revoked. These grants and privileges need to be re-created for the new view.
- The view can be re-created by redefining it with the `create view` statement with the `or replace` optional clause. This method is used to replace the current definition of a view but also preserves all current grants and privileges.

The following example replaces the view emp with a new definition for the view:

```
CREATE or replace view emp_dept_name as
SELECT f_name, l_name, empno, dept.deptno
FROM emp, dept
WHERE emp.deptno = 15;
```

Replacing views has the following effects:

- The view definition in the data dictionary is updated. All underlying objects remain unaffected by the view replacement.

- Any constraints that were in the original view definition but not in the new view definition are dropped.

- All views and PL/SQL programs that are dependent on the replaced view become invalid.

To replace a view, you must have the system privileges to drop and create a view.

Using Views

Views should be treated in the same manner as tables in your SQL statements. For example, the following will query the view emp_dept_name:

```
Select f_name, l_name, empno from emp_dept_name;
```

The following example inserts a new record into the EMP table using the emp_dept_name view:

```
Insert into emp_dept_name
values ('Thomas','Baker',281);
```

You can use a view anywhere you would use a table in any of the following SQL statements:

- select
- insert
- update
- comment
- lock table

There are a few restrictions when using a view. They are as follows:

- You cannot use a view to perform insert, update, or delete operations when the view's query contains a join operation, set or distinct operators, a group by clause, or a group function.

- You cannot use a view to insert or update rows of the underlying tables if the view is defined with the with check option clause.

- A row cannot be inserted into the base table using a view if a not null column is defined without a default value clause.

- Rows cannot be inserted into tables using a view if the view was created using the decode expression.

- A view's query cannot reference the nextval or currval psuedo-columns.

The disadvantage of using a view is that it adds one more processing level when a user is querying or manipulating data. The use of views requires additional processing time before the data is retrieved, thereby slightly reducing the Oracle server response time.

Recompiling Views

Use the `alter view` *viewname* `compile` command to explicitly recompile a view. Recompilation will discover any errors with the view prior to executing the view in a production runtime environment. You might want to recompile the view explicitly after any modification to any of the view's base tables. The following will recompile the emp_dept view:

```
ALTER VIEW EMP_DEPT_NAME COMPILE;
```

The `alter view` command does not change the view's definition or any other object that might depend on it. You can recompile any view in your schema, or you must have the `alter any table` system privilege to recompile a view in another schema.

Dropping Views

To drop a view, use the `drop view` command. The following example drops the emp_dept_name view from the database:

```
DROP VIEW emp_dept_name;
```

You can drop any view in your own schema. You need the `drop any view` system privilege to drop a view in another user's schema.

Essential Summary

What
A view is a logical table that enables you to access data from other tables and views. Views do not contain data. The tables upon which the view is based contain the data and are known as base tables.

Why
Views enable the developer to present information to the user in a way that is different from the base tables but still satisfies the user's data needs. Views also improve database security by masking the actual names and locations of the base tables.

How
Accessing and manipulating data through a view is very similar to working with tables. You can perform `selects`, `inserts`, `deletes`, and `updates` with views in the same way you would with tables, as long as the view references only one table.

Snapshots

What Is a Snapshot?

What A snapshot is a table that contains the results of a query of one or more tables, called master tables, or views that are typically located on a remote node. In essence, it is a local copy of a remote database. One feature of the snapshot is that it is a static picture of data, hence the name snapshot.

A snapshot is a read-only table. No updates can occur on the snapshot; only the master tables can be updated. Once the data is captured in the snapshot, it will remain unchanged until it is refreshed by the snapshot refresh cycle. This means that the master tables may change and the snapshot not reflect the modifications until the refresh occurs.

Internal to the Oracle server, a snapshot is a collection of schema objects. To the users, these objects work together and give the appearance that only one object is present—the snapshot table. The objects created during a snapshot creation include the following:

- On the remote node, a base table is created to hold the results of the snapshot query
- A read-only view is created on this base table to be used when queries are issued against the base tables

■ On the local node, a view is created on the master tables for the periodic snapshot refresh process

Why Use Snapshots?

Why

Data is commonly replicated on the local database for data that is accessed frequently from remote nodes. By having this local copy of data, called a snapshot, the distributed database does not have to send data across the network repeatedly, thus reducing network traffic and improving application performance. Additionally, the snapshot protects you against the loss of access to the remote database by always providing a local copy of the data. For example, if you were replicating data with the select command, you would be out of luck if the network failed to the source database. A local snapshot of the data, however, provides you the opportunity to carry on with your work regardless of the status of the network.

Snapshots provide the most benefit under the following circumstances:

■ When the master tables are rarely updated but accessed heavily
■ When the master tables are accessed by many remote users

The application developer and the database administrator must work together to create the right snapshots. There is a cost to having snapshots. For each master table-to-snapshot association, the Oracle server incurs additional overhead processing to maintain the periodic snapshot refreshes. Also, there are extra storage requirements to hold the snapshot. Unnecessary use of snapshots degrades the server and application performance. However, correct use of snapshots benefits the server and application.

How to Use a Snapshot

How

Taking advantage of the power of snapshots in Oracle involves the creation of the snapshot, using the snapshot, refreshing the snapshot, and establishing the correct privileges.

Two types of snapshots are differentiated by the complexity of the snapshot's defining query: simple snapshots and complex snapshots. The simple snapshot queries only one table, but the complex snapshot can query multiple tables and views.

Preparing for a Snapshot

During database creation, a series of SQL scripts is run that sets up the environment necessary to use snapshots. These scripts are run by default during database creation for databases with the procedural option.

For those databases not running the procedural option, you need to run the following scripts:

■ catsnap.sql
■ dbmssnap.sql

These scripts need to be executed on both the database that holds the master tables and the database that holds the snapshot.

Creating a Snapshot

To create a snapshot, use the `create snapshot` command. The following command creates a snapshot named UK_emp to represent the employees located in the United Kingdom offices. This command establishes the storage parameters for the snapshot, the snapshot refresh rate, and the query that defines the snapshot content.

```
create snapshot UK_emp
pctfree 15
pctused 55
tablespace user_01
storage (initial 50K
next 50k
pctincrease 10)
refresh fast
start with sysdate
next sysdate + 1
as select * from emp@uk
```

Whenever a snapshot is created, it is immediately populated with the results of the query that define the snapshot. This snapshot is a static picture of data until it is refreshed at the specified refresh interval.

Snapshots are created in the user's schema. The name of the snapshot must be unique with respect to the other objects in the schema. To create a snapshot, you must have the `create snapshot`, `create table`, and `create view` system privileges.

You also need `select` privileges on the master tables.

When creating the snapshot, your `create snapshot` command contains a defining query statement. This statement can be any valid query on a table, view, or other snapshot. With a simple snapshot, each of its rows are based on a single remote table. Therefore, the simple snapshot cannot contain any of the following SQL constructs:

- The `group by` clause
- The `connect by` clause
- Subqueries
- Joins
- Set operators

A complex query is one in which the snapshot query contains one or more of the constructs not allowed in the query of a simple snapshot.

Simple snapshots, when compared to complex snapshots, tend to be more efficient when refreshes occur but might be slower during query execution. The complex snapshot is usually more efficient during the query execution but not as efficient as the simple snapshot during its refresh execution.

Setting Storage Parameters

The storage of the snapshot must be determined to ensure proper space availability for the snapshot. In general, the snapshot storage requirements are very similar to the master table's storage requirements. If the snapshot does not include all the columns of its master table, modify the snapshot storage requirements accordingly.

The complex snapshot storage requirements should be the same as the master table's storage requirements. The only difference is that the complex snapshot's pctfree should be set to 0, and the pctused should be set to 100 to obtain maximum efficiency during the complete refresh.

Using a Snapshot

Snapshots are accessed just like tables and views. For example, the following statement queries the snapshot dept:

```
select deptno, dept_name from dept;
```

The snapshot is a read-only object; therefore, you cannot issue the update, insert, or delete statements on a snapshot. Be aware that the base tables of a snapshot can be altered on a continuous basis. A new copy of these updated tables is not captured in your snapshot until a refresh occurs.

You can define a view or a synonym that is based on a snapshot. The following creates the synonym emp based on the snapshot UK_emp:

```
create synonym emp for UK_emp;
```

Snapshot Logs

Snapshot logs are used to decrease the amount of processing and time needed to perform a refresh on a simple snapshot. The use of snapshot logs is reserved for simple snapshots only.

The snapshot log is a table that is associated with the snapshot's master table. This table tracks changes to the master table data. Oracle adds rows into the snapshot log table that describe the changes to the master table. Later, when a refresh occurs, Oracle uses the rows in this table to refresh the snapshot quickly. The process of refreshing the snapshot from the snapshot log is called a fast refresh. Refreshing without the use of the snapshot log means the re-execution of the snapshot's defining query. This is known as a complete refresh.

The snapshot log is located in the same schema as the snapshot's internal master table. You can create only one snapshot log for a master table. Therefore, if you have several simple snapshots querying the same table, all these snapshots would share the same snapshot log.

Snapshot logs are created by using the create snapshot log command. Like the snapshot declaration, you must specify the storage specifications for the log. The following example creates a snapshot log for the UK_emp snapshot:

```
create snapshot log on UK_emp
tablespace emp_o1
storage (initial 20k next 20k pctincrease 25);
```

If you own the master tables, you must have the `create table` and `create trigger` system privileges to create a snapshot log. If you do not own the master tables, you must have the `create any table` and `create any trigger` system privileges.

Space Management for Snapshots

At times the snapshot log will grow very large and will have many extents allocated to it. Purging the log of rows does not reduce the amount of space allocated for the log. You must either purge or drop and re-create the log to reduce the allocated space. Oracle provides a stored procedure in the drop_snapshot package that purges the log. For example, the following command deletes rows from the snapshot log needed to refresh the oldest three (or the three least recent) refreshed snapshots

```
execute dbms_snapshot.purge_log('master_table',3,'DELETE');
```

If you truncate a snapshot log, the first refresh that must be performed is a complete refresh. From then on, fast refreshes can resume.

Any user can purge a snapshot log by executing the purge_log procedure if they have the `delete any table` system privilege.

Indexing a Snapshot

To improve the performance of a query on a snapshot, you can create an index on any of the columns of the snapshot. To create the index, you must use the underlying `snap$...` table created to hold the rows of the snapshot. The following example creates an index on the column deptno in the snapshot UK_emp:

```
create index i_uk_emp on snap$UK_emp (deptno);
```

Refreshing a Snapshot

As defined earlier, a snapshot is a static picture of its master table. The snapshot won't be of much value if the master table changes. In practice, master tables change frequently. That is why the snapshot needs to be updated with fresh data to accurately reflect the master tables. The process of updating the snapshot is called refreshing the snapshot. With the `refresh` clause in the `create snapshot` command, you specify the time and the mode for Oracle to automatically refresh the snapshot.

To allow Oracle to perform the automatic refresh, the following steps must be taken:

1. Specify the `start with` and `next` parameters in the `create snapshot` statement. The `start with` clause establishes the time of the first automatic refresh cycle. The `next` clause defines the interval between automatic refreshes.

2. Oracle evaluates the start with and next parameters and stores this information in the data dictionary. These parameters must evaluate to some time in the future or an error will be generated.

The following example illustrates the statement that creates a simple snapshot. This statement specifies that the snapshot will be refreshed the next day at 9 a.m. and subsequently every Monday at 3 a.m.:

```
create snapshot master_emp
pctfree 15
pctused 25
tablespace user_03
storage (initial 50k next 50k pctincrease 10)
refresh start with round(sysdate + 1) + 9/24
fast next (trunc(sysdate, 'MONDAY') + 3/24
as select * from emp;
```

You can alter the time and mode of the refresh process by using the alter snapshot command. The following example alters the mode of refresh to fast for the snapshot master_part:

```
alter snapshot part_master mode fast;
```

fast and complete are the two refresh modes available. To perform a fast refresh, Oracle uses the entries in the snapshot log to update the snapshot. This is the faster refresh mode. A fast refresh occurs only if the following items are true:

- The snapshot is a simple snapshot
- The master table has a snapshot log
- The snapshot log was created before the snapshot was last refreshed or created

If any of the previous items are false, Oracle does not perform the refresh and returns an error message.

During a complete refresh, Oracle executes the snapshot defining query and places the results in the snapshot. This refresh mode is usually slower than the fast refresh because the entire contents of the master tables are captured, sent over the network, and placed in the snapshot's database.

You can also specify the force option of the refresh statement to allow Oracle to decide how to refresh the snapshot at refresh time. If a fast refresh is possible, Oracle automatically performs the fast refresh. If a fast refresh is not available, Oracle performs the complete refresh.

Dropping a Snapshot

To remove a snapshot from your schema, issue the drop snapshot command like this:

```
drop snapshot UK_emp;
```

If the snapshot is a simple snapshot, all entries in the snapshot log that are needed to refresh the dropped snapshot are purged. Dropping the snapshot commits all pending changes to the snapshot database.

When you drop only the master tables of a snapshot, Oracle does not automatically drop the snapshot based on the tables. Therefore, when Oracle attempts the next refresh, an error will occur because the master tables have been deleted.

You can drop a snapshot in your own schema, or you must possess the `drop any snapshot` system privilege to drop other snapshots.

To drop the snapshot log, issue the `drop snapshot log` command. The following example drops the snapshot log on the `MASTER_EMP` table:

```
drop snapshot log on master_emp;
```

After you drop the snapshot log, Oracle can no longer perform a fast refresh. The snapshot can only be refreshed completely.

To drop a snapshot log in another person's schema, you must have the `drop any table` and `drop any trigger` system privileges.

Essential Summary

You learned that a snapshot is a table that contains the results of a query against one or more other tables. This resultant table holds a static picture of data from the master tables. A snapshot enables you to refresh this data on a repetitive basis.   **What**

Snapshots provide you the benefits of accessing remote data quickly. They also provide you data protection by replicating in your snapshot data that is stored remotely. This security protects you against loss of data when the connecting network fails and goes down.   **Why**

Snapshots are created just like tables, with added parameters specifying storage requirements and data refresh cycle times. Access to the snapshot is much like accessing tables.   **How**

PART III

The Structured Query Language

Structured Query Language (SQL)

What Is Structured Query Language?

What Structured Query Language (SQL) is the standard language for relational database management systems as defined by the American National Standards Institute (ANSI).

SQL is a very simple, yet powerful, nonprocedural language for communicating with the Oracle server. All operations executed within the Oracle database are performed using SQL statements.

SQL provides a comprehensive set of commands for a variety of tasks, including the following:

- Querying data
- Updating, inserting, and deleting data
- Creating, modifying, and deleting database objects
- Controlling access to the database
- Providing for data integrity and consistency

The SQL statement is a simple set of instructions to the Oracle server to perform an action. This statement contains reserved words and has a specific syntax. A partially constructed SQL statement cannot be executed. Oracle returns an error when this is attempted.

Oracle SQL statements are divided into the following categories:

- Data Manipulation Language (DML) statements

  DML statements query or manipulate existing schema objects. For example, they enable you to insert new rows into a table or view.

- Data Definition Language (DDL) statements

  DDL statements define or alter the structure of the schema objects. For example, DDL statements would be used to create a new table.

- Transaction Control statements

  These statements manage all the changes made by the DML statements. For example, the transaction statements commit data.

- Embedded SQL statements

  Embedded SQL statements incorporate DML, DDL, and transaction control statements within a procedural language program. For example, an embedded SQL statement enables you to create and release cursors.

- System Control statements

  There is only one system control statement. The `alter session` statement is used to kill processes and manage other system parameters.

- Session Control statements

  Session control statements manage properties of a user's session. For example, you would enable and disable roles with the session control statements.

Why Use Structured Query Language?

SQL is a very powerful language that benefits all types of users of the Oracle database. You use SQL to perform all tasks with the Oracle database. The following groups of individuals benefit from SQL:

- Database administrators
- Application developers
- Database security administrators
- End users

SQL is a very flexible language that enables you to accomplish your development efforts. SQL enables you to work with large groups of data rather than restricting you to single rows of data. Additionally, SQL allows for the results of one query to be the input to another query statement.

SQL removes from you the burden of deciding on the correct access method. Oracle uses its own internal optimizer to determine the fastest and best means of accessing data. This simplifies your application and reduces development overhead.

By defining SQL as the sole database access language, Oracle eliminates the potential of security and data compromise. You cannot circumvent the SQL language to access any Oracle database.

How to Use Structured Query Language

SQL is used to create and manipulate all Oracle objects. These objects include tables, views, clusters, snapshots, sequences, synonyms, roles, and tablespaces.

The following sections contain reference information on the basic elements of SQL.

SQL Style and Structure

SQL is the primary means of communicating with the Oracle database. As such, several guiding styles and structures must be understood to improve your communication with the Oracle database, including the following:

- SQL*Plus doesn't care if your commands are typed in upper- or lowercase. Both cases are treated equally except when performing a comparison.

- SQL statements begin with the SQL command, followed by the remainder of the statement. For example, the following SQL statement uses the SQL command `drop table` to remove the table object from the database:

  ```
  drop table emp;
  ```

- When the Oracle server generates an error code, it is in the following structure:

  ```
  error: error_code: error description
  ```

Naming Objects

Many of the Oracle objects are made up of parts that must be named by you when you create the object. For example, table columns or sequences are named during their creation. SQL has predefined rules when naming objects. The following rules apply to object names as well as to database usernames:

1. Names must be between 1 and 30 bytes. Database names are limited to eight bytes; database links can be up to 128 bytes.
2. Names cannot be in quotation marks.
3. Names are not case-sensitive. This means that it doesn't make a difference if a name is in upper- or lowercase letters.

4. Names can contain only alphanumeric characters and the characters _, $, and #. Names of a database link can also contain the characters . and @. The name must begin with an alphabetic character.

5. A name cannot be an Oracle or SQL reserved word.

6. The name must be unique across its namespace. Each of the following bullets represents a single namespace. All the objects listed in a particular bullet are contained in that namespace. This is to say, for example, that a table and view are in the same namespace and therefore cannot be named the same. Tablespaces are in a different namespace than indexes and therefore can have the same name.

   - Tables, views, sequences, snapshots, packages, private synonyms, stand-alone procedures, and functions
   - Indexes
   - Constraints
   - Clusters
   - Database triggers
   - Private database links
   - Public database links
   - Tablespaces
   - Rollback segments
   - Public synonyms
   - Users' roles

7. A name can be enclosed in double quotation marks. Following are a few reasons for using double quotation marks:

   - If the name contains blanks
   - If you want the name to be case-sensitive
   - If you want to begin a name with anything other than an alphabetic character

The name you assign to an object should be descriptive and meaningful. Also, you should use the same column name across all tables to describe the same item.

Referring to Oracle Objects

The general syntax for referencing an object or a part is

```
schema.object_name.object_part_name@database_link
```

The schema is where the object is located. The schema can refer to an object in someone else's database. If you omit this qualifier, Oracle assumes the object is in your own schema.

The object_name is the name of the object being referenced.

The object_part_name enables you to refer to a part of an object, such as a column of a table. This is an optional parameter.

The database_link is the name of the database containing the object. This database is not your database—it is someone else's that you need to access. If this parameter is omitted, Oracle assumes that you are referring to an object in your own database.

In your SQL statement that refers to an Oracle object, Oracle evaluates the context of the SQL statement and locates the object in the correct namespace. If Oracle cannot find the object in the appropriate namespace, Oracle returns an error. Oracle always attempts to locate the object in your schema first before considering namespaces outside your schema. If the object is not in your schema, Oracle searches the namespace containing public synonyms. If the object is not found, Oracle returns an error message.

Parsing SQL

When an application issues a SQL statement, a parsed representation of the SQL statement is loaded in a shared SQL area in the server. Parsing accomplishes the following:

- It checks the SQL statements for syntax and semantic accuracy.
- It determines whether the process issuing the SQL has the privileges to execute it.
- It performs data dictionary lookups to check table and column definitions.
- It establishes object locks on required objects so their definitions don't change during execution.
- It determines the best execution plan to be used when executing the statement.

Parsing occurs only if there is not an identical SQL statement already in the shared SQL area. If a copy is already present in the shared SQL area, Oracle uses the copy in memory instead of parsing the copy of the source code you are attempting to execute. If there is not a copy, Oracle proceeds and parses the statement. Parsing of a statement occurs only once no matter how many times the statement is executed. Oracle re-executes the parsed statement for each subsequent reference to the statement.

The syntax and semantic validation that parsing performs catches only the errors that can be found before statement execution. There are some errors that parsing cannot catch. For example, data conversion errors are not caught until statement execution.

Query Processing

Query processing is somewhat different from other types of SQL statements because queries return data as results if the statement is successful. Non-query statements return either success or failure, but a query returns multiple rows of data. This data is presented to the user in table format.

Queries can become implicit queries in some SQL statements. For example, each of the following statements requires a query as part of its execution:

- `update`
- `delete from`
- `create table as`

SQL Execution

The following list specifies the phases of SQL statement execution:

1. A cursor is automatically created in anticipation of a SQL statement.
2. Oracle parses the SQL statements.
3. If the characteristics of a query's results are not known, Oracle determines the characteristics (datatypes and lengths) of the result's data.
4. The output domains are defined by Oracle. These include the location, size, and datatype of the variables defined to receive each of the fetched values.
5. Oracle binds any variables. This is when Oracle defines the values of each variable. For example, Oracle establishes the value of emp_name during the binding process.
6. Finally, Oracle executes the SQL statements.
7. Rows of data are selected (and ordered if requested), and each successive fetch retrieves another row of the result until all rows have been retrieved.

SQL and SQL*Plus

SQL is the native language of the Oracle server. It is the language used to communicate with the database. ANSI has adopted SQL as the standard language for relational database management systems.

SQL*Plus is an Oracle server tool that recognizes and executes SQL statements. SQL*Plus is not an extension or superset of SQL.

SQL*Plus is one of the most common ways to communicate interactively with the Oracle database. One of the benefits of SQL*Plus is that you can edit or save the SQL commands that are in the SQL buffer.

The SQL buffer is a part of memory managed by SQL*Plus that stores one SQL command at a time. A single SQL command remains in the SQL buffer until a new command is issued.

SQL Arrays

Every time your application passes a SQL statement to Oracle, the application makes a function call. These function calls add to the overhead processing and thus reduce server performance. These function calls can significantly reduce performance if they are made over a network.

Array processing enables your application to execute a single SQL statement many times with only a single Oracle call. For example, with array processing your application can make a single call to execute a SQL statement 50 times. Without array processing, your application would have to issue this single SQL statement 50 times. By reducing the number of Oracle calls, the database processing overhead is reduced, and server performance is improved.

Oracle tools such as SQL*Forms, SQL*Plus, and SQL*Loader use array processing automatically.

SQL Sharing

Oracle detects when two or more applications send identical SQL statements to the server. When Oracle identifies that a duplicate SQL statement has been received, it does not parse the second SQL statement.

Oracle checks the SQL shared pool for identical statements. These statements can come from applications, interactive users, or even recursive SQL.

When duplicate SQL statements are detected, the first occurrence of the SQL statement is shared by all other processes that need it. The use of shared SQL reduces memory usage of the database server, thereby improving server performance.

Essential Summary

Structured Query Language is the exclusive language for communicating with the Oracle database. The language has its own structure and syntax, as shown by this chapter.

What

SQL provides an easy way of interacting with the database. It enables you to work with the higher level schema objects rather than just individual rows. Additionally, SQL limits the avenues through which you can interact with the server, thereby improving server security and reducing the risk of data compromise.

Why

You can communicate interactively with the Oracle database by using SQL. Additionally, your applications use SQL to access the database. Using SQL is simple and easy. There are only a few guiding rules to follow when creating your SQL statements, hence giving more flexibility and power to the statements.

How

SQL Operators and Conditions

What Are Operators and Conditions?

What Operators and conditions are used to perform operations, such as addition or subtraction, or comparisons on the data items in a SQL statement. Operators are represented by single characters or reserved words.

A condition is an expression of several operators or expressions that evaluates to True, False, or Unknown.

There are two types of operators: binary and unary. The unary operator operates on only one operand. For example, to indicate a negative 10, use the unary operator to write –10. The binary operator operates on two operands. For example, to subtract two numbers you would write 6–4.

Why Use Operators and Conditions?

Why Operators and conditions are necessary features of any computer language. They enable you to perform arithmetic, data comparisons, and a variety of other data manipulations that are necessary to support your application requirements.

These Oracle tools can assist you in selecting specific sets of rows. For example, you could request a set of rows where deptno = 15. Then you would receive only the rows where the deptno is equal to 15. In this example, the = operator was used.

How to Use Operators

How Operators are used to manipulate individual data items and return a result. The following sections discuss the different types of operators: arithmetic, character, comparison, logical, set, and other types.

Arithmetic Operators

Arithmetic operators are used in SQL expressions to add, subtract, multiply, divide, and negate data values. The result of this expression is a numeric value. Table 11.1 shows the arithmetic operators.

Table 11.1. The arithmetic operators.

Operator	Description
+, -	Denotes a positive or negative expression. These are unary operators.
*	Multiplies. This is a binary operator.
/	Divides. This is a binary operator.
+	Adds. This is a binary operator.
-	Subtracts. This is a binary operator.

The following is an example that uses the unary operator - in an evaluation expression:

```
select city_name
from weather_city
where avg_temp = - 10;
```

The following example is one that uses the + binary arithmetic operator:

```
update orders
set order_qty = order_qty + 100;
```

Never use a double minus sign (—) in an arithmetic expression to indicate a double negative or the subtraction of a negative number. The — is reserved in Oracle to indicate the beginning of comments. Hence, anything after the — on that line will be treated as a comment.

Character Operators

Character strings are manipulated by character operators. The most common character operator is the concatenation operator ¦¦. In the following example, two character strings are concatenated to form a new character string:

```
select  'Part Number is ' ¦¦ part_nbr from master_parts;
```

Sample output:

```
Part Number is QA910233
```

If both strings have the datatype char, the resulting string is char with a default length of 255 characters. If either string is varchar2, the resulting string is varchar2 with a default length of 200 characters. If one of the strings is null, the resulting string becomes equal to the non-null string. It is recommended that you use the nvl function prior to using a null in a concatenation. The nvl function converts the null expression to a zero-length string.

Comparison Operators

Comparison operators are used to compare one expression to another expression. The result of the comparison is True, False, or Unknown. Table 11.2 lists the comparison operators with their descriptions.

Table 11.2. The comparison operators.

Operator	Description
=	Equality comparison
!=, <>, ^=	Inequality comparison
>	Greater than
<	Less than
>=	Greater than or equal to
<=	Less than or equal to
IN	Equal to any member of
NOT IN	Not equal to any member of
IS NULL	Tests for nulls
IS NOT NULL	Tests for anything other than nulls
LIKE	Returns true when the first expression matches the pattern of the second expression. Because this command uses pattern matching, wildcards (%) are allowed, and it is case-sensitive
ALL	Compares a value to every value in a list
ANY, SOME	Compares a value to each value in a list

continues

Table 11.2. continued

Operator	Description
EXISTS	True if a subquery returns at least one row
BETWEEN x and y	Greater than or equal to x and less than or equal to y

The following are several examples that illustrate the use of comparison operators.

This example returns all rows where the order quantity is greater than 10,000:

```
select * from master_orders where order_qty > 10000;
```

The following example returns the customers' names and phone numbers where the comments field is filled in (not null):

```
select cust_name, cust_phone from master_orders where cust_comments is not null;
```

The next example uses the ANY operator to check the existence of a city name in the guest register. This statement equates to True if any rows are returned.

```
select * from register
where city = any (select city_name from emp);
```

This example checks to see if a specific value is between the ranges supplied in the statement:

```
select emp_id, cur_salary from emp
where cur_salary
between 45000 and 60000;
```

One of the more popular and useful operators is the LIKE operator. In this example, the select statement retrieves all rows where the material_name begins with the letters Coppe:

```
select * from raw_materials
where material_name like 'Coppe%';
```

Logical Operators

A logical operator is used to produce a single result from the combining of two separate conditions. The logical operators are shown in Table 11.3.

Table 11.3. The logical operators.

Operator	Description
AND	Returns True if both component conditions are true; otherwise returns False.
OR	Returns True if either component condition is true or unknown; otherwise returns False.
NOT	Returns True if the following condition is false; otherwise returns false. For example, the condition in the following statement is false, therefore the select statement returns true and is executed.

```
select * from emp Where not (hire_date > 01-JAN-2000) (no one has been hired in the
future yet).
```

The following example uses the logical operator OR to select employees that were hired prior to January 1, 1990 or who are assigned to department 31;

```
select * from master_emp
where hire_date < '01-JAN-1990' or
dept_no = '31';
```

Set Operators

Set operators combine the results of two separate queries into a single result. The set operators are described in Table 11.4.

Table 11.4. The set operators.

Operator	Description
UNION	Returns all distinct rows from both queries
UNION ALL	Returns all rows from both queries, including duplicate rows
INTERSECT	Returns all rows that are selected by both queries
MINUS	Returns all distinct rows that are in the first query but not in the second query

The following statement returns only those rows that exist in both sets of query results. Specifically, only those part numbers that are in the MASTER_PART table and also in the NEW_PART table are returned by this example:

```
select part_nbr from master_part
intersect
select part_nbr from new_part;
```

You can have multiple set operators in a single SQL statement. Oracle evaluates these set operators as having equal precedence and therefore evaluates from left to right.

Operator Precedence

Precedence defines the order that Oracle uses when evaluating different operators in the same expression.

Every operator has a predefined precedence. Oracle evaluates the operators with the highest precedence first before evaluating the operators of lower precedence. Operators of equal precedence are evaluated from left to right.

Table 11.5 lists operators and their descriptions in descending order of precedence.

Part III

Table 11.5. Operators in order of precedence.

Operator	Description
-	SQL*Plus continuation command
&	Parameter prefix
&, &&	Substitution prefix
:	Prefix for host variable
.	Variable separator
( )	Surrounds subqueries
'	Surrounds a literal
"	Surrounds a table or column alias
"	Surrounds literal text
@	Precedes a database name
( )	Overrides normal operator precedence
+, -	Positive and negative signs
*, /	Multiplication and division
+, -	Addition and subtraction
¦¦	Character value concatenation
NOT	Reverses the result of an expression
AND	True if both conditions are true
OR	True if either condition is true
UNION	Returns all data from both queries
INTERSECT	Returns only the rows that match both queries
MINUS	Returns only the rows that do not match both queries

Other Operators

Oracle supports two more operators that do not fall into any of the previous groups. They are the `prior` and the `outer join` operators.

`prior` evaluates an expression for its hierarchy in a `connect by` clause. This operator when used in a `select` statement forces the results of the query to be presented in a hierarchical format with the root being displayed first and its child displayed second. The following example illustrates the hierarchy of an organization chart. The president of the company is the root of the chart and the employees are the children.

```
select substr(lpad(' ',2*(level-1))¦¦ename,1,15) ename, empno, mgr, job
from emp
connect by prior empno = mgr
start with job = 'PRESIDENT';
```

Sample output:

ENAME	EMPNO	MGR	JOB
KING	7839		PRESIDENT
JONES	7566	7839	MANAGER
SCOTT	7788	7566	ANALYST
ADAMS	7876	7788	CLERK
FORD	7902	7566	ANALYST
SMITH	7369	7902	CLERK
BLAKE	7698	7839	MANAGER
ALLEN	7499	7698	SALESMAN
WARD	7521	7698	SALESMAN
MARTIN	7654	7698	SALESMAN
TURNER	7844	7698	SALESMAN
JAMES	7900	7698	CLERK
CLARK	7782	7839	MANAGER
MILLER	7934	7782	CLERK

The outer join operator is represented by the plus sign (+). This operator indicates that the preceding column is the outer join column in a join. Refer to Chapter 14, "Advanced Functions," for a complete description of the outer join.

How to Use Conditions

Conditions are used in evaluation statements. They are used as expressions whose value equates to either true or false. Conditions always return a value of True, False, or Unknown. An example of a very simple condition is

```
deptno = deptno
```

Conditions can have one of several forms, depending on their usage. The following is a series of examples that illustrate the various forms of a condition statement.

Form 1: A comparison of expressions

```
amt1 + amt2 > 1500;
```

Form 2: A condition that combines other operators in a single conditional statement

```
 (deptno=15) OR (city = 'Boston');
```

Form 3: A conditional test for inclusion in a range

```
pts_scored between 15 and 20;
```

Form 4: A test for nulls

```
equip_desc is null;
```

Form 5: A test for membership in a list or subquery

```
select * from master_parts
where not (part_code_class = '35A');
```

Form 6: A test for existence of rows in a subquery

```
select * from dept
where exists
(select dept_no, dept_name from emp
where dept.dept_no = emp_dept_no);
```

Usage of Conditions

Conditions can be used in numerous situations. You can use a condition in the where clause of these statements:

- delete
- update
- select

In the select command, you can use a condition with these clauses:

- where
- having
- start with

Conditions can be used in simplistic statements such as part_1 = part_2. They can also be used in more complex situations where logical operators combine several conditions into a single condition. For example, the following statement uses the OR logical operator to combine two different conditions into one conditional statement:

```
(curr_salary >= max_salary) or (hire_date < '01-JAN-1975');
```

Essential Summary

What
Operators and conditions are used by the Oracle user to perform arithmetic and comparisons of data expressions. The operators have a predefined order of precedence that Oracle follows when evaluating statements.

Why
You use operators and conditions in your interaction with the Oracle database and in applications to perform specific tasks. Operators and conditions are a necessary part of the SQL language that enable you to perform comparisons, some data manipulations, and arithmetic.

How
An operator is a character or reserved word used in a SQL statement to perform a task or operation on the elements of the expression. A condition enables you to combine one or more expressions or logical operators with one of the several condition statement syntaxes.

SQL Commands

What Are SQL Commands?

What SQL commands are the statements needed to communicate with Oracle. They direct the Oracle server to perform a specific task. SQL commands are classified in six categories, as follows:

- Data Definition Language (DDL) commands.

  DDL commands are used to manage schema objects and user privileges.

- Data Manipulation Language (DML) commands.

  DML commands assist the user in accessing and manipulating database data.

- Transaction Control commands.

  These commands manage the DML changes.

- Session Control commands.

  Session Control commands manage the user sessions.

- System Control commands.

  These commands manage the properties of the instance.

- Embedded SQL commands.

These commands are used to place DDL, DML, and transaction commands into procedures.

Why Use SQL Commands?

Why
SQL commands provide a predefined and consistent way to manage and administer the Oracle database. These commands have a specific syntax and semantic that enable the user to communicate with the server. These commands ensure that the server understands your commands. Without these formal statements, chaos would prevail because it would be difficult for the server to know or understand any of your commands.

How to Use SQL Commands

How
SQL commands are broken into six categories. The following sections address each of these six types of SQL commands:

- Data Definition Language commands
- Data Manipulation Language commands
- Transaction Control commands
- Session Control commands
- System Control commands
- Embedded SQL commands

Data Definition Language (DDL) Commands

The DDL commands enable you to do the following:

- Create, alter, and drop schema objects
- Grant and revoke user privileges and roles
- Add comments to the data dictionary
- Establish auditing options

Oracle implicitly commits the current transaction before and after every DDL statement. The DDL commands are not supported by Oracle's PL/SQL. The following is a brief description of the most commonly used DDL statements.

Most of the DDL commands begin with create, alter, or drop. The create commands are used to create new Oracle objects and structures. The alter commands enable you to modify existing objects and structures. The drop commands remove the objects and structures from the database.

create DDL Commands

create cluster

This command creates a cluster that can contain one or more tables that all have at least one column in common. The following example creates the cluster mst_parts with the cluster key column being part_nbr:

```
create cluster mst_parts
(part_nbr varchar2(15))
size 512
storage (initial 500k
next 100k
pctincrease 5);
```

create database

This command creates an Oracle database. The following example creates the simple database named products. During creation, all default settings are assumed for memory and space allocations and log file specifications.

```
create database products;
```

create database link

This command creates a link to a remote database. This example creates a database link named emp_lnk that refers to user1 with password 1A2BVC on the database as specified by the string D:emp_master:

```
create database link emp_lnk
connect to user1 identified by 1A2BVC
using 'D:emp_master';
```

Once this database link is created, you can query tables in the remote database user1. The following is an example of a query on the remote database user1:

```
select *
from emp@emp_lnk;
```

create function

This command creates a stored function. The following example returns the account balance for all rows that have a county equal to Hamilton:

```
create function get_balance (acct_id in number)
return number
is
   acc_balance number (11,2);
begin
   select balance
   into acc_balance
   from sales
   where sales_account = acct_id
   return (acc_balance);
end
```

create index

This command creates an index for a table or cluster. This example creates the index i_part_nbr on the column part_number in the table MASTER_PARTS:

```
create index i_part_nbr on master_parts
➡(part_number);
```

create package	This command creates the specification of a stored package. The following example creates the specification for the mst_part package:

```
create package mst_part as
procedure inv_parts (part_nbr varchar2)
end mst_part;
```

create package body	This command creates the body of a stored package. The create package command must be executed prior to this command being executed.

```
create package body mst_part as

function 1....
function 2.....
procedure 1.....
```

create procedure	This command creates a stand-alone stored procedure. In this example, the procedure named payroll is created and will accept hours, pay , and emp_id as input parameters. The emp table is updated directly via the procedure.

```
create procedure user_01.payroll
(hours in number, pay in number, emp_id in number)
as begin
update master_salary
set weekly_pay = hours * pay
where emp_id = account_id
end;
```

create rollback segment	This command creates a rollback segment to store the data necessary to roll back changes made by a transaction. The segment will be stored in the system tablespace and will have an initial space allocation of 100 with the next allocation of 50KB.

```
create public rollback segment  rbs_mst_parts
tablespace system
storage (initial 100k, next 50k optimal 125k);
```

create role	This command creates a role. A role is a set of privileges that can be granted to users or to other roles. This example creates the role name application_developer and is password protected with the password app_dev.

```
create role application_developer
identified by app_dev;
```

create sequence	This command creates a sequence for generating sequential values. The following statement creates the sequence s_emp_no, which starts at the value 1 and has an incremental value of 10:

```
create sequence s_emp_no increment by 10;
```

create snapshot

This command creates a snapshot of data from one or more base tables. In the following example, the snapshot UK_emp is created to hold a copy of the MASTER_EMP table, which is located in the remote database emp_UK;

```
create snapshot uk_emp
pctfree 15
pctused 40
table_space users_01
storage (initial 50k
next 50k
pctincrease 20)
refresh fast next sysdate + 14
as select * from master_emp@emp_uk;
```

create snapshot log

This command creates a snapshot log for fast refreshes. This log is created for the refreshing of the mst_part master table.

```
create snapshot log on mst_part
tablespace user_01
storage (initial 50k next 50k pctincrease 50);
```

create synonym

This command creates a synonym for a schema object. The following example creates the public synonym part for the table PART_OWNER.MASTER_PARTS:

```
create public synonym part for
part_owner.master_parts;
```

create table

This command creates a table. The table MASTER_PARTS is created with the following statement:

```
create table master_parts
(part_id number primary key,
part_number varchar2(15),
part_desc varchar2(50))
tablespace part_02;
```

create user

This command creates a new database user or an account through which you can log into the database. In this example, the user is named pay_admin and has the initial password of Qk91H36. The statement also establishes the storage parameters for the user.

```
create user pay_admin
identified by QK91H36
default tablespace user_01
temporary tablespace user_02
quota 5M on user_01
quota 5M on user_02
profile administrator;
```

Part III

create view

This command creates a view of one or more tables. The following statement creates the view of all columns in the table MASTER_PARTS where the order quantity is greater than 10,000. This view is named v_mst_part.

```
create view v_mst_part
as select * from master_parts
where order_qty > 10000;
```

alter DDL Commands

alter cluster

Use this command to change the storage allocations or to allocate an extent for a cluster. You cannot change the number of columns in the cluster key, change the tablespace of the cluster, or remove tables from the cluster. The cluster c_emp_mst is modified in the following statement so the pctfree is altered to be 60 percent. All other parameters from the create cluster statement remain unchanged.

```
alter cluster c_emp_mst
pctfree 60;
```

alter function

Use this command to recompile the function. The following statement recompiles the function get_balance:

```
alter function get_balance compile;
```

alter index

This command enables you to alter future storage allocations for the index. For example, the following statement establishes the future data block's incremental size at 50KB:

```
alter index i_part_sales
storage (next 50k);
```

alter package

This command is used to recompile a package. For example, the package specification and body search_part_pkg is recompiled with the following statement:

```
alter package search_part_pkg compile package;
```

alter procedure

This command recompiles a stand-alone stored procedure. The keyword compile is mandatory. This command recompiles the invalid procedure named mst_parts.

```
alter procedure mst_parts
compile;
```

alter role

This command alters the authorization needed to enable a role. In this example, the role application_developer is assigned the new password developer.

```
alter role application_developer
identified by developer;
```

alter rollback segment
This command alters the rollback segment in one of the following ways:

- Brings it on-line or off-line
- Alters its storage characteristics

The following three examples use the three possible clauses for this command:

```
alter rollback segment rbs_mst_parts offline;
```

```
alter rollback segment rbs_mst_parts online;
```

```
alter rollback segment rbs_mst_parts storage;
(maxextents 35)
```

alter sequence
This command enables you to change the characteristics of a sequence. This command enables you to do the following:

- Alter the increment value
- Establish or delete the minimum and maximum values
- Specify whether the sequence numbers need to be ordered
- Change the number of cached sequence numbers

In the following example, the sequence s_empno is altered so the cache size is now 35. All other sequence parameters remain unchanged from the way they were established in the create sequence command.

```
alter sequence s_empno
cache 35;
```

alter snapshot
You can change the storage characteristics or the refresh mode with the alter snapshot command. For example, the following example changes the refresh mode to fast for the snapshot UK_emp. All other snapshot parameters remain unchanged from the way they were created:

```
alter snapshot uk_emp
refresh fast;
```

alter snapshot log
This command changes the storage parameters of the snapshot log. This example redefines the storage parameters for the snapshot log snp_mst_part. All other storage parameters remain unchanged.

```
alter snapshot log on snp_mst_part
storage (maxextents 35);
```

alter table
: The `alter table` command can be used to do the following:

- Add a column
- Redefine a column's datatype, size, or default value
- Add, modify, or drop an integrity constraint
- Modify storage characteristics

The following command adds the column `sales_comments` to the table PART_SALES:

```
alter table part_sales
add (sales_comments varchar2(1000));
```

alter user
: Use this command to change any of the following characteristics of the database user:

- Password
- Default tablespace
- Default role
- Limits of database resources

The following example resets the password for `user_01`:

```
alter user user_01 identified by HI8012JQ;
```

alter view
: This command recompiles views. This action is usually taken when a view's base table has been modified. This does not change the view's definition. The following statement recompiles the view `v_emp`:

```
alter view v_emp compile;
```

drop DDL Commands

The `drop` commands remove objects, integrity constraints, users, and roles from the database. The following is the general syntax for all `drop` commands:

```
drop keyword object_name/command
```

keyword can be replaced with any of the following:

- A cluster
- A database link
- A function
- An index
- A package

- A procedure
- A profile
- A role
- A rollback segment
- A sequence
- A snapshot
- A snapshot log
- A synonym
- A table
- A tablespace
- A trigger
- A user
- A view
- A grant

The following statement removes the table OBSOLETE_PART_NBRS and all of its data from the user's schema:

```
drop table obsolete_part_nbrs;
```

The next command drops the cluster parts and all of its tables and integrity constraints:

```
drop cluster parts
including tables
cascade constraints;
```

Other DDL Commands

audit
: Use this command to choose specific SQL statements for auditing in subsequent user sessions. The following statement enables auditing for any statement that queries or deletes from any table:

```
audit select table, delete table;
```

comment
: Use this command to add comments directly into the data dictionary. The following places a comment about the s_remarks column of the table SALES_ORDERS into the data dictionary:

```
comment on column sales_orders.s_remarks
is 'This field is the sales reps subjective
evaluation
of his current sales territory';
```

grant
: Use this command to grant system privileges and roles to specific users and roles. The following grants create session to the database user user_02:

```
grant create session to user_02;
```

The next statement grants `select` privileges on the table MST_PARTS to user `user_02`:

```
grant select on mst_parts
to user_02;
```

revoke

This command revokes system privileges and roles from users and roles. In the following example, the `update` system privilege is revoked from all users of the table MASTER_EMP:

```
revoke update on master_emp from public;
```

truncate

This command removes all rows from a table or cluster and frees up the space that the rows used. The following statement removes all rows from the DEPT table:

```
truncate table dept;
```

Data Manipulation Language (DML) Commands

The DML commands enable you to manipulate and query data that is in your database. The DML commands do not implicitly commit the current transactions.

The following is the list of DML commands with a brief description and example of each:

delete

This command removes the specified rows from a table or from a view's base tables. For example, all rows with deptno equal to 20 are deleted from table MASTER_DEPT:

```
delete from master_dept
where deptno = '20';
```

insert

Use this command to add new rows to a table or to a view's base tables. The following example adds a new row into the PART_NBR table:

```
insert into prt_nbr
values (s_part_nbr.nextval,'43289821','water pump');
```

select

This command is used to retrieve rows of data from tables, views, or snapshots. The default for the `select` command is to retrieve all rows of the selected object. You can elect to use the `distinct` parameter to return only one copy of each set of duplicate rows. Duplicate rows are rows with matching values in the columns specified in the `select` list. The following example retrieves all rows from the EMP table:

```
select * from emp;
```

Here's an example that uses the `distinct` parameter:

```
select distinct part_name, part_number from
master_parts;
```

In the `select` statement, you can also use the `start with`, `group by`, and `where` clauses. These clauses are defined as follows:

`start with`

This identifies a condition that rows must satisfy in order to be selected first in the hierarchical query. The following query returns all rows from the table MST_PART that have the part_name car or any child row of that car row.

```
select * from mst_part
start with part_name = 'CAR';
```

`group by`

This clause groups the selected rows and summarizes them based on the value of the expression so that only a single row of data is returned for each group. For example, the following summarizes the sales for part_type and returns only one row for each type:

```
select part_type,sum(sales_amt)
from open_orders
group by part_type;
```

The output would be

```
part_type      sales_amt
---------------------------
23-wire          3500
27-wire          8090
2x4x8lmbr        12028
```

`where`

The `where` clause enables you to restrict the rows returned by a query. The following example returns the names of employees who live in the state of Ohio:

```
select emp_name from emp
where emp_state = 'OH';
```

`update`

The `update` command is used to change the existing data values in a table or in a view's base table. The following is an example where the value in table PART_NBR is updated:

```
update part_nbr
set part_desc = '23 wire copper, thin twisted'
where part_nbr = '2812300';
```

Transaction Control Commands

commit
: This command makes permanent any changes made by statements that have been executed since the beginning of this transaction. The following statement makes permanent the recent changes:

```
commit;
```

rollback
: This command undoes all changes since the beginning of the current transaction or since the last savepoint. The following example rolls back all changes since the last savepoint:

```
rollback to savepoint sp_daily;
```

savepoint
: This command creates a point in a transaction to which you can later roll back. For example, the following statement creates the savepoint sp_daily:

```
savepoint sp_daily;
```

Session Control Commands

alter role
: This command alters the authorization required to enable a role. For example, the following statement changes the role password to 93213jd1:

```
alter role identified by 93213jd1;
```

System Control Commands

alter system
: This command is used by the Oracle database administrator to alter the Oracle instance. Because this is a very specialized discipline, no example of this statement is included.

Embedded SQL Commands

close
: This command closes a cursor. Refer to Chapter 16, "Selecting and Maintaining Data," for additional information on cursors.

connect
: This command enables you to log in to an open database.

fetch
: This command retrieves one or many rows of data and assigns them to variables.

open
: This command is used to open a cursor. Refer to Chapter 16 for additional information on cursors.

Chapter 12

Essential Summary

SQL commands are the necessary vocabulary you need to communicate with and direct the Oracle server to meet your business needs.

What

The SQL commands provide a standard and structured format in which to communicate with the database. It is necessary to have this predefined method for communicating for the server to completely understand your every command.

Why

You can issue SQL commands through your application or other Oracle tools, such SQL*Plus. Oracle receives these commands and responds accordingly.

How

Functions

What Are Functions?

What Functions are predefined operations that manipulate data items and return a result. Functions can generate two types of output. One type of output is the input file after manipulation, and the other output type tells you something about the input file. For example, one function can change the characters of a string to all lowercase characters; another function can count the number of characters that are in the input string.

There are two types of functions:

- Single row functions
- Multi-row or group functions

The difference between these two types of functions is the number of rows on which they act. As the name implies, the single row function returns a single result row for each row of a queried table or view. The multi-row or group function returns a single result row for a group of queried rows.

When you create a function, you create a stand-alone Oracle object that resides in your schema. Functions are similar to operators except that functions can operate on multiple arguments.

Why Use Functions?

Functions are created to solve a specific problem or to perform a set of related tasks. Functions are created to handle repetitive processing such as calculating the average monthly sales.

Functions offer you advantages in the following areas:

- Performance
- Memory allocation
- Integrity
- Development

Performance of the server is enhanced because the function's compiled form is readily available to the database. No compilation of the function is required to prepare it for execution. Additional performance is gained through the reduction of network traffic because the function is already stored in memory. The application does not have to send SQL statements or PL/SQL packages over the network when using functions. Finally, if the function already resides in the System Global Area (SGA), Oracle does not have to retrieve the function from disk—it executes the SGA copy of the function immediately.

Memory allocation is helped by the use of functions because functions take advantage of the shared memory capabilities of Oracle. This means that only a single copy of the function needs to be loaded into memory for execution by multiple users.

Functions improve the integrity and consistency of your applications. By having all developers use the same set of functions, coding becomes more consistent, and the likelihood of committing coding errors is reduced.

Development productivity is enhanced by designing your applications around a common set of functions. You avoid redundant coding through the use of functions, thereby improving your productivity.

How to Use Functions

The following sections describe each of the functions and their general syntax. Functions follow the general syntax of

```
function (argument1, argument 2,...)
```

These sections are divided according to whether they are single row or group functions.

Single Row Functions

As the name implies, single row functions return a single result row for each row of a queried table or view.

Character Functions

Character functions accept character strings as input and return character values. Functions that return datatypes of varchar2 are limited to a length of 200 bytes. Functions that return char datatypes are limited in length to 255 bytes. If the length of the return value exceeds these limits, Oracle returns a truncated value and does not issue an error.

ASCII   Returns the decimal equivalent to an ASCII character.

Syntax:

```
ascii(char)
```

Example:

```
select ascii('B') from dual;
```

Output:

```
ASCII('B')
----------
        66
```

CHR   Returns the character with the ASCII value of the integer passed to it. For example, the ASCII equivalent of the letter K is 75.

Syntax:

```
CHR(integer)
```

Example:

```
select chr(75) from dual;
```

Output:

```
C
-
K
```

CONCAT   Returns the concatenation of expression 1 to expression 2. This function is equivalent to using the || command in the SQL statement.

Syntax:

```
concat(string1, string2)
```

Example:

```
select concat(region,state) from master_location;
```

Output:

```
concat(region, state)
----------
midwestohio
```

LENGTH   Returns the length of the input string in characters.

Syntax:

```
length(char)
```

Example:

```
select length('ABCDEFGHIJ') from dual;
```

Output:

```
LENGTH('ABCDEFGHIJ')
--------------------
10
```

LOWER   Returns the character string with all letters in lowercase.

Syntax:

```
lower(char)
```

Example:

```
select lower('MISSISSIPPI') from dual;
```

Output:

```
LOWER('MISSISSIPPI')
--------------------
mississippi
```

LPAD   Returns a string that is padded on the left with the sequence of characters in the third argument. This function has three arguments: the first is the input string; the second is the maximum length of the return value; and the third is the characters to pad the string with.

Syntax:

```
lpad(input string, length, padding argument)
```

Example:

```
select lpad('Warning: ',20,'***** ') from dual;
```

Output:

```
LPAD('WARNING:',20,')
--------------------
***** *****WARNING:
```

LTRIM   Returns a string that has all characters removed from the left of the input string. All characters are removed up to the specified set values.

Syntax:

```
ltrim(char[set])
```

Example:

```
select LTRIM ('chicago','ic') from dual;
```

Output:

```
LTRIM(
-------
Chicago
```

REPLACE   Returns a string with every occurrence of the search string replaced with the replacement string.

Syntax:

```
replace(char,search string,replacement string)
```

Example:

```
select replace ('Pete','Pe','123') from dual;
```

Output:

```
REPLA
-----
123TE
```

RPAD   Right pads the input string with values provided in the third argument.

Syntax:

```
rpad(inputstring,length,pad characters)
```

Example:

```
select rpad ('tom',6,'l') from dual;
```

Output:

```
RPAD(
------
tomlll
```

RTRIM   Returns the input string with the final characters removed after the last character that is not in the set argument.

Syntax:

```
rtim(inputstring,in set characters)
```

Example:

```
select rtrim('Tomlll','l') from dual;
```

Output:

```
RTR
- - -
Tom
```

| SUBSTR | Returns a portion of the input string beginning at a specified starting point and has a defined length. |

Syntax:

```
substr(string,start position,length)
```

Example:

```
select substr('ABCDEFGH',5,3) from dual;
```

Output:

```
SUB
- - -
EFG
```

| UPPER | Returns the input string in uppercase characters. |

Syntax:

```
upper(char)
```

Example:

```
select upper('cincinnati') from dual;
```

Output:

```
UPPER('CIN
- - - - - - - - - -
CINCINNATI
```

Number Functions

Number functions receive numeric inputs and return a numeric value.

| ABS | Returns the absolute value of the input value. |

Syntax:

```
abs(n)
```

Example:

```
select abs(3) from dual;
```

Output:

```
ABS(3)
- - - - - -
     3
```

POWER   Returns the input value raised to the nth power.

Syntax:

```
power(value,n)
```

Example:

```
select power(4,2) from dual;
```

Output:

```
POWER(4,2)
----------
        16
```

ROUND   Rounds the input value to the specified number of decimal places.

Syntax:

```
round(input value,precision)
```

Example:

```
select round(123.456,2)from dual;
```

Output:

```
ROUND(123.456,2)
----------------
          123.46
```

TRUNC   Returns the input value truncated to the specified number of decimal places.

Syntax:

```
trunc(input number,precision)
```

Example:

```
select trunc(213.456,2) from dual;
```

Output:

```
TRUNC(213.456,2)
----------------
          213.45
```

Date Functions

Date functions operate on input items with a datatype of date.

ADD_MONTHS   Returns a date that is the specified date plus the specified number of months. In the following example, curr_date is defined as 1-JAN-1995.

Syntax:

```
add_months(date,number of months)
```

Example:

```
select add_months(sysdate,6) from dual;
```

Output:

```
ADD_MONTH
---------
13-FEB-96
```

LAST_DAY   Returns the last day of the month that is specified in the argument.

Syntax:

```
last_day(date)
```

Example:

```
select last_day('1-may-95') from dual;
```

Output:

```
LAST_DAY(
---------
31-MAY-95
```

MONTHS_BETWEEN   Returns the number of months by which date2 precedes date1.

Syntax:

```
months_between(date1,date2)
```

Example:

```
select months_between('1-mar-95','1-jan-95') from dual;
```

Output:

```
MONTHS_BETWEEN('1-MAR-95','1-JAN-95')
-------------------------------------
                                    2
```

SYSDATE   Returns the current system date and time. This function requires no arguments.

Syntax:

```
sysdate
```

Example:

```
select sysdate from dual;
```

Output:

```
SYSDATE
-------
13-AUG-95
```

Conversion Functions

Conversion functions convert the input values from one datatype to another.

TO_CHAR   Converts a date or number into a character string.

Syntax:

```
to_char(input,format)
```

Example:

```
select to_char(sysdate,'mm/dd/yy') from dual;
```

Output:

```
TO_CHAR(SYSDATE,'MM/DD/YY')
--------------------------
08/13/95
```

TO_DATE   Converts a number or character value into a date datatype.

Syntax:

```
to_date(string,format)
```

Example:

```
select to_date('04/21/94','MM/DD/YY') from dual;
```

Output:

```
TO_DATE('
---------
21-APR-94
```

TO_NUMBER   Converts a character to a number format.

Syntax:

```
to_number(char,fmt)
```

Example:

```
select to_number('1234.56') from dual;
```

Output:

```
TO_NUMBER('1234.56')
--------------------
            1234.56
```

Part III

Other Single Row Functions

Several additional functions do not fall into any of the previous groupings.

DUMP
This returns a varchar2 value containing the datatype, value length, and internal representation of the expression. The input arguments include the format code of the return value. The following codes are used to define the format that you desire for the return value:

8	Return octal notation
10	Return decimal notation
16	Return hexadecimal notation
17	Return single characters

Syntax:

```
dump(string,format,start position, end position)
```

Example:

```
select dump('city',16,1,8) from dual;
```

Output:

```
DUMP('CITY',16,1,8)
------------------------
Typ=96  Len=4: 63,69,74,79
```

GREATEST
Returns the greatest value in an input list.

Syntax:

```
greatest(value1,value2,...)
```

Example:

```
select greatest('Tom','Tim','Terry') from dual;
```

Output:

```
GRE
---
Tom
```

LEAST
Returns the least value in an input list.

Syntax:

```
least(value1, value2,...)
```

Example:

```
select least('Tom','Tim','Terry') from dual;
```

Output:

```
LEAST
-----
Terry
```

USER — Returns the name of the current Oracle user. This function requires no additional arguments.

Syntax:

```
user
```

Example:

```
select user from dual;
```

Output:

```
USER
----------
ops$user_1
```

Group Functions

The group functions return a single result row for a group of queried rows.

AVG — Returns the average value for a group of rows.

Syntax:

```
avg(value)
```

Example:

```
select avg(month_sales) from order;
```

Output:

```
AVG(MONTHLY_SALES)
------------------
          80762.13
```

COUNT — Returns the number of rows in a query. You can indicate to the count function the following:

* Indicates to return all rows of the query

distinct — Returns a count of the unique rows as identified in the query.

Syntax:

```
count(indicator expression)
```

Example:

```
select count(*) from orders;
```

Output:

```
COUNT(*)
--------
     281
```

MAX   Returns the maximum value of the expression.

Syntax:

```
max(expression)
```

Example:

```
select max(monthly_sales) from orders;
```

Output:

```
MAX(MONTHLY_SALES)
------------------
          91281.23
```

MIN   Returns the minimum value of the expression.

Syntax:

```
min(expression)
```

Example:

```
select min(monthly_sales) from orders;
```

Output:

```
MIN(MONTHLY_SALES)
------------------
             89.85
```

SUM   Returns the sum of the values in the expression.

Syntax:

```
sum(expression)
```

Example:

```
select sum(monthly_sales) from orders;
```

Output:

```
SUM(MONTHLY_SALES)
------------------
         192438.82
```

Chapter 18

Essential Summary

Functions are predefined routines that manipulate data items and return a result value. Functions return a value that either describes the input to the function or manipulates the input data.

What

There are many benefits to using functions. These benefits include improving the performance of the Oracle server, improving memory allocations, increasing development time, and improving database integrity.

Why

Functions are used in SQL statements to satisfy your processing requirements. Single row functions return a result for each row in a query, whereas group functions return a single result for a group of rows in a query.

How

Advanced Functions

What Are Advanced Functions?

What Advanced functions are similar to simple functions except that these functions handle more complex expressions and are less frequently used than simple functions. Functions are simply a set of SQL and PL/SQL statements that are logically grouped together to perform a specific task. For example, You can have an advanced function that creates a phonetic representation of an input variable. Please refer to Chapter 13, "Functions," for additional information about functions and how they are used.

Functions come in two different types. One type acts only on a single row of data while the second type of functions acts on multiple rows of data. Advanced functions are stand-alone Oracle objects that reside in your own schema. They are similar to operators except that functions can operate on multiple arguments.

Why Use Advanced Functions?

Advanced functions enable you to solve problems and perform specific tasks easily especially if your processing involves repetitive tasks.

Advanced functions, like simple functions, offer you advantages in the following areas:

- Performance—Performance is enhanced because a function is stored in its compiled form and is therefore readily available for execution. No compilation or other preparation is required to execute the function. Additional benefits are also gained because the functions are stored in memory and thereby network traffic is reduced.

- Memory allocation—Advanced functions take advantage of shared memory, which allows multiple users to execute the same copy of an advanced function that resides in memory.

- Integrity—Advanced functions provide users with a single program unit for execution to perform a task. This provides a consistent means to perform the activity.

- Development—Development time is reduced as programs take advantage of a common set of functions. This eliminates the need to create the functions functionality from scratch.

How to Use Advanced Functions

The following sections describe each of the advanced functions and their general syntax. All functions follow the general syntax of

```
function (argument1, argument 2,...)
```

These sections are divided according to whether they are single row or group functions.

Advanced Character Functions

INITCAP   Returns the input string with the first letter of each word in uppercase and all other letters in lowercase. Words are delimited by whitespace or any non-alphanumeric value.

Syntax:

```
initcap(char)
```

Example:

```
select initcap('sales orders') from dual;
```

Output:

```
INITCAP('SAL
-----------
Sales Orders
```

| INSTR | Returns the location of a set of characters in the input string. Evaluation of the input string starts with the specified position and continues until the specified occurrence is met. This function returns the number of characters from the starting point and satisfies the occurrence count. |

Syntax:

```
instr(input string,search string,start,occurence)
```

Example:

```
select instr('Sells Sea Shells by the Seaside','Se',1,3) from dual;
```

Output:

```
INSTR('SELLSSEASHELLSBYTHESEASIDE','Se',1,3)
-------------------------------------------
                                          25
```

| INSTRB | Returns the location of a set of characters in the input string. Evaluation of the input string starts with the specified position and continues until the specified occurrence is met. This function returns the number of bytes from the starting point and satisfies the occurrence count. |

Syntax:

```
instrb(input string,search string,start,occurrence)
```

Example:

```
select instrb('Sells Sea Shells by the Seaside','Se',1,3) from dual;
```

Output:

```
INSTRB('SELLSEASHELLSBYTHESEASIDE','SE',1,3)
-------------------------------------------
                                          25
```

| SOUNDEX | Returns a phonetic representation of the input character string. This function can be used to compare two words that are spelled differently but sound alike in English. |

Syntax:

```
soundex(string)
```

Example:

```
select last_name from emp
where soundex(last_name) = soundex('smith');
```

Output:

```
LAST_NAME
---------
Smith
Smyth
```

TRANSLATE   SQL evaluates the characters in a string, then checks to see if any of the characters exist in a predefined lookup string. If any exist, it substitutes the found characters in the input string with the corresponding positional characters in the substitution string.

Syntax:

```
translate (input string, look up string, replace string)
```

Example:

```
select translate ('abcedfghi','befi','1234567890') from dual;
```

This function has the input string abcdefghi, a lookup string equal to befi, and a replacement string of 1234567890.

Output:

```
TRANSLATE
---------
a1cd23gh4
```

Because the letters acdgh do not exist in the lookup string, they are not translated and retain their original value. The letters befi are in the lookup string and are therefore translated to a new value. The replacement values are positional, so the letter b would be translated to 1, the letter e would be translated to 2, and so on.

Advanced Number Functions

Advanced number functions receive numeric inputs and return a numeric value.

CEIL   Returns the smallest integer that is greater than or equal to the input value.

Syntax:

```
ceil(value)
```

Example:

```
select ceil(23.170) from dual;
```

Output:

```
CEIL(23.170
-----------
         24
```

COS   Returns the cosine of the input value.

Syntax:

```
cos(value)
```

Example:

```
select cos(180*3.14159/180) from dual;
```

Output:

```
COS(180_8.14159/180)
--------------------
                  -1
```

EXP   Returns the value *e* raised to the nth power. Oracle defines the value of *e* as 2.718

Syntax:

```
exp(n)
```

Example:

```
select exp(5) from dual;
```

Output:

```
EXP(5)
----------
148.413154
```

FLOOR   Returns the largest integer that is less than or equal to the input value.

Syntax:

```
floor(value)
```

Example:

```
select floor(20.183) from dual;
```

Output:

```
FLOOR(20.183)
-------------
           20
```

LN   Returns the natural logarithm of the input value.

Syntax:

```
ln(value)
```

Example:

```
select ln(3) from dual;
```

Output:

```
LN(3)
----------
1.09861229
```

LOG   Returns the specified base logarithm of the input value.

Syntax:

```
log(base,value)
```

Example:

```
select log(10,100) from dual;
```

Output:

```
LOG(10,100)
-----------
          2
```

MOD   Returns the remainder of a value divided by a specified divisor.

Syntax:

```
mod(value,divisor)
```

Example:

```
select mod(10,3) from dual;
```

Output:

```
MOD(10,3)
---------
        1
```

SIGN   Returns 1 if the input value is greater than zero, or returns −1 if the
                             value is less than zero. Returns 0 if the value is zero.

Syntax:

```
sign(value)
```

Example:

```
select sign(-70) from dual;
```

Output:

```
SIGN(-70)
---------
       -1
```

SIN   Returns the sine of the input value.

Syntax:

```
sin(value)
```

Example:

```
select sin(30*3.141592653/180) from dual;
```

Output:

```
SIN(30_3.141592653/180)
- - - - - - - - - - - - - - - - - - - - -
                     .5
```

SQRT   Returns the square root of the input value.

Syntax:

```
sqrt(value)
```

Example:

```
select sqrt(16) from dual;
```

Output:

```
SQRT(16)
- - - - - - -
       4
```

TAN   Returns the tangent of the input value.

Syntax:

```
tan(value)
```

Example:

```
select tan(135*3.14159265393/180) from dual;
```

Output:

```
TAN(135*3.14159265393/180)
- - - - - - - - - - - - - - - - - - - - - - - -
                       -1
```

Advanced Date Functions

Advanced date functions operate on input items with a datatype of `date`.

NEW_TIME   Returns a time that is updated to reflect the current time in the
                   specified time zone. The time zones are as follows:

AST   Atlantic Standard Time

CST   Central Standard Time

EST   Eastern Central Time

GMT   Greenwich Mean Time

HST   Alaska-Hawaii Standard Time

MST   Mountain Standard Time

PST   Pacific Standard Time

Syntax:

```
new_time(date time,current time zone,new time zone)
```

Example:

```
select to_char new_time(sysdate,'MST','PST'),'dd-mon-yy hh:mi:ss) from dual;
```

Output:

```
TO_CHAR(NEW_TIME(SYSDATE,'MST','PST),'DD-MON-YYHH:MI:SS')
-----------------------------------------------------
13-aug-95 11:28:21
```

ROUND
: Returns a date that is rounded to the units specified in the input. The rounding units include the following:

cc,scc
: This rounds the date to the nearest century.

year, yy
: This rounds the date to the nearest year. Rounding down occurs for dates ranging from 1-Jan to 30-June. Rounding up occurs for dates ranging from 1-July to 31-Dec.

ww
: Rounds to the nearest Monday.

d
: Rounds to the nearest day. This rounds to the next day if the time is after 12 p.m. (noon).

dy,day
: Rounds up to the next Sunday, which is the first day of the week.

Syntax:

```
round(date,rounding units)
```

Example:

```
select round to_date('12-AUG-93'),'year') from dual;
```

Output:

```
ROUND(TO_
----------
01-JAN-94
```

Advanced Conversion Functions

These functions convert the input string from one datatype to another:

CHARTOROWID
: Returns a value of datatype rowid. This value was converted from a datatype of char or varchar2. This function is normally used to debug source code. Oracle performs this conversion automatically for you; hence, this function is rarely used.

Syntax:

```
chartorowid(char)
```

Example:

```
select dept_mgr from mst_dept
where rowid = chartorowid('0000000D.0002.0002') from dual;
```

Output:

```
DEPT_MGR
--------
Baker
```

CONVERT   Returns a value that was converted from one datatype to another. The character sets are as follows:

US7ASCII	Standard US 7-bit ASCII set
WE8DEC	DEC West European 8-bit character set
WE8HP	HP West European 8-bit character set
WE8PC850	IBM PC Code
F7DEC	DEC 7-bit set for France

Syntax:

```
convert(value,final char set, original char set) from dual
```

Example:

```
select convert('Thomas','us7ascii','we8pc850') from dual;
```

Output:

```
CONVER
------
Thomas
```

ROWIDTOCHAR   Converts a rowid value to a char datatype.

Syntax:

```
rowidtochar(value)
```

Example:

```
select rowid from emp
where rowidtochar(rowid) like '%smyt%';
```

Output:

```
ROWIP
-----------------
00000034.0003.0003
```

Other Advanced Functions

UID — Returns the current user ID of the database user. There are no arguments with this function. uid is a pseudo-column in the database. It cannot be modified by the user.

Syntax:

```
uid
```

Example:

```
select uid from dual;
```

Output:

```
UID
- - - - - - - - -
972A8C32
```

USERENV — This returns information about the current session. The possible arguments for this function are as follows:

entryid	Returns available auditing entry identifier
label	Returns your current session label
language	Returns the language currently used by your session and the database character set
sessionid	Returns your auditing session identifier
terminal	Returns the operating system identifier for your current session's terminal

Syntax:

```
userenv(argument)
```

Example:

```
select userenv('language') from dual;
```

Output:

```
USERENV('LANGUAGE')
- - - - - - - - - - - - - - - - - - - - - - - -
american_america.us7ascii
```

VSIZE — Returns the number of bytes the input value is occupying in storage.

Syntax:

```
vsize(value)
```

Example:

```
select vsize('ORACLE') from dual;
```

Output:
```
VSIZE('ORACLE')
- - - - - - - - - - - - - - -
              6
```

Essential Summary

Advanced functions are predefined routines that can manipulate data items. These advanced functions return a value that either describes the input value or manipulates the input value.

What

Advanced functions help the application developer by decreasing the amount of time it takes for development, improving database performance, and improving data integrity and security.

Why

Advanced functions are used in SQL statements. They can be used to evaluate or manipulate each row from a query or use the group of rows in the results to process them.

How

Joins and Unions

What Are Joins and Unions?

What Joins and unions are two techniques used to bring different groups of data together. Once the data is logically grouped, you can display the data or perform additional processing on the data. Both union and join groupings are established in the select statement.

Why Use Joins and Unions?

Why Joins and unions are used to group together data stored in different tables. These two methods of grouping bring data together from multiple tables that are related to each other. This capability simplifies your querying process.

Part III

How to Use Joins and Unions

How

The various types of joins and unions are discussed in the following sections.

Simple Joins

A simple join is a `select` statement that returns rows from two or more tables. These tables are related, or joined, by columns that they have in common. The tables that are joined by the common columns appear in the `from` clause of the `select` statement. This chapter discusses joins on two tables, but this information also applies to joins with three or more tables.

Oracle places no restrictions on which columns from either table you can actually select. You can select no columns or multiple columns from each table. The columns you specify in the `where` clause do not have to appear in the `select` list.

Joining two tables together without the `where` clause creates a Cartesian product. This product combines every row in the first table with every row of the second table. For example, the Cartesian product of one table with 10 rows and another table with 25 rows would be a join of 250 rows. This result is usually meaningless and is typically not used.

You can substitute a table alias for the actual table name in the `from` clause of your `select` statement. However, Oracle requires that you substitute the table alias for the table name throughout the `select` statement, including the `select` list and the `where` clause.

The syntax for a simple join is as follows:

```
select column(s)
from table1, table2
where table1.column1 = table2.column1
```

The following explains this example:

- `column(s)` represents the column or columns from which data is retrieved
- `table1, table2` represents the tables from which data is retrieved
- `table1.column1 = table2.column1` represents the condition that joins the two tables together

Figure 15.1 shows the two tables joined in the next example. In this example, the tables EMPLOYEE and DEPARTMENT are joined by the column dept_id.

Figure 15.1.
Select data from joined tables (a simple join).

Employee

l name	dept id
Adams	23B
Baker	101
Price	90C
White	90C

Department

dept id	desc
23B	Finance
101	System
90C	Manufacturing
90C	Manufacturing

This statement creates a join for the EMPLOYEE and DEPARTMENT tables:

```
select employee.l_name, employee.dept_id, department.desc
from employee, department
where employee.dept_id = department.dept_id;
```

Sample output:

```
L_NAME                  DEPT_ID   DESC
--------------------    -------   ---------------
Adams                     23B     Finance
Baker                     101     Systems
Price                     90C     Manufacturing
White                     90C     Manufacturing
```

To return specific rows from a join, simply introduce search conditions in addition to the join condition in the where clause:

```
select employee.l_name "Emp. Name",
employee.dept_id "Dept #",
department.desc "Dept. Name"
from employee, department
where employee.dept_id = department.dept_id
and employee.1_name like 'B%';
```

Sample output:

```
Emp. Name               Dept_#    Dept. Name
--------------------    -------   ---------------
Baker                     101     Systems
```

Outer Joins

An outer join is similar to a simple join. An outer join returns all rows that the simple join returns, as well as those rows from one table that have no direct match with any row from the other table.

The syntax for an outer join is

```
select column (s)
from table1, table2
where table1.column1 = table2.column(+)
```

The following explains this example:

- (+) is used to indicate an outer join
- column(s) represents the column or columns from which data is retrieved
- table1, table2 represents the tables from which data is retrieved
- table1.column = table2.column represents the condition that joins the two tables together

The plus sign (+) can be placed on either side of the where clause condition, but not on both sides. You should append this outer join symbol following the name of the table without the matching rows. Oracle generates nulls for the columns of the table whenever the table has no rows to join to a row in the other table.

Figure 15.2 shows the two tables that we performed an outer join on. In this example, all departments are displayed regardless of whether they have any employees currently assigned to them.

Figure 15.2.
Select data from tables without a direct match (an outer join).

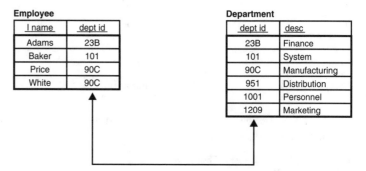

The following statement creates an outer join on the EMPLOYEE and DEPARTMENT tables. Note that the outer join symbol is placed next to the EMPLOYEE table because it does not contain any matching rows to the DEPARTMENT table. Also note that all rows from the DEPARTMENT table are displayed.

```
select employee.l_name, employee.dept_id, department.desc
from employee, department
where employee.dept_id(+) = department.dept_id;
```

Sample output:

```
L_NAME                    DEPT_ID   DESC
--------------------      -------   ----------------
Adams                     23B       Finance
Baker                     101       Systems
Price                     90C       Manufacturing
White                     90C       Manufacturing
                          951       Distribution
                          1001      Personnel
                          1209      Marketing
```

Self Joins

Oracle permits a join on a single table as though it were two separate tables. This type of join is known as a self join.

Figure 15.3 depicts the EMPLOYEE table being viewed as two separate tables: EMP and DEPT.

The following statement performs a self join on the EMPLOYEE table. Logically, the statement establishes that the EMPLOYEE table is viewed as two tables. One table is named EMP and the other is named DEPT.

Figure 15.3.
*Select data from
different rows of the
same table (a self join).*

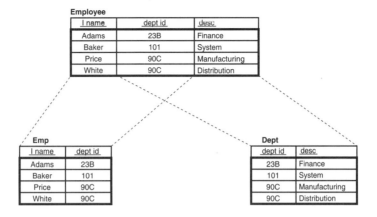

```
select emp.l_name, emp.dept_id, dept.desc
from employee emp, employee dept
where emp.dept_id = dept.dept_id;
```

Sample output:

```
L_NAME                  DEPT_ID   DESC
--------------------    -------   ----------------
Adams                   23B       Finance
Baker                   101       Systems
Price                   90C       Manufacturing
White                   90C       Manufacturing
```

Joins and Views

You can use a join to simplify the creation of a view. For example, you can use a join to define a view that is a collection of related columns or rows in multiple tables. However, the view hides the fact that this information originates from multiple tables.

Joins and Clusters

In the Oracle server, you should cluster only tables that are frequently joined on the clustered key columns in SQL statements. This clustering will improve the performance of the joins but will most likely result in performance degradation of full table scans, table inserts, and update statements that modify the clustered key values. Before clustering the joined columns, consider the pros and cons of this, because it affects server performance.

union

union is a set operator that combines the results of two queries into a single result. This operator returns only distinct values from the queries. Consider the following two lists of data:

```
Part_Name_1            Part_Name_2
- - - - - - - - - -    - - - - - - - - - -
coil                   coil
condenser              motor
motor                  tank
switch                 wire
valve
wire
```

The following statement performs a union on the two lists:

```
select part_name from part_name_1
union
select part_name from part_name_2;
```

Sample output:

```
part_name
- - - - - - - - -
coil
condenser
motor
switch
tank
valve
wire
```

As you can see from the preceding example, all the distinct values from both tables are included in the results of the query.

When the union or union all set operators are used in statements that select character data, the return values have their datatype determined by the following:

- If both queries select char datatype values, the returned values have a datatype of char.
- If either or both queries select varchar2 datatype values, the returned values have a datatype of varchar2.

union all

union all is a set operator that combines the results of two queries into a single result. This operator returns all values from the queries. Consider the following two lists of data:

```
Part_Name_1            Part_Name_2
- - - - - - - - - -    - - - - - - - - - -
coil                   coil
condenser              motor
motor                  tank
switch                 wire
valve
wire
```

The following statement performs a union all on the two lists:

```
select part_name from part_name_1
union all
select part_name from part_name_2;
```

Sample output:

```
part_name
---------
coil
coil
condenser
motor
motor
switch
tank
valve
wire
wire
```

As you can see from the preceding example, all values from both tables are included in the results from the query. This includes duplicate rows of data.

order by

You can use the order by clause in a select statement of a union query. However, within the union statement, you must specify the column number on which you want to order the data. The positional number of the column is required in the select statement, not the column name.

The following statement uses the order by clause to sort the results in ascending order of the dept_id column (dept_id is the third column).

```
select dept_name, dept_plant, dept_id from department
union
select dept_name, dept_location, dept_id from dept
order by 3;
```

Sample output:

```
dept_name       dept_plant   dept_id
--------------  ----------   -------
Packaging       Michigan     101
Shipping        Michigan     198
Pre-assembly    New Mexico   304
Costing         Ohio         668
```

intersect

intersect is a set operator that combines two select statements and returns only those rows that are returned by both queries. Consider the following two lists of data:

```
Part_Name_1        Part_Name_2
-----------        -----------
coil               coil
condenser          motor
motor              tank
switch             wire
valve
wire
```

The following statement performs an `intersect` on the two lists:

```
select part_name from part_name_1
intersect
select part_name from part_name_2;
```

Sample output:

```
part_name
---------
coil
motor
wire
```

This operation returns only those items that exist in both lists.

minus

`minus` is a set operator that combines the results of two queries and returns only those values that are selected by the first query but not the second.

Using the same lists as the previous example, consider the following statement:

```
select part_name from part_name_1
minus
select part_name from part_name_2;
```

Sample output:

```
part_name
---------
condenser
switch
valve
```

In this example, only those rows that are in the first list and not in the second list are returned by the statement.

Essential Summary

In this chapter, you learned that joins and unions are two methods used to logically group data from different tables together. Once grouped, you can display the resulting group or perform additional processing on the group.

Why

Joins and unions are used to bring data together from multiple tables for displaying on the screen or for additional processing. These techniques enable you to query multiple tables that are related by common columns to create a single result set.

Joins and unions use the `select` statement to query multiple databases. By using the various types of joins and unions, you control the exact domain of the return values from the `select` statement.

PART IV

Data Access

Selecting and Maintaining Data

Oracle stores data in tables for some users to read the data, but other users have the privilege to update, delete, and insert new data in the database. This chapter reviews the techniques used to perform these actions.

What Does Selecting and Maintaining Data Mean?

What Selecting data from the Oracle database is synonymous with asking a question of the database. Your goal is to receive information from the database based on the questions you ask Oracle. You can ask many different types of questions of Oracle, and those are covered in this chapter.

Maintaining the data in the Oracle database is paramount to many other tasks in the server. Maintaining the data in the database involves deleting unwanted data, modifying existing data, and inserting new data. This is required to keep the integrity and accuracy of the data intact. The database would serve no purpose and have no need for existence if no user had any confidence in the database data.

Why Select and Maintain Data?

Why

Selecting data from the database is the act of issuing a query to the server and receiving a response to the query. Users, developers, database administrators, and others all have a requirement to select data from the database. Users need access to the data to perform their day-to-day business activities. Developers and database administrators require access to the data to develop new applications, validate existing applications, and assist end users.

Normal business activities require the continuous maintenance of data. For example, a company can add new orders to the database by inserting rows of orders into the server. Additionally, this company can adjust an existing order quantity by modifying the row in the server for that order.

How to Select and Maintain Data

How

This chapter looks at the various ways to access the database data with the `select` command. The commands used to maintain the database data are also described.

Displaying Table Columns

Throughout this chapter, it is vital for you to know exactly which tables and columns you wish to select and which ones to maintain. The `describe` command can help you confirm that you are accessing the correct table, view, or synonym. The `describe` command displays the structure of the table, including column names, datatypes, length, precision, and null or not null status.

The following example uses the `describe` command to display the structure of the EMP table:

```
describe emp
```

The resulting output is this:

```
Name          Null?      Type
------------------------------
EMP_ID        NOT NULL   NUMBER
F_NAME        NOT NULL   VARCHAR2(30)
L_NAME        NOT NULL   VARCHAR2(30)
COMMENTS                 VARCHAR2(5)
```

The Name column in the table layout lists the names of the columns. These are the names you reference in your select and manipulation statements. The Null? column in the layout specifies whether a column must contain data. Data is required in a column only if the Not Null keyword is listed. The Type information lists the datatype for each column.

Selecting Data from Tables

The SQL `select` statement is used to query and display data from the Oracle database. The general syntax for the `select` statement is

```
select column_name(s) from table (or view or snapshot)
```

Oracle left-justifies all character data that is returned from the `select` statement. Likewise, numeric data is right-justified.

Displaying All Rows

Use the asterisk (*) with the `select` keyword to select all rows from a table. The following example selects all rows from the table EMP:

```
select * from emp;
```

You can also display all columns of a table by listing all column names in the `select` statement. For example, the following statement returns the same result as the previous example:

```
select emp_id, f_name, l_name, comments from emp;
```

Displaying Unique Columns of Data

Sometimes you don't want to return all rows from a table. For example, you might want to see what states are represented by visitors to a museum today. You could issue the following command to see every row in the guest registry database:

```
select guest_state from registry;
```

Sample output:

```
GUEST_STATE
- - - - - - - - - -
Alabama
Alabama
Arkansas
California
California
California
     ...
Wisconsin
Washington
Washington
```

As you can see from this example, every row is listed in the database. This makes it somewhat difficult to see precisely what states are represented by the guests. Alternately, you could use the `distinct` clause in the `select` statement to display only the unique states in the database. Using the `distinct` clause removes all duplicate values of the column specified in the `select` statement. The following example uses the `distinct` clause:

```
select distinct guest_state from registry;
```

Sample output:

```
GUEST_STATE
- - - - - - - - - -
Alabama
Arkansas
```

```
California
   ...
Wisconsin
Washington
```

Substituting Column Headings

The results returned from a select statement use the actual column names as the column headers. As shown in the previous example, the column header assumed the column name guest_state.

You can define a substitute column header in the select statement by including the new header after the column header. If the new header contains blanks or special characters, it must be enclosed in quotation marks. The following example changes the column header to Visitor State from the default column header guest_state:

```
select distinct guest_state "Visitor State" from registry;
```

Sample output:

```
Visitor State
- - - - - - - - - - - -
Alabama
Arkansas
California
   ...
Wisconsin
Washington
```

Selecting Specific Rows of Data

To select specific rows from a table, you use the where clause in the select statement. The where clause is composed of column names, comparison operators, constants, and expressions. You can use any of the comparison operators (=, <, >, <=, >=, like, between, in, or null). The following statement selects only those employees that belong to the Finance department:

```
select * from emp
where dept_name = 'Finance';
```

The where clause accepts many different operators. In the following example, the select statement uses the like operator to return only part numbers that begin with the characters CK1. The percent sign (%) wildcard is used in conjunction with the like operator to indicate that pattern matching is to occur on only the first three characters of the data. Oracle tries to match the characters CK1 with the first three characters in the column data. The percent sign is used to indicate that pattern matching will not occur on any character past the third position.

```
select * from master_part "CK1 PARTS"
where part_number like 'CK1%';
```

Sample output:

```
CK1 PARTS
- - - - - - - - -
CK1-0921
CK1-A82
CK1723D
```

The next statement uses pattern matching with the single character wildcard, the hyphen (-). This `select` statement returns only those sales people with a last name matching SM-TH, where the hyphen can be any character:

```
select sales_name from orders
where sales_name like 'SM-TH';
```

Sample output:

```
SMITH
SMYTH
```

Selecting Rows Using Complex Conditions

Oracle permits the use of complex conditions in the `select` statement. This means that you can use any number of conditions in the `where` clause of the `select` statement. For example, the following selects those employees in the Finance department whose commissions are greater than 20 percent and whose hire date is prior to January 1, 1990:

```
select * from emp
where dept_name = 'Finance' and com_perc > 20 and
hire_date < '1-JAN-1990';
```

Ordering Selected Rows

You can place the displayed rows of a query in ascending or descending order. By default, Oracle presents the rows in the same order as they appear in the database. This typically means the rows are not in any order. Use the `order by` clause in the `select` statement to order the rows in the results. You can include the following clauses with the `order by` clause to get the desired result:

- asc orders the rows in ascending order. This is the default mode for the `order by` clause.
- desc orders the rows in descending order.

The following example puts the resulting rows of the query in ascending order:

```
select emp_name "Employee Name"
from emp
order_by emp_name asc;
```

Sample output:

```
Employee Name
- - - - - - - - - - - -
Adams
Archibald
Baker
Cutshall
   ...
Wilson
Young
```

The following statement displays the rows of the query ordered first by the plant_id and then sorted by emp_name:

```
select plant_id, emp_name, dept_no from emp
order by plant_id, emp_name asc;
```

Sample output:

```
PLANT_ID  EMP_NAME    DEPT_NO
------------------------------
10        Baker       20
10        Young       20
15        Cutshall    10
20        Adams       10
30        Archibald   30
30        Wilson      25
```

Manipulating Data

The SQL insert, update, and delete commands are used in SQL statements to maintain the data in the database.

Inserting Data

The insert command adds single rows of data into the Oracle table or the view's base tables. The data to be added in the row is specified in the values clause of the insert statement.

The following example uses a simplistic insert statement to add a row to the EMP table. Note that the sequence generator s_emp_id is used to automatically generate a unique sequential number for the first column in the insert.

```
insert into emp values
(s_emp_id.nextval,'Thomas','Luers','23-B');
```

You can specify certain columns to insert data into and leave the unspecified columns null. For example, in the MASTER_PART table, all columns are explicitly inserted with data except the Comments column. The Comments column remains in an empty or null state.

```
insert into master_part (part_id, part_number, part_name)
values (s_part_id.nextval,'19832-003','Ceiling Fan');
```

The following command uses a subquery to generate the input values for the insert statement. This example copies employee information from the UK_EMP table to the EMP table:

```
insert into emp
select * from uk_emp where region_name = 'UK';
```

Updating Data

Oracle permits you to alter the data values in any column you specify. The update statement accomplishes this task. This part of the chapter describes the update statement and its various clauses.

The following example updates all rows of the table SALES by setting the commission rate to 0.25 for all sales people:

```
update finance.sales
set commission_rate = '.25';
```

The following statement modifies the value of the dept_no column where the emp_id is 10923:

```
update emp
set dept_no = '982-C'
where emp_id = 10923;
```

You can also do multiple updates on a single row at the same time. For example

```
update emp
set dept_no = '982_C', start_date = '1-JUN-1995'
where emp_id = 10923;
```

The following example updates multiple rows of a table. In this example, all employees of the Shipping department have their department numbers changed to 883:

```
update emp
set dept_no = '883'
where dept_name = 'Shipping';
```

Deleting Data

To remove rows from a table or a view's base table, use the SQL delete command. You cannot delete from a view if the view's defining query contains one of these constructs:

- join
- set or distinct operator
- group by clause
- group function

The next statement deletes all rows from the table TRAINING_1:

```
delete from training_1;
```

It is recommended that you use the SQL truncate command to delete all rows from a table. Truncate is more efficient than the delete command.

Sometimes you want to delete only particular rows from a table. To accomplish this, use the delete command with the where clause. For example, the following statement deletes only those rows where the sales quantity is less than 100:

```
delete from orders
where sales_qty < 100;
```

Truncating Tables

Truncating tables removes all rows from that table. Truncate works quicker than the delete command for the following reasons:

- truncate is a DDL command and therefore generates no rollback information. Caution must be exercised when using the truncate command, because you cannot roll back this statement.
- Truncating a table does not activate any of the table's delete triggers.

- If you are truncating the master table to a snapshot, the truncate command does not record any changes in the table's snapshot log.

The truncate command also enables you to optionally deallocate the space freed by the deleted rows. By default, Oracle drops the allocated storage from the table. The following example illustrates the truncate command. In this statement, all rows from the ORDERS table are removed:

```
truncate table orders;
```

In the following example, Oracle keeps the allocation for reuse by that table. The space is not freed up and returned to the server:

```
truncate table orders
reuse storage;
```

Interactive Data Manipulation

Oracle enables you to write a SQL script that queries the user for information to be used in a later database action. For example, you can query the user for values that are to be used in an insert statement. Alternatively, the script can query the user for values to be used in a select statement. This section uses the accept command and the ampersand (&) substitution value.

The accept command forces the server to define the value of a variable as equal to the entered value in an accept statement. The ampersand tells Oracle to substitute the value of the variable with the value that was entered by the user. The following example uses the accept statement to query the user for the dept_no that is used in the select statement.

```
accept dept prompt 'Enter the Department Number: '

select * from master_dept
where dept_no = &dept;
```

The next example uses the accept command and the ampersand to direct Oracle to use the entered values in the insert statement:

```
accept emp_lname prompt 'Enter employees last name: '
accept emp_fname prompt 'Enter employees first name: '
accept emp_ssn prompt 'Enter employees ssn: '

insert into emp (f_name, l_name, emp_ssn)
values (&emp_fname, &emp_lname, &emp_ssn);
```

Essential Summary

What Selecting data from the database is the act of querying the database and receiving rows of data in response. Maintaining data in the database includes updating, inserting, and deleting data from the database to ensure data integrity and completeness.

Why One of the fundamental reasons that databases exist is for people to access and retrieve data from them. To satisfy the requirements of these users, the data must be kept up-to-date and accurate. Maintaining the data is essential to the success of the database.

Displaying the structures of tables is an important aspect of selecting and maintaining the Oracle tables. You need to know the column names, datatypes, and lengths to successfully select and maintain the data.

Cursors

What Are Cursors?

What Cursors are constructs that enable the user to name a private memory area to hold a specific statement for access at a later time. There are two kinds of cursors used in Oracle: implicit and explicit. PL/SQL implicitly declares a cursor for every SQL Data Manipulation Language (DML) statement, such as `insert`, `delete`, and `update`. Explicit cursors are declared by the user and are used to process query results that return multiple rows.

The number of rows returned by a query can be zero, one, or many, depending on the query search conditions. Oracle provides the cursor as the mechanism to be used to easily process these multiple row result sets one row at a time. Without cursors, the Oracle developer will have to explicitly fetch and manage each individual row that is selected by the cursor query.

The multiple rows returned from a query are called the active set. PL/SQL defines its size as the number of rows that have met your search criteria and formed the active set. Figure 17.1 illustrates a cursor that is holding multiple rows. Inherent in every cursor is a pointer that keeps track of the current row being accessed, which enables your program to process the rows one at a time.

Figure 17.1.
A multiple row cursor.

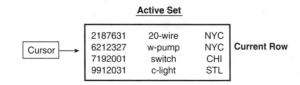

Query:
Select part_nbr, part_name, mfg_plant from master_parts;

Why Use Cursors?

You can view a cursor as a file that needs to be processed from the top to the bottom of the file, one record at a time. Cursors are used to process multi-row result sets one row at a time. Additionally, cursors keep track of which row is currently being accessed, which allows for iterative processing of the active set.

Using several cursors simultaneously can improve system performance by reducing the frequency of parsing and cursor opening. After each iteration of the cursor, the cursor retains enough information about the active set and the SQL statements that it can be re-executed many times. Each iteration is accomplished without having to re-open and parse the cursor every time.

By opening several cursors, the parsed representation of the SQL statements can be saved, thereby eliminating the repeated cost of opening the cursor and parsing.

How to Use Cursors

Oracle SQL*Plus implicitly creates a cursor for every Data Manipulation Language statement executed. This happens whether the query returns one or many rows. Users can explicitly declare a cursor to process the multiple-row active set one row at a time.

Following are the steps to create and use cursors:

1. Declare the cursor
2. Open the cursor
3. Fetch data into the cursor
4. Close the cursor

Each of these steps is covered in detail in the sections of this chapter.

Declaring Explicit Cursors

The cursor must be declared before it is referenced by PL/SQL. Declaring a cursor accomplishes two goals:

- It names the cursor
- It associates a query with the cursor

The name you assign to a cursor is an undeclared identifier, not a PL/SQL variable. The name is used to reference the query. You cannot assign values to a cursor name or use it in an expression. The results of the cursor query become the cursor's active set. In the following example, a cursor named c_parts is declared:

```
declare
cursor c_parts is
select * from master_parts;
```

There is no predefined limit to the number of cursors a session can have. The only constraint that can limit the number of cursors is the availability of memory to manage the cursors. Also, there is a system-wide limit of cursors per system. This limit is defined in the open_cursor parameter and is established by the database administrator.

You can use parameters with cursors to pass different values to the cursor and to override default values. These parameters must be declared at the same time the cursor is declared. Parameters can appear in a query wherever a constant can appear. The following example illustrates the cursor c_parts and the parameter v_part_qty:

```
declare
cursor c_parts (v_part_qty number) is
select * from master_parts where part_qty > v_part_qty;
```

Opening Explicit Cursors

Opening the cursor executes the query and identifies the active set. The active set contains all the rows that meet the query search criteria. For cursors that are declared using the for update clause, Oracle locks the rows that meet the cursor query.

The cursor open statement must have an actual parameter specified for each of the parameters that was specified in the cursor declaration. If it doesn't, the parameters in the declaration assume their default values.

You can associate actual parameters in an open statement with the formal parameters in a cursor declaration using positional notations. The following statement opens the cursor c_parts:

```
open c_parts
```

When the open command is executed, the cursor identifies only the rows that satisfy the query. The rows are not actually retrieved until the cursor fetch is issued. The cursor is initialized to just before the first row of the active set.

Explicit Cursor Attributes

Each cursor you define has four attributes. These attributes can be accessed to obtain useful information about the cursor. These cursor attributes are as follows:

%isopen   This Boolean attribute equates to True if the cursor is already open. The following example checks to see if the cursor named c_cursor is open. If it is already open, the fetch is executed. If the cursor is closed, the open cursor command is issued.

```
begin
if c_coursor%isopen then
fetch c_cursor into v_ord_qty, v_ord_price;
else
open c_cursor;
end if;
end;
```

%notfound   This Boolean attribute equates to True if no rows were returned by the most recent `fetch` execution. The `fetch` statement is expected to fail at some point during execution, so when this happens, no exception is raised. The following example uses this attribute to exit a loop when there are no more rows to process:

```
loop
fetch c_cursor into v_ord_qty, v_ord_price;
exit when c_cursor%notfound;
end loop;
end;
```

%found   This evaluates to True until the most recent `fetch` does not return a row. This attribute is the logical opposite of the %notfound attribute. The %found attribute equates to Null when a cursor is opened prior to the first `fetch`. Once the first `fetch` is executed, this attribute equates to True until the `fetch` returns no rows. This example uses the %found attribute to control the execution of the `insert` command:

```
begin
loop
fetch c_cursor into v_ord_qty, v_ord_price;
if c_cursor%found then
insert into master_orders values (v_ord_qty, v_ord_price);
else
exit;
end if;
end loop;
end
```

%rowcount   This is a numeric attribute that equates to the total number of rows returned by the `fetch`. This attribute equates to zero when a cursor is opened prior to the first `fetch`. Once the first `fetch` is executed, it equates to the number of rows returned so far. The following example uses %rowcount to halt execution after the first 100 rows have been processed:

```
begin
loop
fetch c_cursor into v_ord_qty, v_ord_price;
exit when c_cursor%rowcount > 100;
end loop;
end;
```

Using Explicit Cursors

The `fetch` command retrieves the rows in the active set one at a time. The first `fetch` statement sorts the active set, if necessary. The cursor advances to the next row in the active set each time the `fetch` command is executed. You can move through the active set only with the `fetch` command. For each column value returned by the cursor query, there must be a corresponding variable in the into list. The following example illustrates the use of the open and fetch commands as well as the %notfound attribute:

```
begin
open c_guests
loop
fetch c_guests into master_guests;
exit when c_guests%notfound;
end loop;
end;
```

In the preceding example, each row of the active set as defined by the cursor c_guest is processed one row at a time. The iterative loop keeps reading and processing individual rows until all the rows in the active set have been processed.

The following example is a complete PL/SQL script that uses a cursor to process rows of data individually. In this example, you will be reading in records of sales data. The records are processed and data is inserted into the master_order file.

If you want to revisit a previously fetched row, you must close and reopen the cursor and then fetch each row in turn. If you want to change the active set, you must assign new values to the input variables in the cursor query and reopen the cursor. This re-creates the active set with the results of the revised query statement.

```
declare
v_ord_qty number(7,2):=0;
v_ord_price number (7,2):=0;
ord_total number(11,2):=0;

cursor c_orders is           -- cursor declaration
select qty, price from master_order;

begin
open c_orders               -- opening cursor
loop
fetch c_orders into v_ord_qty, v_ord_price;

exit when c_orders%notfound;

  -- calculate order total from cursor values
  -- then insert result into sales order table

v_ord_total = v_ord_price * v_ord_qty;
insert into s_orders values (v_ord_total);
end loop;

close c_orders;                -- close cursor
commit;                        -- commit/save work
end;                           -- program end
```

Closing Explicit Cursors

To close a cursor, you execute the close statement. The following statement closes the cursor c_orders:

```
close c_orders;
```

Oracle implicitly closes a cursor when the user's program terminates its connection with the server.

Implicit Cursors

Oracle implicitly creates and opens a cursor for every SQL statement that is not part of an explicitly declared cursor. The most recent implicit cursor can be referred to as the SQL cursor. You cannot use the open, close, and fetch commands with implicit cursors. However, you can use cursor attributes to access information about the most recently executed SQL statement via the SQL cursor.

Implicit Cursor Attributes

The implicit cursor has four attributes: %isopen, %found, %rowcount, and %notfound. These are the same four attributes as the explicit cursors. You can use these cursor attributes in procedural statements, but not in SQL statements. These attributes, shown in the following list, let you access information about the most recent execution of the insert, select into, update, and delete commands.

%isopen	This always equates to False in an implicit cursor. Oracle always closes the implicit cursor automatically after executing its associated SQL statements.
%notfound	This Boolean attribute equates to True if an insert, update, or delete affected no rows or a select into returned no rows.
%found	Until a SQL data manipulation statement is executed, this attribute evaluates to Null. It equates to True if an insert, update, or delete affects one or more rows. Otherwise, %found equates to False.
%rowcount	This returns the number of rows affected by an insert, update, or delete statement or returned by a select into statement. %rowcount returns zero if the SQL statement affects or returns no rows.

The value of the cursor attributes always refers to the most recently executed SQL statement. This holds true no matter where the statement appears in the program.

Package Cursors

Oracle enables the specification of a cursor to be stored in a package. In this specification, the return clause must be used. This approach to cursors enables you to change the cursor body without changing the cursor specification. The following example illustrates a packaged cursor named c_emp_sal:

```
create package emp_monthly as
cursor c_emp_sal return emp%rowtype;
end emp_monthly;

create package body emp_monthly as
cursor c_emp_sal return emp%rowtype;
select emp_id, emp_salary from master_emp where hire_date > '01-JAN-1986';
end emp_monthly;
```

A cursor specification has no `select` statement because the `return` clause defines the datatype of the result value. In the preceding example, the `%rowtype` attribute is used in the `return` clause to provide the record type that represents a row in a database table.

A cursor body must have a `select` statement and the same `return` clause as its corresponding cursor specification.

Cursor *for* Loops

As a shortcut to fetching rows in a cursor, you can use the `for` loop. The `for` loop is iterated once for each row returned by the query. The cursor itself determines when the cursor `for` loop is exited as well as all other cursor operations. The cursor `for` loop simplifies coding by performing the following:

- An implicit `open` is executed when the loop is initiated
- An implicit `fetch` is executed for each iteration of the loop
- An implicit `close` is executed when the loop is exited

The following PL/SQL example uses the cursor `for` loop to accumulate total orders for each product line:

```
accept p_order prompt 'Please enter your order number: '

declare
v_ord_id   s_item_ord%type :=p_order;
v_order_total number (11,2):=0;

cursor c_cursor is                -- Cursor Declaration
select part_id, price, qty from master_part
where order_id = v_ord_id;

begin                             -- Implicit Open
for order_rec in c_cursor loop    -- Implicit Fetch
v_order_total := v_order_total +
((order_rec.qty * order_rec.qty)*.95);
insert into master_order (part_id, order_total) values
(order_rec.part_id, v_order_total);
end loop;                         -- Implicit Close
commit;                           -- Save Work
end;
```

Cursor Aliases

The fields in an implicit cursor hold the same name as the corresponding fields in the query statement. A problem arises when the query statement contains an expression. For example, how would you refer to the column name in the following query?

```
cursor is ytd_sales
select sales_id, (sales_total/12)*.015 from master_sales
```

In this type of situation, use an alias to refer to the select list item `(sales_total/12)*.015`. In the following example, the same cursor as before is used, except that the alias sales_comm is established:

```
cursor is ytd_sales
select sales_id, (sales_total/12)*.015 sales_comm
from master_sales
```

From this point on, you simply need to refer to the alias sales_comm:

```
if sales_comm > 5000 then ...
```

Cursor Performance

The speed of execution calls within cursors can be improved by adjusting the value of the `cursor_space_for_time` parameter. This parameter specifies when a shared SQL area can be deallocated to make room for a new SQL statement. The default value for this parameter is False. This means that Oracle can deallocate a SQL shared area from the library cache regardless of whether an application cursor associated with its SQL statements is open. The value of True means that a shared SQL area can be deallocated only when all application cursors associated with its SQL statements are closed.

If the value of this parameter is False, Oracle must spend the time and resources to check that the shared SQL area containing the SQL statement is in the library cache. Setting the parameter to True saves Oracle a small amount of time and might improve performance of the execution calls. This is because Oracle does not need to check the shared SQL area because it can never be deallocated while an application cursor is associated with it.

Essential Summary

What Cursors are PL/SQL constructs that enable you to process, one row at a time, the results of a multi-row query. Implicit cursors are created for every SQL Data Manipulation Language statement, whereas explicit cursors are created by users to process queries that return multiple rows.

Why Cursors enable the user to process, one row at a time, the results of a multi-row query. Cursors also improve code processing by reducing the need to parse code repeatedly. Furthermore, you have to open a cursor for processing only once, thereby helping the server performance as well.

How This chapter reviewed the four necessary steps for proper use of cursors. These steps are the cursor declaration, cursor opening, data fetch, and cursor closing.

You also learned the difference between implicit and explicit cursors and saw some practical applications of each.

Formatting Query Results with SQL*Plus

What Is SQL*Plus?

What SQL*Plus is an Oracle product that provides an open window into the Oracle database. It provides developers and end users with the ability to interact directly with the database. SQL*Plus has a command-line interpreter where users can directly submit SQL and SQL*Plus commands and PL/SQL blocks.

SQL commands and PL/SQL blocks are submitted in SQL*Plus to query, manipulate, or delete data in the Oracle databases. In fact, using SQL*Plus is the most common method used to interact with the Oracle database. SQL*Plus commands are issued to control the SQL*Plus environment and to format the database information returned by the SQL commands.

Some of the environmental variables you can control include the session page and line sizes, the displaying of server feedback messages, and whether you want headings on your displayed data.

Why Use SQL*Plus?

SQL*Plus provides Oracle users, whether you are an end user, database administrator, or developer, with a convenient way to interact with the database. Through SQL*Plus you can do the following:

- Manage every aspect of the database
- Enter, edit, retrieve, and run SQL statements and PL/SQL blocks
- Create well-polished, formatted reports
- Display column definitions for any table
- Access and copy data between databases
- Send messages to and accept responses from an end user
- Generate SQL and SQL*Plus code dynamically

SQL*Plus is most commonly used for executing SQL commands and for formatting query results. It is not the only way to interact with the Oracle server. Other Oracle products such as Case*Designer, Data Browser, and SQL*Forms offer you alternate ways to interact with the database.

How to Use SQL*Plus

SQL*Plus is used in the command-line environment to control various features of your Oracle session. The following sections describes SQL*Plus and its many uses.

Environment Commands

The SQL*Plus environment commands define the system parameters that you work within. The set and show commands are used to control these parameters. The set command is used with an extensive number of options that control the interaction of the user's terminal with other SQL commands. The show command is used to display the current setting of the various parameters that have been established by the set command. The general syntax of the set command is

```
set parameter value
```

The following sections go into detail on the various specific SQL*Plus commands.

Session Controls

These parameters establish the general look and feel of your SQL*Plus session. You establish the parameter values with the set command. The following are the options that are to be used with the session commands:

feedback *n*   This defines the number of records returned by a query, where the query selects at least *n* records. The default value is 6.

`feedback on/off`	This determines whether the feedback display is on or off. The default is on.
`pause msg`	This displays a message after scrolling through one screenful of output when running reports. When the message is displayed, the user responds by pressing Enter. There is no default value.
`pause on/off`	This determines whether the pause feature is on or off. The default is on.
`pagesize n`	This sets the number of lines per page to *n*. The default value is 14.
`linesize n`	This sets the number of characters per line to *n*. The default value is 80.
`heading on/off`	This determines if column headings are displayed. The default is on.
`space n`	This sets the number of spaces between columns. The maximum value is 10. The default value is 1.
`echo on/off`	This determines whether each command in a text file is displayed on the screen as it is being executed. The default is off.
`verify on/off`	This determines whether each command in a SQL statement is displayed before and after SQL*Plus substitution parameters are replaced by actual values. The default value is on.

The following example highlights a few of these parameters:

```
set pagesize 6
set pause 'Press <return> to continue...'
set pause on
select city_name from city_index;
```

Sample output:

```
CITY_NAME
---------
charlotte
chicago
clarion
davidson
donaldston
dover

Press <return> to continue...
```

Display Controls for Headers and Footers

The following parameters control the header and footer formats of the output reports:

`ttitle`	This defines the header text. By default, this command centers the header. Insert a vertical line in the text to split the header across several lines.
`ttitle off`	This turns the header off.

`btitle`	This defines, the footer text. By default this command centers the footer.
`btitle off`	This turns the footer off.

All parameter settings remain in effect until they are explicitly changed or the SQL*Plus session ends. Therefore, it is always a good idea to clear the header and footer after each report. The following SQL*Plus commands place a header and footer in the output report:

```
set pagesize 22
set linesize 60
set feedback off
ttitle 'Monthly Sales¦for June'
btitle 'Confidential'

select sales_region, sales_totals from master_sales
where sales_month = '06';
```

Sample output:

```
-------------

          Monthly Sales
            For June

SALES_REGION      SALES_TOTALS
------------      ------------

North East              99204
South East              72900
Mid West               921892
Plains                  69916
South West              98421
West                  1027653
North West              87367

Confidential


ttitle off
btitle off
```

Display Controls for Columns

The `column` parameter enables you to change the heading and formats of the report columns.

`column column_name`	This displays the current settings for the specified columns
`column`	This displays the settings for all columns
`column column_name clear`	This clears all settings for the specified columns
`clear columns`	This clears the settings for all columns

All parameter settings remain in effect until they are explicitly changed or the SQL*Plus session ends. Therefore, it is always a good idea to clear the column parameters after each report. The following example is similar to the previous example except that column headers are specified.

```
set pagesize 22
set linesize 60
set feedback off
ttitle 'Monthly Sales¦for June'
btitle 'Confidential'
column sales_region heading 'Sales Region' format A15
column sales_totals heading 'Total Sales' format $99,999,999

select sales_region, sales_totals from master_sales
where sales_month = '06';
```

Sample output:

```
-------------

          Monthly Sales
            For June

Sales Region        Total Sales
-----------         ----------

North East             $99,204
South East             $72,900
Mid West              $921,892
Plains                 $69,916
South West             $98,421
West                $1,027,653
North West             $87,367

Confidential


column sales_region clear
column sales_total clear
ttitle off
btitle off
```

In the preceding example, the format clause was used to control the positions of certain punctuation marks as well as output character suppression. Use the following formats to meet your requirements:

9	Represents a single zero-suppression digit
,	Represents the position of a comma
.	Represents the position of a period
$	Represents a floating dollar sign
n	Defines a display width of n for character and date columns

Saving and Retrieving Command Files

SQL*Plus enables you to store your commands in an external file known as a command file. After you create a command file, you can retrieve it, edit it, and run it many times, unlike the interactive SQL*Plus commands.

To create the command file, simply type the command `edit file_name` at your SQL*Plus prompt. This starts up the host environment editor. From this point on, type the SQL and SQL*Plus commands that you want in the command file. When you are finished, save the file. By default, the filename extension is .sql.

You can retrieve the command file by entering the `edit file_name` command. Once retrieved, you can edit and save the file as needed.

To run the command file, use the `start` or the `@` command. For example, the following two statements are equivalent, and both run the `sales_setup.sql` command file:

```
start sales_setup
```

```
@sales_setup
```

With the `start` and the `@` commands, the last line of the SQL or PL/SQL block that was executed remains in the session's buffer.

You can also run a command file at the same time you log in to SQL*Plus. This is accomplished by following the `sqlplus` command with your username and password and the `@` command and filename. In the following example, the `sales_setup` command file is executed at the same time the login to SQL*Plus is executed.

```
> sqlplus user_01/password @sales_setup
```

Editing Commands

SQL*Plus commands are stored in the buffer. Therefore you either edit these commands with the backspace key as you type them or you reenter the entire command.

SQL*Plus has numerous commands you can use to edit the SQL or PL/SQL block that is currently stored in the buffer. The following commands can be used to edit the code that resides in the buffer:

`append`	Adds text to the end of the line
`change/old/new/`	Changes old to new in a line
`del`	Deletes a line
`list`	Lists the contents of the buffer
`list n`	Lists line n of the buffer
`input`	Adds one or more lines to the buffer

These commands can be abbreviated to the first letter of the command. The following examples illustrate the usage of the editing commands. Note that an asterisk (*) appears next to the current line of the buffer. By default, the last line in the buffer is the current line. This first example renames a column heading:

```
select sales_region
from master_sales
where dept_no > '203';
```

Sample output:

```
SALES_REGION
------------
North East
South East
North West
```

Now edit the buffer's first line:

```
SQL> l
1  select sales_region
2  from master_sales
3* where dept_no > '203'

SQL> l 1
1* select sales_region
SQL>a "Region"
```

Now list the buffer again to confirm the change to line 1:

```
SQL> l
1  select sales_region "Region"
2  from master_sales
3* where dept_no > '203';
```

Now issue the change command to change the value of dept_no:

```
SQL>l 3
3* where dept_no > '203'

SQL>c/203/205/
```

Again, issue the list command to confirm the changes:

```
SQL> l
1  select sales_region "Region"
2  from master_sales
3* where dept_no > '205';
```

To run the contents of the buffer after editing, issue the run or the slash (/) command. The / command executes the buffer contents, whereas the run command displays the buffer contents and then executes the buffer.

Building a Simple Break Report

A break report is a report where duplicate values are suppressed in the specified column. Additionally, in the break report, a line is skipped every time a value changes in the break column. The following is the normal (non-break) output from the MASTER_SALES table:

```
        Monthly Sales
          For June


sales_region    sales_totals
------------    ------------
North East             55100
North East             43104
North East              1004
```

```
South East              72900
Mid West               811460
Mid West               110432
Plains                  69916
North West              31012
North West              21101
North West               5243
North West              30011
```

Confidential

The following SQL*Plus commands are issued to create a break report:

```
set pagesize 22
set linesize 60
set feedback off
ttitle 'Monthly Sales|for June'
btitle 'Confidential'
column sales_region heading 'Sales Region' format A15
column sales_totals heading 'Total Sales' format $99,999,999
break on sales_region skip 1

select sales_region, sales_totals from master_sales
where sales_month = '06'
order by sales_region;
```

Sample output:

```
        Monthly Sales
          For June


Sales Region        Total Sales
------------        -----------
North East             $55,100
                       $43,104
                        $1,004

South East             $72,900

Mid West              $811,460
                      $110,432

Plains                 $69,916

North West             $31,012
                       $21,101
                        $5,243
                       $30,011

Confidential
```

Summary Computations

Once you have your report broken into subunits with the break command, you can perform additional operations on the rows within each subset. You do this with the compute command. There are eight summary functions that you can use in a break report. Following is the syntax for the compute command:

```
compute function of compute_column on break_column
```

The eight functions to be used with the compute function are as follows:

sum	Computes the sum of the values in the column
count	Counts the number of not null values in the column
num	Counts the number of rows in the column
min	Computes the minimum value in the column
max	Computes the maximum value in the column
avg	Computes the average of the values in the column
std	Computes the standard deviation of the values in the column
var	Computes the variance of the values in the column

Continuing the example from the previous section, the compute command with the sum function is added to display the total sales for each region:

```
set pagesize 22
set linesize 60
set feedback off
ttitle 'Monthly Sales¦for June'
btitle 'Confidential'
column sales_region heading 'Sales Region' format A15
column sales_totals heading 'Total Sales' format $99,999,999
break on sales_region skip 1
compute sum of sales_totals on sales_region

select sales_region, sales_totals from master_sales
where sales_month = '06'
order by sales_region;
```

Sample output:

```
              Monthly Sales
                For June


Sales Region          Total Sales
------------          -----------
North East               $55,100
                         $43,104
                          $1,004
************          -------
sum                      $99,204

South East               $72,900
************          -------
sum                      $72,900

Mid West                $811,460
                        $110,432
************          -------
sum                     $921,892

Plains                   $69,916
************          -------
```

```
sum                          $69,916

North West                   $31,012
                             $21,101
                              $5,243
                             $30,011
************                 -------
sum                          $87,357
```

Confidential

To calculate the grand total for a column, use the report clause with the break and compute commands. The order by command is included in this example to order the output in ascending order.

```
set pagesize 22
set linesize 60
set feedback off
ttitle 'Monthly Sales¦for June'
btitle 'Confidential'
column sales_region heading 'Sales Region' format A15
column sales_totals heading 'Total Sales' format $99,999,999
break on sales_region skip 1 on report
compute sum of sales_totals on sales_region on report

select sales_region, sales_totals from master_sales
where sales_month = '06'
order by sales_region, sales_totals
```

Sample output:

```
              Monthly Sales
                For June


Sales Region             Total Sales
-----------              -----------
Mid West                    $111,460
                            $810,432
************                 -------
sum                         $921,892

North East                   $55,100
                             $43,104
                              $1,004
************                 -------
sum                          $99,204

North West                   $31,012
                             $31,101
                             $20,243
                              $5,011
************                 -------
sum                          $87,357

Plains                       $69,916
************                 -------
sum                          $69,916
```

```
South East                    $72,900
************                   -------
sum                           $72,900

sum                        $1,251,269

              Confidential
```

spool

The spool command is used to store the results of a query in an external flat file. This flat file can be saved for future use or it can be printed on your printer. The following command directs SQL*Plus to place all results of queries in the external flat file named regional_sales.rpt:

```
spool regional_sales.rpt
```

SQL*Plus continues to spool information to the flat file until you turn spooling off. Issue the spool off command to do this.

To print the query results immediately, spool them to a file as described by the spool command. Then, issue the spool out command. This command stops spooling and copies the contents of the spooled file to your host computer's default printer. spool out does not delete the spooled file after printing.

Besides spooling reports or query results to a flat file, it is common to spool columns of data to flat files. This act is usually performed to transfer data from one database to another. Normally, you would spool the necessary columns to a flat file, then use SQL*Loader to load them into the destination tables.

Prior to creating a flat file of data, you should issue the following commands. These commands turn off column headers and other information that results in column data only:

```
set pagesize 0
set linesize 80
set newpage 0
set echo off
set feedback off
set verify off
```

Essential Summary

SQL*Plus is an Oracle product that provides a direct and easy way to interact with the Oracle database. With SQL*Plus, you can control the environment you are working in as well as format the results of a query.

What

As you learned in this chapter, SQL*Plus provides an easy way to create a well-formatted report. Additionally, SQL*Plus assists you with data transfer from one database to another, managing all aspects of the database, and entering and running all SQL commands.

Why

How

Through an interactive session or the use of a command file, you issue commands to Oracle through SQL*Plus that control the working environment, session parameters, and formatting of query results.

Additional SQL*Plus Commands

What Are Additional SQL*Plus Commands?

What SQL*Plus is a tool that enables you to interact directly with the Oracle database. SQL*Plus enables you to manipulate SQL and PL/SQL block commands, format query results, copy data between tables, and execute SQL and PL/SQL code. You can also use SQL*Plus to define your environment, which controls the area you work within. These controls include defining page sizes and line sizes, determining whether you want headings on the query results, and defining the level of server information feedback you would like.

This chapter discusses the more advanced commands that were not covered in Chapter 18, "Formatting Query Results with SQL*Plus," as well as some lesser-known commands.

Why Use Additional SQL*Plus Commands?

Why

SQL*Plus commands provide the user, developer, and database administrator the necessary tools to access the Oracle database efficiently and easily. Some of the benefits of using SQL*Plus include the following:

- It has an online text editor that enables you to save, retrieve, and run SQL and PL/SQL block commands
- It formats and performs calculations on query results
- It displays column information for tables

How to Use Additional SQL*Plus Commands

How

This chapter presents the more advanced SQL*Plus topics that enable you to tailor your output to meet many diverse needs.

Page Formatting

In SQL*Plus, a page refers to a screenful of information on your computer display, or a page of spooled printed report. You can place titles at the top and bottom of each page, set the number of lines per page, and establish the width of each line.

As described in Chapter 18, you can include a title at the top and bottom of each page by using the ttitle and btitle commands, respectively. This section describes the options you can use with these two title commands.

The clauses that can be used with the ttitle and btitle commands are as follows:

col *n*	Makes the next character value appear in the specified column of the line.
skip *n*	Skips to a new line *n* times. If *n* is greater than 1, *n*–1 blank lines appear before the next character value.
left	Left justifies the following character value.
right	Right justifies the following character value.
center	Centers the following character value.
bold	Makes the line bold. Bold is represented on your screen by repeating the line three times. When it is printed, the line is printed once and is bolded.
	This is the line continuation marker. Place the hyphen at the end of a line that is continued on the following line.

Additionally, you can include any of the following system parameters in the title statements:

SQL.LNO	Represents the current line number
SQL.PNO	Represents the current page number
SQL.RELEASE	Represents the current Oracle release number
SQL.SQLCODE	Represents the current error code
SQL.USER	Represents the current username

The following example uses several of these clauses and parameters to create meaningful and appealing reports. The skip, center, left, and right SQL*Plus clauses and the sql.pno system parameter are used in the following example:

```
ttitle center 'XZY Corporation' skip 1 -
center '***************' skip 2 left 'Region Sales Report' -
right 'Sales Totals for June' skip 2
btitle left 'Confidential' right 'Page: ' format 999 -
sql.pno
set line size 60

column sales_region heading 'Sales Region' format A15
column sales_totals heading 'Total Sales' format $99,999,999
break on sales_region skip 1

select sales_region, sales_totals from master_sales
where sales_month = '06';
```

Sample output:

```
                    XYZ Corporation
                    ***************

Region Sales Report                  Sales Totals for June


Sales Region        Total Sales
------------        -----------
North East             $55,100
                       $43,104
                        $1,004

South East             $72,900

Mid West              $811,460
                      $110,432

Plains                 $69,916

North West             $31,012
                       $21,101
                        $5,243
                       $30,011


Confidential                             Page: 1
```

Bind Variables

Bind variables are variables that are created in SQL*Plus. These variables can then be referenced in a PL/SQL program as if they were a declared variable in the PL/SQL program. Bind variables are necessary because variables declared in PL/SQL programs are not accessible to SQL*Plus. Bind variables are used frequently to manage subprogram return codes.

To create a bind variable, use the `variable` command. The syntax is

```
variable variable_name number
```

To reference the bind variable in a PL/SQL subprogram, precede the bind variable with a colon (:). For example, the following statement references the bind variable sales_total by assigning the value of 0 to it in a PL/SQL program:

```
:sales_total :=0;
```

To display the value of the sales_total bind variable, use the SQL*Plus `print` command. The syntax for this is

```
print sales_total
```

Substitution Variables

A substitution variable is a user-defined variable name that is preceded by an ampersand (&). SQL*Plus treats the substitution variable as though it were the value of the substitution variable, rather than the variable itself. You can use substitution variables anywhere in SQL and SQL*Plus commands, except as the first command entered during a SQL*Plus session. If you do not supply a value for the substitution variable, SQL*Plus prompts you for a value. This occurs when the substitution variable is encountered during execution.

In the following example, the variable sort1 is defined as position and the variable table1 is defined as master_parts.

The first example uses substitution variables, whereas the second example uses the values of the substitution variables. Both examples produce the same results.

```
break on &sort1
select * from &table1
order by &sort1 asc;

break on position
select * from master_parts
order by position asc;
```

The following system variables affect substitution variables:

set scan	Turns substitution on and off.
set define	Defines the substitution character. By default it is the ampersand (&).

set escape	Defines the escape character you would use before the substitution character. This character instructs SQL*Plus to treat the substitution character as an ordinary character.
set verify on	Defines whether each line of the command file is listed before and after substitution.
set concat	Defines the concatenation character. By default it is the period (.).

The following example uses the set concat command. SQL*Plus automatically queries the user for the value of sales because it is not previously defined.

```
SQL> select * from master_parts
where parts_codes = '&c_parts.001';

Enter value for c_parts: 21345
```

This is interpreted as

```
SQL> select * from master_sales
where sales_region = '21345001';
```

Now look at a realistic example where the order by clause is used with the substitution variable. Notice in the following example that SQL*Plus queries the user for input for every substitution variable.

```
SQL> select * from master_personnel
SQL> where job = '&c_job'
SQL> order by '&c_job';

Enter value for c_job: teacher
old where job = '&c_type'
new where job = 'teacher'


Enter value for c_job: teacher
old order by &c_job
new order by 'teacher'
```

Note from the preceding example that you had to enter the value twice for the substitution variable c_job. SQL*Plus prompts you for every substitution variable. You can avoid being prompted repeatedly for the same values by using the double ampersand (&&). This directs SQL*Plus to automatically define the substitution variable with && as equal to the substitution variable with one ampersand (&). This way, you can recode the previous statement to avoid the reprompting as follows:

```
select * from master_personnel
where job = '&c_job'
order by &&c_job;
```

Database Connections

SQL*Plus enables you to connect to your default database or to a remote database. Use the connect command to accomplish the remote connections. Normally, when you start SQL*Plus, you connect to your default database.

Once you are logged in to your default database, SQL*Plus allows you to connect to the same database under a different user name. For example, to connect user_01 to the current default database using the password 0823KYQ, your statement would look like this:

```
SQLPLUS> connect user_01/0823KYQ
```

SQL*Plus prompts you for your username and password if you omit them from the connect string.

You can also access remote databases through SQL*Plus. This is particularly important when you have a distributed environment. SQL*Plus enables you to connect to a remote database in one of two ways:

- Connect to the remote database from within your current SQL*Plus session
- Connect to the remote database at the same time you issue the sqlplus command

Either way, you must have a valid username and password on the database to which you wish to connect.

To connect to a remote database from within SQL*Plus, issue the connect command, username and password, and the remote database specification. For example, the following statement establishes a connection to the remote database california_sales using the user_01 username:

```
SQLPLUS> connect user_01/0823KYQ@california_sales
```

The exact database specification you entered in the connect statement depends upon the SQL*NET protocol and operating system of your computer. Check with your SQL*NET manual and system administrator for the correct database string to use.

To connect to a remote database from the command line, issue the sqlplus command along with your database specification. If you omit the username and password, SQL*Plus prompts you for these. The following example is similar to the previous one, except that this statement connects to the remote database when you start up SQL*Plus:

```
>sqlplus connect user_01/0823KYQ@california_sales
```

You will remain connected to the database until you do one of the following:

- Issue a connect command to connect you to a different database
- Issue the disconnect command
- Exit SQL*Plus

Using SQL*Plus to Copy Data

SQL*Plus permits you to copy data in any of the following ways:

- From one remote database to another remote database
- From your default database to a remote database
- From a remote database to your default database

The syntax of the SQL*Plus command is as follows:

```
copy from database_name to database_name -
action -
destination_table (column_name, column_name,...) -
using query
```

Let's take a look at each of the pieces of the SQL*Plus command. You must know the exact database specification for the from and to database_names as well as have a valid username and password.

The copy command acts differently depending on the action clause you supply and whether the destination table already exists. The four clauses that you can use are create, insert, append, and replace.

The create clause results in the following actions:

- If the destination table already exists, an error is generated and processing stops.
- If the destination table does not already exist, the copy command creates the table using the copied data.

The insert clause results in the following actions:

- If the destination table already exists, the copy command inserts the data into the table.
- If the destination table does not already exist, an error is generated and processing stops.

The append clause results in the following actions:

- If the destination table already exists, the copied data is inserted into the table.
- If the destination table does not already exist, the copy command creates the table and inserts the copied data.

The replace clause results in the following actions:

- If the destination table is already present, the copy command drops the existing data and replaces it with the copied data.
- If the destination table does not exist, copy creates it using the copied data.

Miscellaneous SQL*Plus Commands

The following is a summary of many SQL*Plus commands in addition to those presented earlier in this chapter.

@   Runs the specified command file. By default the file has an extension of .sql and is expected to be in the current default directory. The following executes the file part_copy.sql:

```
@part_copy.sql
```

@@ Runs a nested command file. By default, the command file is expected to be sql and be located in the same path as the calling command file. The following example is the command file part_copy.sql. When processing reaches @parts_pre, that file is expected to be found in the current default directory. When @@parts_cross_xref is executed, this file is expected to be located in the same directory as the part_copy.sql file.

```
Select * from master_parts;
@parts_pre
@@Parts_cross_xref
```

/ The slash executes the SQL command or PL/SQL block that is currently stored in the buffer. This command is similar to the run command but does not display the commands on your screen.

accept Reads a line of data input from the terminal and stores it in a specified variable. You can include the option hide clause at the end of the statement to suppress the displaying of the user's input. A practical example of the hide clause is when you are prompting the user for a password. You would not want this to be echoed back to the screen.

Syntax:

```
accept variable datatype prompt text
```

The following is an example where the user is prompted to enter the social security number of the employee:

```
accept emp_ssn char prompt 'Enter Employee's SSN: '
```

define Assigns a character value to a user-specified variable. This command can also be used to display the value of the specified variable. The first example assigns a character value to the variable text:

```
define text_1 = 'your text string goes here'
```

This example lists the value of the variable text_1:

```
SQL>define text_1
```

```
define text_1     = 'your text string goes here' (char)
```

describe Lists the columns, datatypes, and lengths of the columns in the specified table, view, or synonym. This can also be used to display the specifications for the specified function, procedure, package, or package contents. The following describes the MASTER_PART table:

To describe the table, issue

```
describe master_part
```

This command lists

```
NAME                NULL?      TYPE
-------------------------------
PART_ID             NOT NULL   NUMBER
PART_NUMBER         NOT NULL   VARCHAR2(15)
```

```
PART_NAME                    VARCHAR2(50)
PART_CODE                    VARCHAR2(10)
```

disconnect   Logs the user off the Oracle database and commits all pending changes to the database. The user is not disconnected from SQL*Plus. This command is issued at the sqlplus command line.

exit   Logs the user off the Oracle database, exits the user from SQL*Plus, and commits all pending changes to the database. This command is issued at the sqlplus command line.

help   Accesses the help system for SQL*Plus.

host   Executes a host operating system command without leaving SQL*Plus. The following requests a directory listing of the current directory:

```
SQL> host directory
```

remark   Begins a user comment. This comment is not interpreted as a command by SQL*Plus.

runform   Invokes SQL*Forms from within SQL*Plus

timing   Records timing information for an elapsed period of time. Lists timing information with the show clause. The following statements create a timing area named time_test, display the time data, display timing information, and remove the timing area from memory:

```
timing start time_test
set timing on
timing show
timing stop
```

undefine   Deletes a specified user variable from the database. The following removes the variable cost_count from the database:

```
undefine cost_count
```

whenever oserror   Exits SQL*Plus if an operating system error occurs. The default for SQL*Plus is to continue processing when this command is omitted. The following clauses can be included with this command:

exit	Forces SQL*Plus to exit when an operating system error is detected. You can direct the exit to return the SQL*Plus failure code, operating system failure code, a number, or a variable.
continue	Turns the exit option off.
commit	A commit is executed when an operating system error is detected.
rollback	Executes a rollback when an operating system error is detected.
none	Directs SQL*Plus to take no action when an operating system error is detected.

The following code example rolls back all changes to the last savepoint when an operating system error is detected. The operating system error code returns when SQL*Plus exits.

```
whenever oserror exit oscode rollback;
insert into nightly_costs (select
* from master_costs where nightly_costs.id =
master_costs.id);
```

`whenever sqlerror` Exits SQL*Plus if a SQL command or PL/SQL block generates an error. The default for SQL*Plus is to continue processing when this command is omitted. The following clauses can be included with this command:

`exit`	Forces SQL*Plus to exit when a SQL or PL/SQL error is detected. You can direct the exit to return the SQL*Plus failure code, operating system failure code, a number, or a variable.
`continue`	Turns the exit option off.
`commit`	A commit is executed when a SQL or PL/SQL error is detected.
`rollback`	Executes a rollback when a SQL or PL/SQL error is detected.
`none`	Directs SQL*Plus to take no action when a SQL or PL/SQL error is detected.

The following code example rolls back all changes to the last savepoint when a SQL or PL/SQL error is detected. The operating system error code returns when SQL*Plus exits.

```
whenever sqlerror exit oscode rollback;
insert into nightly_costs (select
* from master_costs where mightly_costs.id =
master_costs.id);
```

Essential Summary

What SQL*Plus is an Oracle tool that enables users to interact with the Oracle server directly. This chapter described several of the environment commands that control how your terminal interacts with SQL*Plus. Additionally, the copy command and advanced SQL*Plus commands were presented in this chapter.

Why SQL*Plus is needed to enable the user to issue SQL and PL/SQL block commands to insert and manipulate the data in the database. Also, this tool allows for formatting, performing calculations on, storing, and printing query results.

How Through an interactive session with SQL*Plus, you issue your SQL, PL/SQL block, or SQL*Plus commands to obtain your desired results. These commands can also be contained in a command file that is executed within SQL*Plus.

PART V

Data Integrity

Data Integrity

What Is Data Integrity?

What A critical issue in database management is ensuring that the data in the database adheres to a predefined set of rules. These rules will be consistent with the business processes the system supports. The database administrator, application developer, and business area representative are responsible for designing and creating the rules.

In essence, data integrity involves defining the rules that restrict the valid values for a column in a table. Integrity constraints are defined on tables, and as such all views and table synonyms are subject to the integrity constraints. If an attempt is made by a DML statement that violates an integrity constraint, an error is generated and the transaction is rolled back.

Why Use Data Integrity?

Why Data integrity constraints are a means that Oracle uses to prevent invalid data entry into the database tables. These integrity constraints are defined to enforce the business rules that are associated with the information in a database. Oracle never violates these rules, thereby guaranteeing data integrity.

The various types of integrity constraints enable you to customize and tailor your database to meet your business needs. The different types of integrity constraints are discussed in this chapter.

How to Use Data Integrity

How Integrity constraints are defined on the tables of the database. Views and table synonyms are subject to the integrity constraints defined in the underlying base tables. This chapter reviews the types of integrity and how to use each type.

Where to Use Data Integrity

You should define the data integrity rules in the database rather than in an application. It is less costly to do it at the database level than to create equivalent logic in your application. One of the biggest reasons for doing it at the database level is that the data integrity at this level is optimized for fast performance. Also, all applications can take advantage of these global constraints, rather than building similar logic in each individual application.

Naming Integrity Constraints

All constraints have a name. You can name the constraint during its creation. If you don't name the constraint, Oracle provides a name for it. This user-provided name must be unique with respect to other constraints that you own.

Types of Integrity Constraints

In the Oracle relational database, the following are the different types of data integrity constraints:

- Null
- Unique
- Primary key
- Referential
- Check

The integrity constraint for a table is established when the table is created or altered. You can include the `constraint` clause in the `create table` or `alter table` command to establish an integrity constraint. The following example illustrates the general syntax format for the constraint clause:

```
constraint constraint_name constraint_type
```

The constraint types are discussed in the following sections.

Null Integrity Constraint

By default, all columns in a table allow nulls. In other words, they permit the absence of a value in every column. By setting the not null integrity constraint, you require the specified column to have a value for every row in the table.

The following statement creates a table where the l_name column has the not null constraint on it. That means for every row added to the table, a value must exist for the l_name column.

```
create table emp
(emp_id    number(7),
 l_name    varchar2(20)
 constraint  s_emp_l_name_nn not null,
 f_name    varchar2(20),
 dept_id   varchar2(5));
```

Use the describe command to view the null constraints on a table. The following describe command shows the not null constraint on the EMP table.

```
describe emp
```

Sample output:

```
Name           NULL?      Type
----           -----      ----
EMP_ID                    NUMBER(7)
L_NAME         NOT NULL   VARCHAR2(20)
F_NAME                    VARCHAR2(20)
DEPT_ID                   VARCHAR2(5)
```

Unique Integrity Constraint

This constraint requires that all values in a column be unique. There cannot be any duplicate values in a column that has the unique integrity constraint. The column defined in the unique key constraint is known as the unique key column. Oracle permits you to place this constraint across several columns. This is commonly known as a composite unique constraint. A composite unique constraint requires that the combination of the unique key column is unique and that the combination does not repeat.

The following statement creates a unique constraint on the emp_id column in the EMP table:

```
create table emp
(emp_id    number(7)
 constraint s_emp_emp_id_uk unique,
 l_name    varchar2(20)
 constraint  s_emp_l_name_nn not null,
 f_name    varchar2(20),
 dept_id   varchar2(5));
```

The previous example used the describe command to confirm the null integrity constraint. However, to display other types of constraints on a table, you have to take a different approach. Refer to the section titled "Displaying Integrity Constraints" later in this chapter for methods to confirm a table's constraints.

The unique integrity constraint considers a column with a null value as unique. All nulls are considered different and unique in the eyes of the unique integrity constraint. Therefore, it is always a good idea to place the not null constraint on the unique column. This ensures that a value is entered for that column and that all values are truly unique. The following table declaration adds the unique and not null constraints on the emp_id column:

```
create table emp
(emp_id      number(7)
constraint s_emp_emp_id_uk unique
constraint s_emp_emp_id_nn not null,
l_name      varchar2(20)
constraint  s_emp_l_name_nn not null,
f_name      varchar2(20),
dept_id     varchar2(5));
```

Primary Key Integrity Constraint

The primary key integrity constraint designates that a column or combination of columns is the table's primary key. The primary key uniquely identifies every row in the table. This constraint also implicitly creates not null and unique constraints on the column. Although Oracle does not require that every table have a primary key, you should get in the habit of creating one. Also, you should choose a column or combination of columns for the primary key whose data values never change.

The following statement creates a primary key constraint on the emp_id field in the EMP table:

```
create table emp
(emp_id      number(7)
constraint s_emp_emp_id_pk primary key,
l_name      varchar2(20)
constraint  s_emp_l_name_nn not null,
f_name      varchar2(20),
dept_id     varchar2(5));
```

You can use a second syntax to create table constraints, known as the table_constraint syntax. With this syntax, the constraints are placed at the bottom of the create table statement. The following example creates the same table as the previous example, using the table_constraint syntax:

```
create table emp
(emp_id      number(7),
l_name      varchar2(20),
f_name      varchar2(20),
dept_id     varchar2(5),
constraint s_emp_emp_id_pk primary key (emp_id));
```

Oracle restricts each table to having only one primary key. The primary key cannot have a datatype of long or long raw. You cannot designate the same column or combination of columns as both a primary key and a unique key or as both a primary key and a cluster key. If this is attempted, Oracle generates an error.

The following example adds a composite `primary key` constraint on the `l_name` and `f_name` columns of the EMP table:

```
alter table emp
add primary key
(l_name, f_name);
alter table emp enable primary key;
```

Referential Integrity Constraint

Referential integrity constraints are used to enforce the business rules that govern the relationships between columns of different tables. With this type of constraint, you develop a parent-child relationship between tables. The parent table contains the referenced key, and the child table contains the foreign key.

For example, you have a parent table that contains a list of the 50 states. The child table can be an address table that contains names and addresses of people you know. The address table has a referential constraint on it that says the only valid addresses are those where the state is one that exists in the parent state table. If you tried to add a new address where the state abbreviation is ZZ, the insert would fail because ZZ does not exist in the parent 50 state table. The following example creates this referential integrity constraint on the address table:

```
alter table address
add constraint fk_state_abbr
foreign key (state_abbr)
references state_abbr(state_abbr)
```

The following is a summary of the main terms used when establishing referential integrity:

Foreign key	The column or set of columns included in the referential constraint definition
Referenced key	The unique key or primary key of the same or different table that is referenced by the foreign key
Dependent table	The table that contains the foreign key
Referenced table	The table that is referenced by the foreign key

Oracle places several restrictions on the actions you can take on referential keys. You cannot alter or delete the referenced key if the resulting key values violate the referential integrity constraints. For example, you could not delete the referenced key value because the dependent would then violate the referential constraints. However, you could delete the reference key value if there were no dependent rows.

Cascading Delete of Foreign Key

There are legitimate times when you do want to delete a reference key value. When there are no foreign key values referencing the value, you can proceed with the delete. However, many times there are rows with the `foreign key` constraint on them that prevent you from deleting the reference key value.

Establish the on delete cascade constraint on the referenced key to resolve this issue. on delete cascade allows the deletion of referenced key values in the parent table that have dependent rows in the child table. When the parent table delete occurs, Oracle automatically deletes the corresponding rows in the child table.

Check Integrity Constraint

The check integrity constraint explicitly defines a condition that must be true. To satisfy this constraint, every row in the table must make the condition true. The condition can also evaluate to Unknown to accommodate the null value. If a statement is attempted that causes a condition to be false, the statement is rolled back.

The check constraint has the following limitations:

- It cannot contain subqueries
- It cannot contain the sysdate, uid, user, or userenv functions
- It cannot use the psuedo-columns currval, nextval, level, or rownum

The following example creates a check constraint on the column city in the table OFFICE_LOCATION:

```
create table office_location
(office_id      number (5),
office_name     varchar2(50),
city            varchar2(50)
constraint check_city
check (city in ("Dallas","Denver","Indianapolis"),
state           varchar2(50));
```

There are no limits to the number of check constraints permitted on a column. A single column can have multiple check constraints.

Displaying Integrity Constraints

In previous sections, the describe command was used to display whether the null constraint was used for a particular column. The USER_CONSTRAINTS table contains comprehensive information about all the constraints on a given table.

The following are the columns in the USER_CONSTRAINTS table:

owner	The user who owns the constraint definition.
constraint_name	Name of the constraint definition.
constraint_type	The type of constraint. The different types are C for check, P for primary key, U for unique key, and R for foreign key.
table_name	Name of the table associated with the constraint definition.
search_condition	Text of the search condition for a check condition.
r_owner	Owner of the table referenced in a referential constraint.

r_constraint_name	Name of primary key constraint definition on the referenced column of a referential constraint.
delete_rule	Action to take with foreign keys that reference a deleted primary or unique key. The two options are delete cascade and no action.
status	Value used internally by the Oracle server.

To confirm the constraints on a particular table, perform a select on the USER_CONSTRAINTS table for your specified table. For example, the following checks the constraints on the MST_PARTS table:

```
select constraint_name "Name",
constraint_type "Type"
from user_constraints
where table_name = 'mst_parts';
```

Sample output:

```
Name              Type
----------------  ----
S_PARTS_CODE_FK    R
S_PARTS_NUMBER_UK  U
S_PARTS_ID_PK      P
```

The USER_CONS_COLUMN table provides additional information that helps you confirm the constraints on a table. The following are the columns of the USER_CONS_COLUMN table:

owner	User that owns the constraint definition
constraint_name	Name of the constraint definition
table_name	Name of the table associated with the constraint definition
column_name	Name of the column specified in the constraint definition
position	Original position of the column in the constraint definition

The following statement displays the column constraint information for the table CUSTOMER:

```
select constraint_name "Constraint",
column_name "Column"
from user_cons_column where table_name = "customer";
```

Sample output:

```
Constraint            Column
----------------      ------
S_CUST_ID_PK          CUST_ID
S_CUST_SALES_REG_FK   SALES_REGION
```

Displaying Integrity Constraint Exceptions

To assist you in debugging your constraint exceptions, include the exceptions option in the enable clause of a create table or alter table command. This exceptions option places the rowid, table owner, table name, and constraint name of all exception rows into a predefined

EXCEPTIONS table. Oracle provides a script, named `utlexcpt.sql`, that creates the EXCEPTIONS table.

The following statement alters a table to add a new constraint with the `exceptions` option:

```
alter table personnel,
enable primary key
exceptions into exceptions;
```

Once the EXCEPTIONS table is created, you can perform a select on it to obtain the rows that are in violation of a constraint. The following example uses a join to create an output that displays the rows of data that are in violation of the table rules. In this example, a duplicate unique key value exists in the table DEPT.

```
select dept_no, dept_name, dept_mgr from dept, exceptions
where exceptions.constraint = "s_dept_name_uk"
and dept.rowid = exceptions.row_id;
```

Sample output:

```
DEPT_NO   DEPT_NAME   DEPT_MGR
-------   ---------   --------
     11   Packaging   Riley
     11   Packaging   Riley
```

Enabling and Disabling Integrity Constraints

An integrity constraint defined on a table can be in either of two states: enabled or disabled. When a constraint is enabled, the constraint rules are enforced as defined in the constraint definition. Likewise, when the constraint is disabled, the constraint rules are not enforced.

If an attempt is made to enable a constraint on a table that does not adhere to the rules of the integrity constraint, Oracle generates an exceptions error and the issuing statement is rolled back. If an exception exists, you cannot enable the constraint until it is updated or deleted.

The `create table` and `alter table` commands are used to enable and disable constraints. The following example disables the constraints on the table MST_PARTS:

```
alter table mst_parts
disable constraint s_parts_code_fk;
```

There are several legitimate times when you want to temporarily disable constraints. Some examples are during data loading via SQL*Loader and during importing and exporting processes. In both of these cases, temporarily turning off the constraints can improve the performance of the operation.

System Views of Integrity Constraints

All constraint information is stored in the data dictionary. Oracle provides several views that can be used to see how the data dictionary currently has integrity constraints defined. These views are as follows:

`all_constraints`	Constraint definitions for all accessible tables
`all_cons_columns`	Information about accessible columns in constraint definitions
`user_constraints`	Constraint definitions on the user's tables
`user_cons_columns`	Information about columns in constraint definitions owned by the user
`dba_constraints`	Constraint definitions on all tables in the database
`dba_cons_columns`	Information about all columns in constraint definitions

Dropping Integrity Constraints

To drop an integrity constraint, issue the `alter table` command with the `drop` clause. In the following statement, the constraint is dropped from the MST_PARTS table:

```
alter table mst_parts
drop constraint s_parts_code_fk;
```

Essential Summary

Data integrity ensures that the database data adheres to a predefined set of rules as determined by the database administrator and the application developer. Both the administrator and the developer receive these rules from the business areas the database supports. It is truly the business process that drives and defines data integrity. **What**

Data integrity and integrity constraints are mechanisms used by the Oracle server to prevent invalid data from entering the database. These constraints on data help ensure that the business rules are strictly enforced. **Why**

In this chapter, you learned the various types of integrity constraints and how to apply them at the table level. This chapter also presented the ways to manage and administer the constraints. **How**

Transactions

What Is a Transaction?

What A transaction is one or more SQL statements that make up a single logical unit of work. The transaction begins with the first SQL statement being executed and ends when the effects of the transaction are saved or backed out.

For every transaction, Oracle allows two situations to occur. If the SQL statements in a transaction complete normally, the effects of the transaction are made permanent in the database. This is called committing the transaction. The other situation is if any of the SQL statements are unable to complete for some reason. In this case the effects of the transaction are removed from the database and the transaction ends. This removal of the effects of a transaction is called rolling back the transaction.

Why Use Transactions?

Why Transactions provide the user of the Oracle server, application developer, or database administrator the capability of guaranteeing data consistency and data concurrency. Data consistency provides the user with a consistent view of the data, which consists of data committed by other users as well as changes made by the user. Data concurrency provides the user access to data concurrently used by many other users.

Without transactions coordinating data concurrency and data consistency, the user would experience inconsistent data reads, lost updates, and nonrepeatable reads. Additionally, DDL statements issued by all users could destroy your operations. For example, you could be executing a table update while another user is simultaneously trying to delete the same table.

To help solve problems associated with data concurrency and consistency, multi-user databases use some form of data locking. Locks are ways to prevent destructive interaction between users accessing the same table or row of a table.

How to Use Transactions

Executing a transaction successfully is not the same as committing the transaction. A successful execution of the transaction means that the SQL statement was executed without any errors. However, the effects of the successfully executed transaction can still be rolled back until it is committed.

This chapter goes over the different aspects of transactions and different ways to manage these transactions.

The *set transaction* Command

The set transaction command is an integral part of transaction management. This command performs one of these operations on the current transaction:

- It establishes the transaction as either a read-only or a read-write transaction
- It assigns your current read-write transaction to a specified rollback segment

The read-only transaction is the default mode of all transactions. With this mode, you do not have a rollback segment assigned. Additionally, you cannot perform an insert, delete, or update command during this transaction.

The read-write transaction mode provides no restrictions on the DML statements allowed in the transaction.

The set transaction command enables you to explicitly assign a particular rollback segment to the read-write transaction. This rollback segment is used to undo any changes made by the current transaction if a rollback is executed. If you do not specify a rollback segment, Oracle assigns one to the transaction.

Committing a Transaction

Committing a transaction is simply the user either explicitly or implicitly permanently saving the transaction changes to the database. Until you perform a commit, the following characterize the state of your transaction:

- Data Manipulation Language operations affect only the database buffer. Because the changes have affected only the buffer, these changes can be backed out.
- A rollback segment buffer is created in the server.
- The owner of the transaction can view the effects of the transaction with the `select` statement.
- Other users of the database cannot see the effects of the transaction.
- The affected rows are locked and other users cannot change the data within the affected rows.

Once the commit is executed, the following steps occur:

1. Locks held on the affected rows are released.
2. The transaction is marked as complete.
3. The internal transaction table of the server generates a system change number, assigns this number to the transaction, and saves them both in the table.

Use the `commit` statement to explicitly make permanent the changes from a transaction. The following example shows a simple transaction being executed, with a commit issued after the transaction is executed:

```
SQL>insert into table raw_material values
SQL>(part_id, part_name)
SQL>values (s_raw_mat.nextval, "18g Copper Wire");

1 row created

SQL> commit;

Commit completed
```

You can use the `comment` clause with the `commit` statement to place a text string in the data dictionary along with the transaction ID. You may, at a later time, view the comments in the data dictionary through the dba_2pc_pending data dictionary view.

To make an explicit commit, you must have the `force transaction` system privilege. To manually commit a distributed transaction that was originated by another user, you must have the `force any transaction` system privilege.

Oracle performs an implicit commit before and after every Data Definition Language (DDL) command.

Two-Phase Commits

Oracle manages the commits and rollbacks of distributed transactions and maintains data integrity for all the distributed databases participating in the distributed transaction. Oracle performs these tasks by a mechanism known as a two-phase commit.

In a nondistributed environment, all transactions are either committed or rolled back as a unit. However, in a distributed environment, commits and rollbacks of a distributed transaction must be coordinated over a network so that the participating databases either all commit or all roll back the transaction. This must be true even if the network fails during the distributed transaction. The two-phase commit guarantees that the nodes participating in the transaction either commit or roll back the transaction, thus maintaining complete data integrity of the global database.

All implicit DML operations performed by integrity constraints, remote procedure calls, and triggers are protected by Oracle's two-phase commit.

Rolling Back a Transaction

Rolling back a transaction means undoing any changes the current transaction has made. The `rollback` command undoes the entire transaction. To execute a rollback of the entire transaction, issue the `rollback` command at the `sqlplus` command line. Alternately, you can roll back a portion of a transaction with the `rollback to savepoint` command. Savepoints are discussed in the next section of this chapter.

When you roll back an entire transaction, the following steps occur:

1. All changes made by the current transaction are undone using the corresponding rollback segment.
2. All locks on the rows caused by the transaction are released.
3. The transaction is ended.

When you roll back a transaction to a savepoint, the following steps occur:

1. Only the SQL statements executed after the last savepoint are rolled back.
2. The specified savepoint in the `rollback` command is preserved, but all other savepoints after that savepoint are removed from the database.
3. All locks established since the specified savepoint are released.
4. The transaction is still active and can continue.

No privileges are required to roll back your own transactions. Oracle requires that you have `force transaction` system privileges to roll back any in-doubt distributed transaction owned by you. An in-doubt transaction is a transaction that is executed on one or more nodes of a distributed database. The transaction becomes 'in-doubt' when the connecting network fails or one of the nodes is unable to complete the processing of the transaction. Please refer to Chapter

40, "Distributed Databases and Processes," for more information on distributed databases. If the distributed transaction is owned by someone else, you are required to have the `force any transaction` system privilege.

Oracle performs an implicit rollback if there is a severe failure with the host computer or the application program.

Savepoints

A savepoint is like a bookmark in the transaction. You explicitly place this bookmark for reference at a later time. Savepoints are used to break up a large transaction into smaller pieces. This enables you to roll back your work to intermediate points in the transaction rather than rolling back the entire transaction. For example, if you are performing a large number of updates, and an error occurs, you need to roll back only to the last savepoint; therefore, you would not need to reprocess every statement.

The following example creates the savepoint master_credit:

```
savepoint master_credit;
```

Savepoint names must be unique within a given transaction. If you create a second savepoint named the same as an earlier savepoint, the previous savepoint is erased. Either of the following statements rolls back a transaction to the savepoint master_credit:

```
rollback to savepoint master_credit;
rollback to master_credit;
```

Rollback Segments

Every transaction requires an associated rollback segment. This rollback segment holds the information necessary to undo the changes made by the transaction. Oracle normally assigns a rollback segment to a transaction. However, you can explicitly assign a rollback segment to a transaction by using the `set transaction` command. Transactions are explicitly assigned to rollback segments for the following reasons:

- The storage requirements of the rollback segment can be better managed to ensure sufficient storage capacity in the existing extents.

- System performance is minimally affected by the rollback segments because additional extents are not dynamically allocated. Subsequently, these extents for the rollback segments have to be truncated as well.

Use `set transaction` with the `use rollback segment` parameter to explicitly assign the rollback segment. The following statement assigns the rollback segment named rbs_mst_credit to the current transaction:

```
set transaction
use rollback segment rbs_mst_credit;
```

Using multiple rollback segments distributes rollback segment contention across many segments and improves system performance. Multiple rollback segments are required in the following situations:

- When a database is created, Oracle creates a rollback segment named `system` in the system tablespace. If the database is to have multiple tablespaces, you must have at least one rollback segment in addition to the system rollback segment.
- With the Oracle parallel server, each instance requires its own rollback segment.

When there are multiple rollback segments, Oracle tries to use the system rollback segment only for special system transactions and distributes the other transactions over the other rollback segments. If there are too many transactions for the nonsystem rollback segments, Oracle uses the system rollback segment.

The `rollback_segments` initialization parameter defines which rollback segments will be acquired by an instance. Modify this parameter to force an instance startup process to acquire a particular rollback segment. You might want to do this to ensure that a segment is acquired of the proper size or located in a particular tablespace.

The rollback segment size might affect transaction performance. The segment must be large enough to hold the rollback entries for your transactions. You should avoid dynamic space management with the rollback segments.

The size of the segment is defined by the rollback segment's storage parameters. Total rollback segment size should be set based on the typical transaction size issued against the database. Typically, rollback segments can handle transactions of any size easily. However, in an extreme case where the transaction is very small or very large, you might want to use an appropriately sized rollback segment.

If the application is running very short transactions, rollback segments should be small enough so they are always cached into memory. This significantly improves performance. The main disadvantage of this approach is the increased chance of receiving the error `snapshot too old` when running a large transaction. You should design the application to use short transactions whenever possible.

You want to set a high `maxextents` value for rollback segments. This allows a rollback segment to allocate subsequent extents as needed.

Use the `create rollback segment` or the SQL*DBA utility to create a rollback segment. You need the `create rollback segment` system privilege to create the segment. Once the rollback segment is created, it is not available for use until it is brought online. Bring the segment online with the `alter rollback segment` command with the `online` clause. You can also use the SQL*DBA utility to bring the segment online.

Data Locking

Oracle automatically locks a row on behalf of a transaction to prevent other transactions from acquiring a lock on the same row. You don't want simultaneous row manipulations by two separate transactions. Data locks prevent destructive interference of simultaneous conflicting DDL and DML statements. For example, Oracle prevents a table from being dropped if there are uncommitted transactions on the table. These data locks are automatically released when the transaction completes.

DML operations can obtain data locks for specific rows and for specific tables. Row locks are acquired automatically by the transaction when a row is modified with the following commands: insert, delete, update, or select. These row locks stay in effect until the transaction is completed or rolled back. The DML-Locks initialization parameter defines the number of locks permitted by all users on a single table.

A transaction acquires a table lock when a table is modified with the following DML statements: insert, update, delete, select, or lock table.

Implicit data locking occurs automatically for all SQL statements, so users of the database do not have to explicitly lock any rows. By default, Oracle locks resources at the lowest level possible.

In the multi-user database, locks have two levels:

Exclusive	This prohibits the sharing of the associated resource. The first transaction that acquires the resource is the only transaction that can alter the resource until the lock is released.
Share	This lock allows the associated resource to be shared, depending on the operations involved. Several transactions can acquire shared locks on the same resource. Shared locks provide a higher degree of data concurrency than exclusive locks.

Discrete Transaction Management

Performance of short, nondistributed transactions can be improved by using the bundled procedure begin_discrete_transaction. This procedure is included in the Oracle server with the procedural database option. This procedure allows short transactions to be executed more rapidly.

During a discrete transaction, all changes made to any data are deferred until the transaction commits. Redo information is generated but is stored in a separate location in memory. When a commit is issued, the redo information is written to the redo log and the database blocks are written directly to the database file. This eliminates the need to generate undo information because the database block is not actually modified until the transaction is committed.

The `begin_discrete_transaction` procedure must be called prior to the first transaction. This called procedure is only in effect for the duration of the transaction. Any follow-up transactions must recall the procedure.

Transactions that use the discrete transaction procedure cannot participate in distributed transactions.

Essential Summary

What

Transactions are logical groups of SQL statements. Each transaction terminates with either a commit or a rollback operation. Commits permanently save to the database the changes made by the transaction. Rollbacks undo all changes made to the database by the transaction.

Why

Transaction management provides all users of the database the guarantee of data concurrency and data consistency. Without this management, the quality and accuracy of the data would plunge—thereby rendering the database nearly worthless.

How

In this chapter, you learned the various components of transaction management, including commits, rollbacks, rollback segments, and data locking. You also learned that many of the features of transaction management are inherent in the Oracle server. Oracle enables you to customize some of the transaction parameters to suit individual needs and requirements.

PART VI

Oracle Constructs

PL/SQL

What Is PL/SQL?

What PL/SQL is Oracle's Procedural Language extension to Oracle Structured Query Language. PL/SQL is a block-structured language that enables developers to code procedures, functions, and anonymous (unnamed) blocks that combine SQL with procedural statements. Related procedures, functions, cursors, and variable declarations can be grouped and stored together in packages. Parameters can be passed to these blocks, enabling procedures and functions to accept and return values.

PL/SQL fully supports ANSI/ISO SQL data manipulation language commands and SQL datatypes. Complex data is easily handled with PL/SQL's Boolean and composite datatypes.

With blocks, you can group logically related declarations and statements. The declarations are local in state and cease to exist when the block completes. PL/SQL blocks can appear anywhere that SQL blocks can appear.

PL/SQL is processed by its own PL/SQL engine. This engine is incorporated into the following Oracle products:

- Oracle Server with Procedural Option
- SQL*Forms

- SQL*Menu
- SQL*Report Writer
- Oracle Graphics

Why Use PL/SQL?

Why

PL/SQL is a complete transaction processing language that provides the following advantages:

- PL/SQL supports SQL. SQL is a nonprocedural language, which means that you state what you want and Oracle determines the best way to accomplish it. PL/SQL fully supports SQL data manipulation, cursor control, and transaction management statements.

- PL/SQL improves server performance by reducing the number of calls from your application to Oracle.

- Your application can pass numerous SQL statements to Oracle at once, which improves network traffic and throughput.

- All PL/SQL code is portable to any operating system and platform on which Oracle runs.

- Recompilations are minimized because packages don't need to be recompiled if you redefine procedures within the package.

- Disk I/O is reduced because related functions and procedures are stored together.

- PL/SQL enables conditional, iterative, and sequential control structures, thereby providing tremendous programming flexibility.

- Modularity is promoted because PL/SQL lets you break an application down into manageable, well-defined logic modules.

- Errors are easily detected and handled.

How to Use PL/SQL

How

Without PL/SQL, the Oracle server must process each SQL statement individually. Each statement results in high performance overhead due to the additional call for each statement.

With PL/SQL, an entire block of statements can be sent to Oracle at one time. This reduces the network traffic between your application and the Oracle server. PL/SQL can also add procedural processing power to Oracle tools, such as Developer 2000, to improve performance.

PL/SQL is composed of blocks, control structures, attributes, variables, and cursors. The following sections provide information on how to use the procedural language extensions of SQL.

PL/SQL Blocks

PL/SQL is a block-structured language with procedural and error-handling capabilities. These blocks are composed of procedures, functions, and anonymous blocks that are logically grouped together to solve a specific problem.

A PL/SQL block has three parts to it:

- Declaration—All objects of the block are declared
- Execution—The objects are defined to manipulate data
- Exception—Error-handling logic is placed here

Figure 22.1 illustrates a generic PL/SQL block.

Figure 22.1.
Format of a generic PL/SQL block.

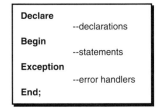

PL/SQL Block

```
Declare
          --declarations
Begin
          --statements
Exception
          --error handlers
End;
```

PL/SQL Architecture

PL/SQL is a technology and an integrated part of Oracle. It has its own processing engine that executes PL/SQL blocks and subprograms. This engine can be installed in the server or in any of the development tools, such as SQL*Forms. If the host program does not have a PL/SQL engine, the blocks of code are sent to the Oracle server for processing. Figure 22.2 shows the PL/SQL engine as an integrated component of the Oracle 7.2 server. The engine executes procedural statements and passes SQL statements to the SQL statement executor in the Oracle server.

When Oracle tools come with a PL/SQL engine, the tools process the PL/SQL blocks directly. Figure 22.3 illustrates the SQL*Form tool processing PL/SQL blocks directly with its own PL/SQL engine and passing the SQL statements to the Oracle server for processing.

Figure 22.2.
Oracle server PL/SQL engine.

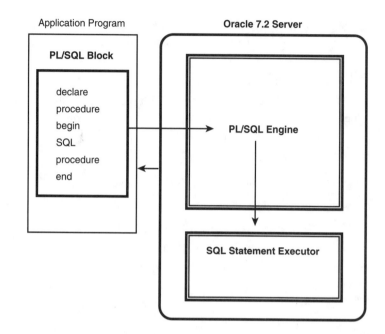

Figure 22.3.
*SQL*Form processing PL/SQL blocks.*

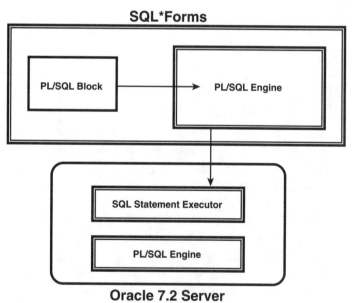

PL/SQL and SQL*Plus

PL/SQL does not support interactive input and output. Therefore, you need a tool like SQL*Plus or OCI environments to use PL/SQL.

In SQL*Plus, you can use PL/SQL in the following ways:

- To input, store, and run PL/SQL blocks
- To create, load, and run a script containing PL/SQL blocks
- To call a stored procedure

Every PL/SQL block begins with the reserved word `declare` or `begin`. `begin` is used as the starting point of the block if the block contains no declaration. Beginning a block instructs SQL*Plus to clear the SQL buffer, enter the input mode, and ignore semicolons. Ending the block with a period stores the block in the SQL buffer.

You save the contents of the buffer with the `save` command. Use the `save` command with the `replace` clause to save the buffer after you have edited it.

To retrieve and load in the buffer a previously saved PL/SQL block, use the `get` command. The following statement retrieves and loads into memory the PL/SQL script `monthly_parts`:

```
SQL> get monthly_parts
```

To execute a PL/SQL block that is stored in the buffer in SQL*Plus, use the `/` or the `run` command. For example, the following statements illustrate both ways to execute the buffer:

```
SQL> RUN
```

or

```
SQL> /
```

SQL Support

By definition, PL/SQL is SQL's procedural language extension. PL/SQL supports all of SQL's data manipulation language commands (except `explain plan`), transaction control commands, functions, pseudo-columns, and operators. PL/SQL does not support SQL's data definition commands, session control commands, or the system control commands.

PL/SQL lets you take advantage of Oracle power and ease of use. In PL/SQL you can access remote databases, manage transactions, customize the optimizer, manage cursors, use distributed global names, and use triggers.

PL/SQL Basics

PL/SQL is similar to any other programming language in that it has its own structure, syntax, and semantics. The following sections examine the various aspects of PL/SQL.

Variables and Constants

You can define variables and constants and use them in SQL and procedural statements anywhere an expression can be used. The only restriction is that forward references are not allowed. This means that you must declare all variables and constants before referencing them in other statements.

PL/SQL variables have the same datatypes as SQL, including char, number, long, date, and varchar2. Additionally, PL/SQL has several of its own datatypes, including Boolean and binary_integer. The following are examples of variables and constants being defined:

```
part_nbr varchar2(15);
part_back_log boolean;
```

You can assign values to variables with the assignment operator (:=). The variable is placed to the left of the assignment operator and the expression is placed to the right:

```
price := qty * (cost*2.5);
part_back_log := true;
```

A second way to assign a value to a variable is to use the select statement to fetch a value into the variable. The following example selects a value into the variable named prt_name:

```
select mst_parts.part_name into prt_name where part_nbr = :part_id;
```

To declare a constant, you include the keyword constant in the variable declaration statement. The following statement defines the constant cost_plus:

```
cost_plus := constant real:= 2.5;
```

Variable and Constant Attributes

Each PL/SQL variable and constant has attributes associated with it. These attributes are properties of the variable or constant that you can reference. Following are descriptions of the PL/SQL attributes:

%type
Describes the datatype of the variable, constant, or table column. You can declare a variable using the %type attribute as shown in the following statement:

```
prt_nbr := mst_parts.part_id%type;
```

In this example, the variable prt_nbr is declared with the same datatype as is defined for the column part_id in the MST_PARTS table.

%rowtype
Describes a record type that represents a row in a table. The following example creates a record named part_rec that has fields with the same name and datatypes as the columns that appear in the table MST_PARTS:

```
declare
part_rec mst_parts%rowtype;
```

Now use the dot notation to access any field in the rowtype record. The next statement assigns the field part_name to the variable part_desc:

```
part_desc := part_rec.part_name;
```

The Character Set

The PL/SQL character set includes the following:

- The alphabet, upper- and lowercase

  PL/SQL is not case-sensitive except within character and string literals.

- Numbers 0 through 9
- Spaces, tabs, and carriage returns
- Special symbols, including ( ) + - _ * / & ^ % $ # @ ! ; : " ' { } [ ] ? / > < |

PL/SQL Sentence Structure

Every sentence of PL/SQL text is structured to improve readability and enforce PL/SQL's syntax. For example, let's evaluate the following statement:

```
select part_name from mst_parts where part_price>= (part_cost*2.5); — high value
➥part names
```

This PL/SQL sentence includes the following:

- Symbols—The symbols * and >= have predefined meanings within PL/SQL
- Labels or identifiers—part_name, mst_parts, part_price, and part_cost are names of database or program objects
- Literals—2.5 is a literal
- Comments—Anything after the — comment indicator is evaluated as a comment

Be careful not to use PL/SQL reserved words incorrectly. For example, the following statement uses a PL/SQL reserved word incorrectly:

```
declare
values number
```

The reserved word values cannot be used in a declaration. All reserved words have a predefined special syntactic meaning and cannot be redefined.

Comments

Comments are a vital part of any computer program. They promote program readability and understanding. Comments are for people, not computers. Oracle ignores comments. They are there simply for your benefit.

The single-line comment begins with the double hyphen (--). This comment indicator can begin anywhere on a line and continues to the end of that line. An example of single-line comments follows:

```
Declare
part_desc varchar2(50) — generic name for the part
— Begin main processing
select
```

The multi-line comment indicator begins with /* and terminates with */. This comment can span multiple lines.

A multi-line comment is shown in the following example:

```
/* Select the high value part names by using the cost based times mfg markup
approach.
Use the mst_inv table if you want to use the WIP based approach for valued parts */
➥select part_name from mst_parts where part_price>= (part_cost*2.5);
```

The use of comments comes with the following restrictions:

- You cannot nest comments
- You cannot use single-line comments if the block is processed dynamically by a precompiler program

Datatypes

PL/SQL variables and constants have datatypes. The datatype specifies a storage format, constraint, and a valid range of values. The following list shows the valid PL/SQL datatypes:

Scalar datatypes:

- `binary_integer`
- `dec`
- `decimal double precision`
- `float`
- `int`
- `integer`
- `string`
- `natural number`
- `numeric`
- `positive`
- `real`
- `smallint`
- `char`
- `character`
- `long`
- `long raw`
- `raw`
- `rowid`
- `string`

- varchar

- varchar2

- date

- boolean

Composite datatypes:

- record

- table

Scalar datatypes have no internal components, whereas composite datatypes have internal components you can manipulate. Scalar datatypes are similar to SQL datatypes. Refer to Chapter 4, "Datatypes," for a discussion of scalar datatypes.

PL/SQL provides two composite datatypes: table and record. The table datatype is used to give an array-like access to table rows. The table datatype is similar to a database but not exactly the same.

A record datatype is similar to a table record except that the column names are unique to the record.

PL/SQL and Precompilers

Oracle permits you to embed PL/SQL blocks within programs written in any of the following languages: C, COBOL, FORTRAN, Ada, Pascal, or PL/I. After writing your program in any of these languages, you precompile the source code. This precompilation checks for errors and creates a modified source code file that can be compiled, linked, and executed.

To embed a PL/SQL block in your program, you must precede the block with the exec SQL execute statement. The PL/SQL block must end with the end-exec command. The following example illustrates the syntax for embedding PL/SQL in a high-level language program:

```
exec SQL execute
begin
end
end-exec
```

Use host variables to pass values to and from the host program and the PL/SQL block. Variables declared inside the PL/SQL block are global in scope.

All references to host variables in a PL/SQL block must be prefaced with a colon (:). This notation enables the precompiler to distinguish between host and PL/SQL variables.

Oracle enables you to use an optional indicator variable when referencing a host variable. This indicator variable is an integer variable that indicates the value or condition of a host variable. The indicator variable is used to detect nulls and truncate values in output host variables and to assign nulls to input variables.

For output variables, the following values can be assigned to the indicator variable:

−1   This indicates to the host program that the value of the variable is null. Therefore, the host program must have logic included to trap for such conditions.

0   Oracle passes the value of the variable to the host program without modification.

>0   Oracle assigns a truncated value to the host variable.

For input variables, the following values can be assigned to host variables by your program:

−1   Oracle ignores the value of the input host variable and assigns a null to it.

>=0   Oracle accepts the value of the host variable as is without modification.

The indicator variable must be declared as a 2-byte integer. In use with a SQL statement, the variable must be prefaced with a colon and appended to its host variable.

The following example illustrates the use of the indicator variable:

```
/* PL/SQL block follows */
exec SQL execute
begin
select part_qty, part_price, part_name
into :prt_qty:qty_ind, :prt_price, :prt_name
from mst_parts;
end;
end-exec
/* host program logic follows */
if qty_ind = -1
then
else
```

PL/SQL Errors

The Oracle server and the PL/SQL engine generate an error message and code for every runtime execution error and hardware failure. The format of the PL/SQL error message is

```
PLS-00000 error message
```

The error code is prefaced with PLS and followed by a unique number. This number should be used to assist you in finding the error definition in either the *PL/SQL User's Guide and Reference* or the *Oracle Messages and Codes Manual.* Please refer to both these manuals for a comprehensive list of PL/SQL error codes and messages. An example of an actual PL/SQL error message you might encounter is shown here:

```
PLS-00111 end-of-file in comment
```

Like most programming languages, a PL/SQL program normally stops processing when an internal runtime error is detected. An exception to this is when you take advantage of PL/SQL's exception-handling capabilities. With this, your program does not have to stop processing when an error occurs. You can program your code to handle errors so that processing continues even after runtime errors are detected.

PL/SQL enables users to define exceptions on their own. These user-defined exceptions have to be declared and must be raised explicitly by the raise command.

Please refer to Chapter 36, "Handling Runtime Exceptions in PL/SQL," for additional information on the PL/SQL exception-handling mechanism.

PL/SQL Wrapper Utility

In a client-server application, it is common to find PL/SQL blocks on both the client side and the server side of the application. To protect the client side of the software, Oracle enables the PL/SQL block to be written (or "wrapped") in binary format, thereby protecting the source code from modification or misuse.

Essential Summary

PL/SQL is Oracle's procedural extension to its Structured Query Language. This extension enables developers to incorporate functions, procedures, cursors, and exception handlers into logically grouped procedural statements.

What

PL/SQL provides many benefits to the developer and user of the database. Included in these is a reduction in network traffic because PL/SQL enables you to process blocks of statements at once rather than sending each individual statement to the server one at a time.

Why

This chapter showed you the various aspects and building blocks of PL/SQL. It also presented the environment PL/SQL operates in and can interact with.

How

PL/SQL Structures

What Are PL/SQL Structures?

What With PL/SQL, you can use SQL statements to manipulate Oracle data and flow control statements to process the data to meet all your requirements. PL/SQL combines the data-manipulating power of SQL with the data-processing power of procedural languages. PL/SQL provides many different structures to control the flow of your statement execution and data handling. These structures include the following:

- Cursors
- Procedures
- Functions
- Packages

Why Use PL/SQL Structures?

Why Control structures are the most important PL/SQL extensions to SQL. Not only does PL/SQL let you manipulate data, it lets you process the data using conditional, iterative, sequential, and unconditional flow-control statements such as if-then-else, for-loop, while-loop, exit-when, and goto. Collectively, these statements can handle any situation. Additionally, PL/SQL provides benefits in the following areas:

- Improved productivity—PL/SQL adds functionality to nonprocedural tools such as Oracle Reports and Oracle Forms.
- Better performance—PL/SQL enables a block of SQL statements to be transmitted through the network to the server all at one time. Transmission of individual statements is not necessary with PL/SQL.
- Portability—PL/SQL is portable to any operating system that is running Oracle RDBMS.
- Integration—SQL and PL/SQL enable you to combine or integrate the two languages so that your program can benefit from both.

How to Use PL/SQL Structures

This chapter acquaints you with the basic parts and concepts of PL/SQL. Also, the basic format of a PL/SQL program and its procedure programming language are presented.

Simple Blocks

PL/SQL is a block-structured language. Blocks are the most fundamental logical units of work that make up a PL/SQL program. These blocks include such structures as procedures, functions, and cursors. Blocks can themselves contain other blocks or nested blocks.

Blocks of PL/SQL code are created to solve a specific task or problem. For example, you can have a PL/SQL block that simply counts the daily invoices received per hour.

Blocks are made up of three distinct parts:

- Declaration and initialization of variables
- Executable PL/SQL code

  This is the only mandatory part of a block. The other two parts are optional.
- Exceptions handler

The declaration portion of the block accomplishes the following:

- Declares the name of an identifier
- Declares whether the identifier is a variable or a constant
- Establishes the datatype for the identifier
- Establishes whether the identifier is nullable
- Initializes the identifier, if applicable

The following are examples of identifiers being declared in a PL/SQL block:

```
declare

-- variable to store part name
v_part_name    varchar2(50);

-- variable to store the order date, initialize it to
-- current system date.
v_order_date   date not null :=sysdate;

-- variable to count orders processed, initialized to zero
v_orders_count      binary_integer:=0;

-- creates a flag or indicator as to validity of order
v_valid_order       boolean not null := true;
```

The identifiers are local to the block and cease to exist when the block terminates its processing. By default, the identifiers assume a null value if they are not initialized.

The following is a typical PL/SQL block:

```
declare
new_part_id           s_part_id%type;
hold_part_id          s_part_id%type;

begin
select id
into new_part_id
from mst_part
where id = :p_part_id;
commit;

exception
when no_data_found then
rollback;
commit;

end;
```

Control Structures

Control structures enable the program to change the logical flow of statements within PL/SQL with a number of control structures. PL/SQL supports four basic programming control structures: conditional, iteration, sequential, and unconditional branching. These four structures can be combined in any way to solve a given problem.

The following sections cover these structures in more detail.

Conditional Control

You can execute a statement or sequence of statements conditionally with the if-then statement. Sometimes it is necessary to take alternative actions, depending on a condition or circumstance.

If-Then Statements

The simplest form of the conditional control statement is the `if-then` statement. The syntax for the `if-then` statement is as follows:

```
if condition then
statement(s);
end if;
```

The statements that immediately follow the conditional `if` statement are executed only if the condition evaluates to True. If the condition evaluates to False, the statements are not processed and are passed over.

If-Then-Else Statements

A more likely scenario is that you will have different distinct sets of statements to execute depending on the conditional statement. The `if-then-else` statement provides a means to always execute statements in a conditional statement.

The syntax of the `if-then-else` structure is very similar to the `if-then` syntax. The following example uses the `if-then-else` structure:

```
if max_bal > 100000 then
update mst_audit     -- executed only if condition is true
set comments = 'sell no more';
else
update mst_audit     -- executed only if condition is false
set comments = 'sell more';
end if
```

You can even nest `if-then-else` statements, as shown in the next example:

```
if max_bal > 100000 then
update mst_audit
set comments = 'sell no more';

/* The following is executed only if the condition from the previous statement is
false             */

else
if max_bal = 10000
update mst_audit     -- executed only if condition is true
set comments = 'phone client';

/* The following is executed only if the condition from the previous statement is
false             */

else
update mst_audit
set comments = 'sell more';

end if
end if
```

Each `if-then` statement can have only one `else` statement and must end with an `end if` statement.

If-Then-Elsif Statements

In some situations you need a means to select an action from several mutually exclusive alternatives. The next form of the if-then statement provides an answer for you. The if-then-elsif statement enables you to have several mutually exclusive conditions. The syntax for this statement is as follows:

```
if condition1 then
statement1(s);

elsif condition2 then
statement2(s);

else
statement3(s);
end if;
```

This is how this structure works. PL/SQL evaluates the first condition. If it is True, statement1 is executed and the remainder of the structure is passed over and not executed. If condition1 evaluates to False or Null, the elsif clause is tested. Again, if condition2 evaluates to True, statement2 is executed and the remainder of the structure is passed over. If condition2 is False or Null, control goes to statement3. statement3 is executed and the structure is finished.

You can have only one else clause. However, you can have as many elsifs as you need. To improve the clarity of a program, use the elsif clause instead of nesting ifs.

Iterative Control

Iterative control statements enable you to execute a sequence of statements multiple times. The simplest form of an iterative statement is the loop.

Loop Statements

The syntax for the loop statement is

```
loop
statement(s)
end loop;
```

Each time the loop is processed, control is always resumed at the top of the loop structure, and statements are executed. The exit statement provides a way to stop the iterative loop. The exit statement must be placed inside the loop. The next example uses the loop-exit format to process records:

```
begin
loop                -- top of loop
total=total + 1;

if total >=100 then -- conditional exit statement
exit;               -- explicitly forces an exit
end if;

end loop;
```

For Loop Statements

The `for` loop is a mechanism to cycle through a loop a fixed number of times. A `for` loop iterates over and over for a specified number of times. The syntax for the `for` loop is as follows:

```
for counter in lower-bound..upper-bound loop
statement(s)
end loop;
```

The range of valid integers for the counter is evaluated when the loop is first entered and is never reevaluated. After each iteration, the counter is implicitly incremented. Also, the counter is implicitly declared so you do not have to declare it. If the upper-bound value becomes less than the lower-bound value, the statements are not executed. The following example shows a simple `for` loop:

```
for I in 1..50 loop
statements        -- statements will be executed 50 times
end loop;
```

The lower- and upper-bound values can be literals, variables, or expressions, but they must evaluate to integers. Additionally, the loop range can be determined dynamically at runtime. For example, the following code sets the upper bound of the loop range equal to the number of employees in the company:

```
select count(*) into upper_counter
from employee
where emp_status = 'A';

for I 1..upper_count loop
salary = salary*1.1;
end loop;
```

You can also include the `reverse` clause to decrement the counter. In the next example, the counter begins with the value 10 and is decreased by 1 each time the loop is executed:

```
for I in reverse 1..10 loop
statements;      - statements will be executed 10 times
end loop;
```

When the loop is finished, the counter variable becomes undefined. Likewise, while the loop is active, the counter variable is local and cannot be referenced outside the loop.

Loop Labels

In PL/SQL, you may attach a label name to a loop. This label, which is an undeclared identifier, must appear at the beginning of the loop and must be enclosed in double-angle brackets. Optionally, this label may be placed at the end of the looping statement without angle brackets.

The following example uses labels to clearly mark the beginning and end of the looping structure:

```
<< inventory_loop >>    -- loop label

loop
```

```
...
end loop inventory_loop;
```

While Statements

The while-loop structure repeats a statement until a condition is no longer true. The syntax for the while loop is as follows:

```
while condition loop
statement(s)
end loop
```

Before each iteration, the condition is evaluated. If the condition is True, the statements are executed. Otherwise, the statements are passed over and not executed. The following example illustrates the while loop:

```
declare
v_counter     number(2) := 1;

begin
while v_counter <=50 loop
select cust_name into guest.name
from register
v_counter := v_counter + 1;
end loop;
end;
```

The number of iterations that will be performed by a while loop is unknown until the loop ends. It depends on the condition statement. Because the condition is evaluated at the top or beginning of the loop, the statements might be executed zero times.

Sequential Control

By default, all PL/SQL blocks are executed in a top-down or sequential process. The process begins with the begin statement and terminates with the end statement. The developer can deviate from this default control structure by introducing one of the other control structures discussed earlier in this chapter.

Unconditional Control

Two of the least-used control structures are the goto and null unconditional control statements.

The goto statement forces the flow of processing to branch to a label unconditionally. When executed, the goto statement transfers control to the labeled statement or block. The syntax for the goto statement is:

```
goto label_name;
```

In the following example, the goto statement is used to transfer processing control to the label new_part:

```
select count(*) part_id into part_count
from mst_part;
```

```
for counter 1..part_count loop

select part_nbr from mst_inventory;
if part_nbr like 'AU%'
then goto new_part;
else insert into mst_part values (part_nbr);
end if;

<<new_part>>
insert into part_audit values (:user_name, part_nbr);
insert into mst_part values (part_nbr);

end loop;
```

goto statements cannot do the following:

- Branch into an if or loop statement or subblock
- Branch out of a subprogram
- Branch out of an exceptions handler into the current block

The null statement does nothing other than pass control to the next statement. Specifically, the null statement explicitly specifies inaction. The following shows a typical example of the null statement:

```
if qty<= 50000 then
...             -- perform processing
else
null            -- do nothing;
end if;
```

PL/SQL Tables

PL/SQL provides two composite datatypes: table and record. PL/SQL tables are objects of type table, which look similar to database tables but aren't quite the same. These tables give you an arraylike access to rows of data.

PL/SQL tables are declared in the declaration portion of a block. They can contain one column and a primary key, neither of which can be named. The primary key must be defined with the binary_integer datatype.

To declare a PL/SQL table, you first declare a table type and then declare variables of that type. For example, the following declares a PL/SQL table type:

```
declare
type emp_table_type is table of varchar2(35)
indexed by binary_integer;
```

Once the table type is declared, declare variables of that type. For example, the following declares variables using the table type defined earlier:

```
emp_table    emp_table_type
```

To reference a PL/SQL table, specify a primary key value using the arraylike syntax. For example, to reference the twelfth row in the PL/SQL table created in the previous example, your statement would look like this:

```
emp_table(12);
```

Taking this example one step further, you could assign values directly to a row in the PL/SQL table. The following assigns a value to the emp_table:

```
declare
type emp_table_type is table of varchar2(35)
indexed by binary_integer;
i     binary_integer:=0;

begin
for new_emp in
(select emp_name from personnel where status_code = 'N');

loop
i:=i+1;
emp_table(i) :=new_emp.emp_name -- insert new employee names;
end loop;

end
```

The following rules apply when using PL/SQL tables:

- A loop must be used to insert values from a PL/SQL table into a database column.
- A loop must be used to fetch data from a database column into a PL/SQL table.
- You cannot use the delete command to delete the contents of a PL/SQL table. You must assign an empty table to the PL/SQL table being deleted.

PL/SQL Records

The second of the two composite datatypes is record. A record represents a row in a table or a row fetched by a cursor. Records have uniquely named fields and can belong to different datatypes.

To declare a PL/SQL record, you first declare a table record type and then declare variables of that type. For example, the following declares a PL/SQL record type:

```
declare

type emp_rec_type is record
(emp_id   number(5) not null,
emp_name  varchar2(35),
hire_date date,
dept_no   varchar2(5));
```

Once declared, you can declare records of that type:

```
emp_rec    emp_rec_type
```

The following example shows the declaration and usage of PL/SQL records:

```
declare

type emp_rec_type is record       -- declare record type
(emp_id   number(5) not null,
emp_name  varchar2(35),
hire_date date,
dept_no   varchar2(5));
emp_rec   emp_rec_type;           -- declare variable
...
begin
select ssn, ename, hire_date, dept
into emp_rec
from mst_personnel;

end;
```

The following rules apply when using PL/SQL records:

- Records of different types cannot be assigned to each other.
- You cannot assign a list of values to a record by using the assignment statement.
- Records cannot be tested for equality or inequality.

Essential Summary

What
PL/SQL structures enable you to explicitly control the flow of your programs, thereby making it easy to meet your requirements of data manipulation. PL/SQL combines the power of SQL with its own procedural structures to provide the developer with many alternatives and flexibility to meet the requirements at hand.

Why
PL/SQL structures such as cursors and packages provide the conditional, iterative, sequential, and unconditional flow-control mechanisms needed to meet all your development needs. Also, these structures improve overall server performance, enhance development productivity, and promote code portability.

How
In this chapter, you learned about the basic components of PL/SQL structures and the benefits gained from their use. Also, this chapter presented the basic structure and methodology of using these PL/SQL structures.

Packages

What Is a Package?

What A package is an encapsulated collection of related schema objects. These objects can include procedures, functions, variables, constants, cursors, and exceptions. A package is compiled, then stored in the database's data dictionary as a schema object.

Packages contain stored subprograms, or stand-alone programs, which are called package subprograms. These subprograms can be called from other stored programs, triggers, precompiler programs, or any of the interactive Oracle programs, such as SQL*Plus. Unlike the stored subprograms, the package itself cannot be called, passed parameters, or nested.

A package usually has two components to it: a specification and a body. The specification declares the types, variables, constants, exceptions, cursors, and subprograms that are available for use. The body fully defines cursors, functions, and procedures, and so implements the specification.

The package specification and body are stored separately in the database. This allows other calling objects to depend on the specification only, not on both. This separation enables you to change the definition of a program object in the package body without causing Oracle to invalidate other objects that call or reference the program object. Oracle invalidates the calling or referencing schema objects if you change the package specification.

Why Use Packages?

Packages offer the following advantages:

- The capability to organize your application development more efficiently into modules. Each package and its modules are easily understood, which aids in the development of applications.
- Packages enable you to grant privileges more efficiently.
- Packages' public variables and cursors persist for the duration of the session. Therefore, all cursors and procedures that execute in this environment can share them.
- Packages enable you to perform overloading on procedures and functions. Creating more than one procedure or function with the same name in the same package with different arguments is called overloading the procedure or function.
- Packages improve performance by loading multiple objects into memory at once. Therefore, subsequent calls to related subprograms in the package require no I/O.
- Packages promote code reuse through the use of libraries that contain stored procedures and functions, thereby eliminating redundant coding.

How to Use Packages

How Packages are created interactively using tools such as SQL*DBA and SQL*Plus. The remainder of this chapter reviews the steps necessary to create and manage Oracle packages.

Package Helpful Hints

The following are a few helpful hints you should follow to make your use of Oracle packages more successful:

- Avoid writing packages that replicate existing Oracle functionality.
- Keep packages simple and general to promote their reuse in future applications.
- Design your package body after you design the application. Place only those objects you want to be visible to all users in the package specification.
- Avoid placing too many items in the package specification, specifically those that need compiling. Changes to a package body do not require Oracle to recompile dependent procedures. However, changes to the specification of a package require Oracle to recompile every stored subprogram that references the package.

Package Specifications

The package specification contains public declarations of the name of the package and the names and datatypes of any arguments. These declarations are global in scope to the entire package and local in scope to your database. This means that the declared objects in your package are accessible from anywhere in the package. Therefore, all the information your application needs to execute a stored subprogram is contained in the package specification.

The following is an example of a package declaration. In this example, the specification declares a function and a procedure:

```
create package inv_pck_spec as

function inv_count(qty number, part_nbr varchar2(15))
return number;

procedure inv_adjust(qty number);

end inv_pck_spec
```

Sometimes a specification declares only variables, constants, and exceptions, so that a package body is not necessary. The following example is a package specification for a package that does not have a package body:

```
create package inv_costings is

type inv_rec is record
(part_name varchar2(30),
part_price number,
part_cost number);

price number;
qty   number;
no_cost exception;
cost_or exception;
END inv_costings;
```

The Package Body

The body of a package contains the definition of the public objects you declared in the specification. The body also contains other object declarations that are private to the package. The objects declared privately in the package body are not accessible to other objects outside the package. Unlike the package specification, the declaration portion of the package body can contain subprogram bodies.

A package body is not always necessary. For example, if the specification declares only constants and variables, the package body is not necessary.

Once the package is written, applications can reference its types, call its subprograms, use its cursors, or raise its exceptions. Once the package is created, it is stored in the database for all to use.

Creating Packages

The first step to creating a package is to create its specification. The specification publicly declares the schema objects that are continued in the body of the package.

To create a specification, issue the create package command. The following illustrates the syntax necessary to create a package specification:

```
create or replace package inv_pck_spec as

function inv_count(qty integer, part_nbr varchar2(15))
return integer;

procedure inv_adjust(qty integer);

end inv_pck_spec;
```

Note that the or replace clause was used. This re-creates the package specification without losing any grants that already exist.

After the specification is created, you create the body of the package. The body of a package is a collection of schema objects that were declared in the specification. These objects, or package subprograms, are accessible outside the package only if their specifications are included in the package specification.

In addition to the object definitions for the declaration, the package body can also contain private declarations. These private objects are for the internal workings of the package and are local in scope. External objects cannot reference or call internal declarations to another package.

If you perform an initialization on the package body, it is executed only once when the package is initially referenced.

The following is an example of the body of the package that was specified in the previous example's specification.

```
create or replace package body inv_control is

function inv_count
(qty integer,
part_nbr varchar2(15))
return integer is ;
new_qty integer;
begin
new_qty:= qty*6;
insert into mst_inv values
(new_qty,part_nbr);
return(new_qty);
end inv_count;


procedure inv_adjust(qty integer);
begin
delete from user_01.mst_inv
where inv_qty<10000;
end;
```

```
begin  -- package initialization begins here
insert into inv_audit values
(sysdate, user);
end inv_control;
```

The final part of the procedure body in the preceding example is the package initialization. By definition, this runs only once when the procedure is referenced the first time.

To create a package specification or body in your own schema, you must have the create pro-cedure system privilege. To create a package in another user's schema, you must have the cre-ate any procedure system privilege.

Calling Package Subprograms

When a package is invoked, Oracle performs three steps to execute it:

1. It verifies user access: it confirms that the user has the execute system privilege for the subprogram.

2. It verifies procedure validity: it checks with the data dictionary to determine whether the subprogram is valid. If the object is invalid, it is automatically recompiled before being executed.

3. The package subprogram is executed.

To reference the package's subprograms and objects, you must use the dot notation. The gen-eral syntax for the dot notation is as follows:

```
package_name.type_name
package_name.object_name
package_name.subprogram_name
```

To reference the variable max_balance in the package named inventory, the referencing state-ment would look like this:

```
declare
max_balance number;
begin
...
if inventory.max_balance < curr_balance then
...
end_if
...
```

When Oracle executes a packaged subprogram, an implicit savepoint is created. If the subpro-gram fails with an unhandled exception, before returning to the host environment Oracle rolls back to the savepoint, thereby undoing any changes made by the packaged subprogram.

Synonyms for Packages

Synonyms can be created for stored packages to do the following:

- Hide the identity of the name and owner of a package
- Provide location transparency for remotely stored packages

Synonyms can be used to invoke packages and other subprograms. Synonyms cannot be created for individual procedures that are defined within a package. You can create a synonym that references a package, however.

Recompiling Packages

To recompile a package, use `alter package` with the `compile` keyword. This explicit recompilation eliminates the need for any implicit runtime recompilation and prevents any associated runtime compilation errors and performance overhead. It is common to explicitly recompile a package after modifications to the package.

Recompiling a package recompiles all objects defined within the package. Recompiling does not change the definition of the package or any of its objects.

In the following example, the first statement recompiles just the body of a package. The second statement recompiles the entire package, including the body and specification:

```
alter package inventory_pkg compile body;

alter package inventory_pkg compile package;
```

All packages can be recompiled using the Oracle utility dbms_utility:

```
execute dbms_utility.compile_all;
```

The packages and package objects must be in your schema or you need to have the `alter any procedure` system privilege.

Dropping Packages

Dropping a package removes the stored package from the database. When a package is dropped, the local objects that depend on the package specification become invalidated. If a program tries to reference one of these invalid local objects, Oracle implicitly attempts a recompile of the package. An error is generated unless the package was re-created.

In the following example, the first statement drops the body of the package inventory. The second statement drops the entire package:

```
drop package body inventory;

drop package inventory;
```

When you drop just the body of a package but not its specification, all dependent objects remain valid. However, you cannot call any of the procedures or stored functions declared in the package specification until you re-create the package body.

You cannot directly drop a subprogram from the body of a package. You must re-create the package body without the undesired object.

To drop a package, the package must be in your schema or you need to have the `drop any procedure` system privilege.

Debugging Packages

To aid in debugging, Oracle provides a public package named `dbms_output` that contains debugging information about your package. You can produce debugging information from within an application by issuing the `put` or `put_line` commands. These commands place the debugging information into a buffer that was created by the `dbms_output` package. To display the contents of the buffer, simply type the `set server output on` command at the SQL*Plus prompt or from within SQL*DBA.

The following example illustrates the `put_line` command that you can include inside your packaged procedure:

```
/* Packaged stored procedure specification.        */

create package user_01.parts as

/* The packaged subprogram body begins here.        */

procedure part (qty integer, part_id integer)
as begin
update journal
put_line ('Original Qty =' || journal.qty) /*Debug Line */
set journal.qty = journal.qty + qty
where journal_id = part_id
put_line ('New Qty =' || journal.qty)        /*Debug Line */
```

The following statements are issued at the SQL*DBA command line to execute the parts procedure and to display the debugging information:

```
SQLDBA> set server on
SQLDBA> execute user_01.parts
```

The following are the results of these statements being executed. This information is generated from the dba_output buffer area:

```
Orignal Qty = 100
New Qty = 200
Original Qty = 200
New Qty = 325
... and so on
```

Private Versus Public Package Objects

Within the body of a package, you are permitted to define subprograms, cursors, and private declarations for types and objects. Objects that are declared inside the package body are restricted to use within that package. Therefore, PL/SQL code outside the package cannot reference any of the variables that were privately declared within the package.

Any items declared inside the package specification are visible outside the package. This allows PL/SQL code outside the package to reference objects from within the package. These objects declared in the package specification are called public.

Variables, Cursors, and Constants

Variables, cursors, and constants can change their value over time and exist only for a specific amount of time. This life duration can vary depending on where the declaration is located. For stand-alone procedures, variables, cursors, and constants persist only for the duration of the procedure call. They lose their value when the procedure has finished executing.

If the variable, constant, or cursor is declared in a package specification or body, its values exist for the duration of the user's session. The values are also lost when the package is recompiled.

Package States

A package is always either valid or invalid. A package is considered valid if none if its source code or the objects it references have been dropped, replaced, or altered since the package specification was last recompiled.

The package is considered invalid if its source code or any object that it references has been dropped, altered, or replaced since the package specification was last recompiled. When a package becomes invalid, Oracle also makes invalid any objects that reference the package.

Package Dependency

During the recompiling of a package, Oracle invalidates all dependent objects. These objects include stand-alone or package subprograms that call or reference objects declared in the recompiled specification. If another user's program calls or references a dependent object before it is recompiled, Oracle automatically recompiles it at runtime.

During package recompilation, Oracle determines whether objects on which the package body depends are valid. If any of these objects are invalid, Oracle recompiles them before recompiling the package body. If recompilation is successful, the package body becomes valid. If any errors are detected, the appropriate error messages are generated and the package body remains invalid.

Overloading

Oracle permits several procedures in the same package to have the same name. This is known as overloading. This technique is very useful, especially when you want to execute the same procedure several times but with arguments that have different datatypes. One example of using procedure overload is with the package `dbms_output`. In this package, the `put_line` procedure is called numerous times to produce output lines of different datatypes.

Listing Package Information

Oracle provides several data dictionary views that provide information about packages:

all_errors	A list of current errors on all objects accessible to the user
all_source	Text source of all stored objects accessible to the user
dba_errors	Current errors on all stored objects in the database
dba_object_size	All PL/SQL objects in the database
dba_source	Text source of all stored objects in the database
user_errors	Current errors on all a user's stored objects
user_source	Text source of all stored objects belonging to the user
user_object_size	User's PL/SQL objects

The following example queries the user_errors view to obtain information about the current errors in a package:

```
select line, type, name, text from user_errors;
```

Sample output:

```
LINE  TYPE    NAME    TEXT
----  ------  ------  -------------------------------------------
  4   PROC    PST_QTY PL/SQL-00387: into variable cannot be a database object
                      PL/SQL: SQL statement ignored
```

Essential Summary

A package is a database object that is a logical unit of related PL/SQL types, objects, and sub-programs. The package can be called or referenced by other packages, stand-alone programs, and triggers.

What

In this chapter, you learned the many benefits a package has over stand-alone procedures and functions. One of these benefits is the reduction of server overhead by allowing multiple objects to be stored into memory at once.

Why

Packages are first declared and then defined. Once the creation of a package is successful, the package is stored in the database. Packages can contain both public and private objects. Public objects are available for all to call and reference, but private objects are for internal package use only.

How

Triggers

What Is a Trigger?

What A trigger is a procedure that is implicitly executed when an `insert`, `update`, or `delete` command is issued against the associated table.

Triggers can contain SQL and PL/SQL statements that are executed as a unit and can invoke other procedures and triggers. The trigger is invoked either before or after the `insert`, `update`, or `delete` command is executed. The creator of the trigger specifies when the trigger is executed in relation to the DML statements.

Triggers are defined on tables, but not on views or synonyms of tables. However, triggers on the base tables of a view are executed when the DML statements are issued against the view.

Why Use Triggers?

Why Triggers enable you to execute a stored procedure implicitly when an `insert`, `update`, or `delete` statement is executed against a predefined table.

Triggers are frequently used to do the following:

- Automatically generate derived column values
- Enforce security authorizations and constraints
- Provide transparent event logging
- Gather statistics on table access

You can use triggers to supplement the Oracle internal auditing system. Triggers enable you to record information similar to that recorded by the audit command. For example, you can use triggers to provide value-based auditing on a per-row basis. You should use triggers in this way only when you need more data than the auditing feature provides.

Triggers can be used to synchronously maintain replicated tables located on different nodes of a distributed database. One example of using triggers in this fashion is with snapshots. Refer to Chapter 9, "Snapshots," for additional information on snapshots.

How to Use Triggers

This chapter discusses the many features of creating and managing database triggers. A trigger is a procedure that is stored in the database and executed implicitly when a table is modified.

Guidelines for Triggers

The following items should guide you when preparing to create a trigger:

- Use a trigger only when you want to perform a specific operation every time another predefined operation is executed.
- Use triggers for centralized, global operations that should be executed for triggering statements.
- Never use triggers to replicate an operation that the Oracle server already makes.
- Be careful not to create recursive triggers.
- Exercise restraint in creating the trigger, so that the code is as small as possible.
- When a SQL statement processes rows in a table, Oracle does not guarantee the order in which they are processed. Because of this, do not create a trigger that depends on the order of the rows being processed.

Trigger Parts

A trigger has three main components:

- A triggering statement—This specifies what SQL statements cause Oracle to fire the trigger. This triggering statement can be the update, insert, or delete statement. You must specify at least one and no more than three of these commands.

- A trigger restriction—This specifies a condition that must be true for the trigger to fire. This condition must be a SQL condition and not a PL/SQL condition. The condition can reside in a when clause.

- A trigger action—This specifies the PL/SQL block that Oracle executes when the trigger is fired.

Types of Triggers

When designing and creating the trigger, you specify the number of times the trigger action is executed. There are two types of triggers, defined by the number of times the trigger execution occurs:

- Row trigger—A row trigger is executed every time the table is affected by the triggering statement. For example, if an update statement is executed and it updates 30 rows, the trigger is fired 30 times. If the update statement affects no rows, the trigger is not fired.

- Statement trigger—A statement trigger is fired only once for the triggering statement. For example, if an update statement is issued and it updates 30 rows, the trigger is fired only once. It does not matter how many rows are affected by the triggering statement.

Trigger Timing

When you define a trigger, you specify when you want the trigger to fire. You can specify the trigger action to happen before the trigger statement or after the statement.

before triggers are executed before the triggering statement. This type of trigger is commonly used for the following:

- To derive column values before completing a triggering insert or update statement.

- To determine whether the trigger action should be executed. This can help server performance by eliminating unnecessary processing.

after triggers execute the trigger action after the trigger statement is executed. These triggers are commonly used for the following:

- When you want the triggering statement to complete prior to the trigger action

- To execute additional logic in addition to the before trigger actions

Creating a Trigger

The create trigger command is used to create a trigger. Following is the general syntax for creating a trigger:

```
create trigger 'trigger command'
```

The following are the keywords that can appear in the `trigger` command parameter:

before	Indicates that the trigger is fired before executing the triggering statement.
after	Indicates that the trigger is fired after executing the triggering statement.
delete	Indicates that the trigger is fired after a row is deleted from the table.
insert	Indicates that the trigger is fired whenever a row is inserted.
update	Indicates that the trigger is fired whenever a value changes in any column specified by the of clause. If the of clause is missing, the trigger is fired whenever any value in the row is updated.
of	Details the specific column(s) on which the trigger can be triggered.
on	Defines the schema and name of the table on which the trigger is to be created.
for each row	If specified in the create trigger statement, it establishes the trigger as a row trigger. If this clause is missing in the create trigger statement, the trigger becomes a statement trigger.
when	Defines the trigger restriction. This means that the when clause defines the circumstances in which the trigger is fired.
or replace	This re-creates the trigger if it already exists. This enables you to modify the trigger definition without dropping and re-creating the trigger.

To create a trigger in your own schema, you must have the create trigger system privilege. To create a trigger in someone else's schema, you need the create any trigger system privilege. The name of the trigger must be unique with respect to other triggers you own.

The following is an example that creates the after row trigger named parts_delete. This trigger is fired after the deletion of each row that meets the restrictions as defined.

```
create trigger parts_delete
after delete on mst_parts
for each row
when (part_price < 100)
declare
- insert your procedure block here
end;
```

The next example creates a before statement trigger. Note the multiple DML commands in the trigger statement.

```
create trigger parts_snp
before insert and delete on mst_parts
when (parts_qty > 5000)
declare      /* procedure declaration    */
begin
            /* procedure goes here      */
end;
```

Given the definitions earlier in this section, the following 12 trigger types can exist per table. Please note that earlier versions of Oracle restricted you to having only one trigger type per table. This restriction does not apply to Oracle version 7.1 or higher. You may now create multiple triggers of the same type on the same type. It is strongly recommended that you only create multiple triggers of the same type for use for snapshots. Other uses of this may lead to program logic confusion.

- `before update row`
- `before delete row`
- `before insert row`
- `before update statement`
- `before delete statement`
- `before insert statement`
- `after update row`
- `after delete row`
- `after insert row`
- `after update statement`
- `after delete statement`
- `after insert statement`

Enabling and Disabling Triggers

A trigger must be either enabled or disabled. When enabled, the trigger fires whenever the trigger restriction is true and the trigger statement is issued.

If the trigger is disabled, Oracle does not fire the trigger when the trigger statement is issued and the conditions of the trigger are satisfied.

A trigger is automatically enabled when it is created. You can also enable and disable the trigger with `alter table` with the `enable` or `disable` clause or `alter trigger` with the `enable` or `disable` clause.

The following example disables the trigger t_inv_count:

```
alter trigger t_inv_count disable;
```

To enable and disable triggers with the `alter trigger` command, you must own the trigger or posses the `alter any trigger` system privilege. To enable and disable triggers using the `alter table` command, you must either own the table or possess the `alter any table` system privilege.

Trigger Execution

A single SQL statement can execute up to four triggers. These four are the `before row` trigger, `after row` trigger, `before statement` trigger, and `after statement` trigger. When these triggers are fired, several integrity constraints can be checked. Additionally, these four triggers can cause other triggers to be fired. The follow-up triggers are called cascading triggers. To help keep the firing sequences in the proper order, the following execution model is used:

1. Execute `before` `statement` triggers
2. Loop for each row affected by the SQL statement
   a. Execute `before` `row` triggers
   b. Lock and change rows, check for integrity constraints
3. Complete deferred integrity constraint checking
4. Execute `after` `statement` triggers

This model is a general guideline of the proper sequence of trigger activities. The model can vary slightly, or become recursive, depending on cascading triggering and the type of trigger fired.

One important property of this model is that all actions and checks done as a result of a SQL statement must succeed. If an exception is raised within a trigger and the exception is not explicitly handled, the trigger is halted and all changes as a result of the trigger are rolled back.

Figure 25.1 illustrates a typical use of a trigger. It shows the view v_parts, which has the base tables MST_PARTS and MST_INV. The MST_INV table has a trigger named t_inv_count.

Figure 25.1.
Illustration of a trigger used to track insert activity.

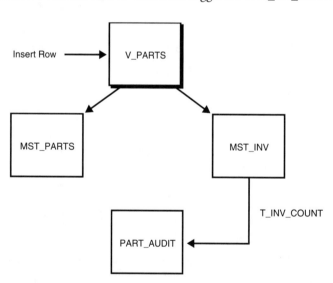

When the user performs an insert on the base tables through the view v_parts, a trigger is fired to perform an insert in the table PART_AUDIT. The following is the code for this example:

```
create trigger t_inv_count    /* defines trigger name    */
after                         /* defines trigger statement*/
insert on mst_inv             /* defines trigged action   */
for each row
```

```
begin
insert into part_audit.part_name
values (mst_inv.part_name);
end;
```

Altering Triggers

You cannot explicitly alter a trigger. You must replace the trigger with a new definition. When replacing a trigger, you must include the or replace clause in the create trigger command. The or replace clause replaces the old trigger with the new trigger without affecting any grants made for the original trigger.

Alternately, triggers can be dropped and re-created. When you drop a trigger, all grants associated with the trigger are dropped as well. The grants must be re-created when the new trigger is created.

Dropping a Trigger

The drop trigger command removes the trigger structure from the database. The trigger must reside in your own database or else you need the drop any trigger system privilege.

The following command deletes the trigger parts_delete from your own schema:

```
drop trigger parts_delete
```

Recompiling a Trigger

For triggers, only their source code is stored in the database. Upon first execution, the source code of the trigger is compiled and cached in the shared pool. If the trigger is flushed from the shared pool, the source code must be recompiled when used again.

Use the alter trigger command to force a recompile of an existing trigger. The trigger can be either enabled or disabled when being recompiled. The alter trigger command does not change the definition of the existing trigger.

Snapshot Log Trigger

When a snapshot log is created for a table, Oracle implicitly creates an after row trigger on that table. Therefore, a user-defined after row trigger cannot be created on this same table. This also means that a snapshot log cannot be created on a table that already has an after row trigger on it.

References to Package Variables

If an update or delete command detects a conflict with a concurrent update, Oracle rolls back to a savepoint and restarts the update. This process can happen several times before the delete is successfully completed. Each time the statement is restarted, the before statement trigger is fired. If any package variables are referenced in a trigger, the rollback to savepoint does not undo any changes to these variables.

Mutating or Constraining Tables

Oracle prevents row triggers from reading or modifying a mutating table. A mutating table is one that is currently being modified by an update, insert, or delete statement. If an attempt is made by a trigger to read or modify a mutating table, an error is generated and any changes caused by the trigger are rolled back.

Also, Oracle prevents a row trigger from changing the primary, foreign, or unique key columns of a constraining table of the triggering statement. If this action is attempted, Oracle generates an error, and the changes made by the trigger are rolled back.

To get around these restraints, you might be able to use a temporary table, PL/SQL table, or a package variable.

Essential Summary

What Triggers are a unit of SQL and PL/SQL code that is executed implicitly by Oracle. Triggers can trigger other triggers as well. Triggers are defined on tables but not on views. However, any insert, update, or delete statement issued on a view fires off the trigger on the base table.

Why Triggers enable you to execute units of code implicitly to automatically derive column data, enforce security authorizations and constraints, and generate transparent event logging.

How This chapter presented the methods users take to create the various types of triggers. In the trigger definition, you define the trigger statement, timing, and action.

Stored Procedures

What Is a Stored Procedure?

What A stored procedure is a logically grouped set of SQL and PL/SQL statements that performs a specific task. This procedure is considered by Oracle as a schema object and is stored in the database. A procedure is executed interactively using Oracle tools such as SQL*DBA or explicitly through an application.

Stored procedures have several parts to them. The declarative part contains declarations of types, cursors, constants, variables, exceptions, and nested subprograms. The executable part contains statements that control execution and manipulate data. Occasionally, the procedure contains an exception-handling part to deal with exceptions raised during execution.

Procedures can be defined using any Oracle tool that supports PL/SQL, such as SQL*Plus. Procedures can be declared in PL/SQL blocks, packages, and other procedures. Procedures must be declared at the end of a declarative section after all other program objects.

Why Use Stored Procedures?

Why Procedures are created to solve a specific problem or task. These stored procedures offer the following advantages:

- PL/SQL enables you to tailor your procedure to suit your specific requirements.
- These procedures are modular. That is, they let you break a program down into manageable, well-defined units.
- Because they are stored in the database, procedures are reusable. Once validated, procedures can be used repeatedly without recompiling or distributing them over the network.
- Improved database security. You can restrict database access by enabling users to access data only through stored procedures.
- You can improve memory by taking advantage of shared-memory resources.

How to Use Stored Procedures

How A stored procedure is an Oracle subprogram that performs a specific task. The following sections discuss the necessary steps to create, alter, and maintain stored procedures.

Prerequisites

The database administrator is responsible for running the catproc.sql script. This script automatically runs all the scripts required for, or used within, the Oracle procedural option.

Parts to a Stored Procedure

A stored procedure has two parts: a specification and a body. The specification declares the procedure and includes the name of the stored procedure and the names and datatypes of any arguments. The body defines the procedure, which consists of the PL/SQL block of code.

Creating Stored Procedures

The create procedure command creates a stand-alone procedure. The following is a list of the parameters that can be used in the create statement:

in
: This parameter specifies that you must pass a value to the subprogram being called. The in parameter cannot be assigned a value because it acts like a constant. The actual value that corresponds to the parameter can be a constant, literal, initialized variable, or expression.

out
: This specifies that the procedure return a value to the calling program. This parameter acts like an uninitialized parameter; therefore, its value cannot be assigned to another variable. The actual value that corresponds to the parameter must be a variable. It cannot be a literal,

constant, or expression. Within your subprogram, the out parameter must be assigned a value.

inout   This specifies that you must pass a value to the procedure and that the procedure return a value back to its calling environment after execution.

or replace   This re-creates the procedure if it already exists.

The following example creates a simple stored procedure. This procedure accepts two arguments, part_id and qty:

```
/* Stored procedure named: user_01.parts. The next line */
/*of code is the stored procedure specification.        */

create procedure user_01.parts (part_id number, qty number)

/* The procedure body begins here.                       */

as begin
update journal
set journal.qty = journal.qty + qty
where journal_id = part_id;
end;
```

Normally procedures are created as stand-alone schema objects. However, you can create a procedure as part of a package. Refer to Chapter 24, "Packages," for additional information about packages.

return Statements

The return statement causes a subprogram to immediately complete its execution and return to the calling program. Execution in the calling program resumes with the statement following the procedure call.

In procedures, the return statement cannot contain an expression. Its sole purpose is to return control back to the calling program before the end of the procedure is reached.

Recompiling a Stored Procedure

To explicitly recompile a stored procedure, issue the alter procedure command. This command must be used only in stand-alone stored procedures and not in procedures that are part of the package.

Recompiling a procedure does not change the procedure's declaration or definition. You must use create procedure with the or replace clause to do this.

If Oracle successfully recompiles a procedure, the procedure becomes a valid procedure that can be executed without runtime compilation. If compilation fails, the procedure becomes invalid and must be debugged. To aid in debugging, Oracle provides a public package named dbms_output that contains debugging information.

You can use the `alter procedure` command to explicitly recompile a procedure that is invalid. Once a procedure is compiled, it does not need to be recompiled implicitly during runtime processes. This leads to reduced overhead and elimination of runtime compilation errors.

You can produce debugging information from within an application by issuing the `put` or `put_line` commands. These commands place the debugging information into a buffer created by the dbms_output package. To display the contents of the buffer, type the `set server output on` command at the SQL*Plus prompt or from within SQL*DBA.

The following example illustrates the `put_line` command line that you can include inside your procedure:

```
create or replace procedure parts(part_id number, qty_in number)
as
qtyw number(5);
begin
select qty into qtyw
from journal
where journal_id = part_id;
dbms_output.put_line('Original Qty = ' ¦¦ qtyw);
update journal
set journal.qty = journal.qty + qty_in
where journal_id = part_id;
select qty into qtyw
from journal
where journal_id = part_id;
dbms_output.put_line('New Qty = ' ¦¦ qtyw);
```

The following statements are issued at the SQL*DBA command line to execute the parts procedure and to display the debugging information:

```
set serveout on
execute user_01.parts(id,qty)
```

The following are the results of these statements being executed. This information is generated from the dba_output buffer area:

```
Orignal Qty = 100
New Qty = 200
Original Qty = 200
New Qty = 325
... and so on
```

Re-creating a Stored Procedure

A stand-alone procedure cannot be altered; it must be either replaced with a new definition or dropped and re-created.

For example, you cannot simply slightly alter one of the PL/SQL statements in the procedure. Instead, the procedure must be re-created with the modification.

When replacing a procedure, the `or replace` clause must be included in the `create procedure` statement. The `or replace` clause is used to replace an older version of a procedure with a newer version of the procedure. This replacement keeps all grants in place; therefore, you do not have to re-create the grants. However, if you drop the procedure and re-create it, the grants are dropped and consequently have to be rebuilt. If you attempt a `create procedure` command for a procedure that already exists, Oracle generates an error message.

The following example re-creates the procedure named "parts" in the user_01 schema:

```
/* Stored procedure named: user_01.parts. The next line */
/*of code is the stored procedure replacement           */
/* specification.                                        */

create or replace procedure user_01.parts
(part_id number, qty number)

/* The procedure body begins here.                       */

as begin
update journal
set journal.qty = (journal.qty*.05) + qty
where journal_id = part_id;
end;
```

Invoking Stored Procedures

Procedures can be invoked from many different environments, including SQL*Plus and SQL*Forms. Also, procedures can be invoked from within another procedure or trigger.

For example, the procedure parts_sum can be called from within another procedure or trigger with the following statement:

```
parts_sum(qty, wip_nbr);
```

Another example where the same procedure is executed from within SQL*DBA is this:

```
execute parts_sum(qty, wip_nbr);
```

The following example shows a procedure being called from within a precompile program:

```
exec sql execute
begin
parts_sum(qty, :wip_nbr);
end
end-exec
```

To execute a procedure, you must possess the execute privilege for stand-alone procedures or you must have the execute any procedure system privilege.

To invoke a procedure on a remote database, include the appropriate database link in the statement, as illustrated in the next example. This example uses SQL*DBA to execute the procedure:

```
execute parts_sum@prod_011(:qty, wip_nbr);
```

Forward Declarations

A forward declaration is simply a procedure declaration terminated by a semicolon. Oracle requires all identifiers to be declared before using them. This means that procedures must be declared before calling them. Normally you declare the procedure prior to calling it. However, in some circumstances you need mechanisms like forward declarations. Forward declarations enable you to define procedures in logical or alphabetical order as well to group procedures in a package. Forward declarations enable you to define mutually recursive procedures. These are procedures that call each other.

The following example illustrates recursive procedures that use forward declarations. This example shows only a portion of the actual code:

```
declare
procedure calc_pay (...)        -- forward declaration

/* Group subprograms together logically             */

procedure annual_bonus (...) is
begin
calc_pay(...)
...
end


/* Declarations is in annual bonus procedure  */

procedure calc_pay (...) is
begin
...
end
```

Parameters

Procedures use parameters (variables or expressions) to pass information. When a parameter is being passed by a procedure, it is known as an actual parameter. However, parameters declared internal to a procedure are known as internal or formal parameters.

The actual parameter and its corresponding formal parameter must belong to compatible datatypes. For example, PL/SQL cannot convert an actual parameter with a datatype of date to a formal parameter with a datatype of long. In this case, Oracle would return an error message. This compatibility also applies to the return values.

When passing parameters, a problem may arise if you use a parameter twice in a procedure call and both occurrences of that parameter are not formal parameters. For example, a problem could arise if a global variable appears in a procedure call and then is referenced within the procedure. This can cause an indeterminate result.

Parameter Definitions

When a procedure is invoked, you must pass in a value for each of the procedure's parameters. If you pass values to the parameter, they are positional and must appear in the same order as they appear in the procedure declaration. If you pass argument with their names, they can appear in any order. You can have a combination of values and names in the argument values. If this is the case, the values identified in order must precede the argument names.

If the default option has been used to define the argument values of a subprogram, you pass a different number of parameters to the subprogram. If an actual value is not passed to the procedure, the corresponding default value is used.

Variables, Cursors, and Constants

Variables, cursors, and constants can change their value over time and have a specific life span. This life duration can vary depending on where the declaration is located. For stand-alone procedures, variables, cursors, and constants persist only for the duration of the procedure call and are lost when the procedure execution terminates.

If the variable, constant, or cursor was declared in a package specification or body, its values persist for the duration of the user's session. The values are lost when the current user's session terminates or the package is recompiled.

Synonyms for Stored Procedures

Synonyms can be created for stored procedures to do the following:

- Hide the identity of the name and owner of a procedure
- Provide location transparency for remotely stored procedures

Synonyms can be used to invoke procedures and other subprograms. Synonyms cannot be created for individual procedures that are defined within a package. However, you can create a synonym that references a package.

Listing Stored Procedure Information

Oracle provides several data dictionary views that provide information about procedures:

all_errors	A list of current errors on all objects accessible to the user
all_source	Text source of all stored objects accessible to the user
dba_errors	Current errors on all stored objects in the database
dba_object_size	All PL/SQL objects in the database
dba_source	Text source of all stored objects in the database
user_errors	Current errors on all a user's stored objects
user_source	Text source of all stored objects belonging to the user
user_object_size	User's PL/SQL objects

The following example queries the user_errors view to obtain information about the current errors on all the stored procedures owned by the current user:

```
select line, type, name, text from user_errors
```

Sample output:

```
LINE  TYPE   NAME     TEXT
----- ------ ------   -------------------------------------
   4  PROC   PST_QTY  PL/SQL-00387: into variable cannot be a database object
                      PL/SQL: SQL statement ignored
```

Dropping a Stored Procedure

Issue the SQL statement drop procedure to drop a procedure's objects. The following statement drops the procedure parts_qty:

```
drop procedure parts_qty;
```

To drop a procedure, the object must be in your schema or you must have the drop any procedure system privilege.

Overloading

Oracle permits you to call the same procedure name in a package but with different arguments. This is known as overloading. This technique is very useful, especially when you want to execute the same procedure several times but with arguments that have different datatypes. One example of using procedure overload is with the package dbms_output. In this package, the put_line procedure is called numerous times to produce output lines of different datatypes.

Overloaded procedure's names can appear only in a block, subprogram, or package. You cannot overload a stand-alone procedure. You cannot overload two procedures if their parameters differ only in name or in mode. For example, the following example of overloading the calc_pay procedure is illegal. The only difference in the second procedure is the parameter mode.

```
procedure calc_pay (hours in number, rate number) is
begin
...
end calc_pay

procedure calc_pay (hours out number, rate number)
begin
...
end calc_pay
```

Recursion

A recursive procedure is a procedure that calls itself. Each recursive call creates a new instance of any object declared in the procedure, including parameters, variables, cursors, and exceptions. Also, new instances of SQL statements are created at each level in the recursive procedure.

With the recursive logic, the procedure must be able to terminate itself at some predefined point or it would last forever. This point of termination is defined in a terminating condition. This example uses a conditional statement to terminate the recursive cycle:

```
function inv_calc
begin
if qty = > :max_qty then -- terminating condition
return 1
else
return qty * inv_calc (qty * :part_qty) -- recursive call;
...
end if;
end inv_calc;
```

Be careful with recursion and where you place the recursive call. If you place the recursive call inside a cursor for loop or between open and close statements, a cursor is opened at each call. This can open enough cursors to violate the maximum number of open cursors permitted by the open_cursor initialization parameter.

Essential Summary

A stored procedure is a group of SQL and PL/SQL statements that you can call by name. In this chapter, you learned the components of a procedure and how to create and use procedures.

What

Procedures are used to provide program extensibility, modularity, and reusability and to improve maintainability.

Why

Procedures, like many other PL/SQL subprograms, can be created as stand-alone schema objects or as part of a package. Procedures can be called by functions, packages, or other procedures.

How

PART VII

Database Utilities

Import and Export

What Are Import and Export?

What Import and export are two complementary programs. The export utility enables users to extract data from an Oracle database, whereas the import utility reads the exported data into the Oracle database.

Import and export are Oracle utilities. These utilities are used to move Oracle data in and out of Oracle databases. The export utility creates a copy of all the table objects in an Oracle database and places them in an external file. This export file is transportable and is used as the sole input to the import utility. The import utility reads into the Oracle database a copy of the table objects from the export file.

Why Use Import and Export?

Why The import and export utilities facilitate the following database activities:

- Archiving data
- Upgrading to new releases of Oracle
- Moving data between Oracle databases
- Dropping a tablespace
- Defragmenting the database

Data archival is one of the most powerful features of the import and export utilities. Database administrators may use the export utility to make complete and incremental backups of the databases. This is often done to supplement the normal operating system backup procedures. If needed, the import utility is used to restore the database from the archived export files.

These utilities enable you to store inactive, historical, or obsolete data in external files. These export files can then be stored in the appropriate storage facility for safekeeping.

The import and export utilities provide an easy and convenient method to move data from an older version of the database to a newer version. These utilities are compatible between versions of Oracle.

In a typical programming shop, the developers have a development instance, testing instance, and production instance. Data that is developed in one of these instances can be moved to any of the other instances via the import and export utilities. Additionally, the data can be moved to a remote or different owner's database with these utilities.

You can have Oracle import all table objects from the export file into the object owner's own default tablespace rather than your own tablespace. Oracle first attempts to import them into your own tablespace, but this effort can be redirected to the owner's tablespace by creating a zero-block tablespace with the same name as the tablespace you want to drop. During the import, the `create tablespace` command will fail due to the zero-block tablespace. The net result of all this is that the original tablespace is dropped.

Over time, the database will become fragmented. This means the database has many small blocks of unused storage space scattered about it. This is a natural phenomenon that occurs with many databases. By using the import and export utilities to create full backups of the database, you can re-create the database with no fragmentation.

How to Use Import and Export

The following sections take you through the steps necessary to export the database objects and then import those objects.

Export

You have two different modes you can choose from when exporting data. The table mode enables you to export specified tables in your schema rather than all tables. The user mode enables you to export all objects in your schema.

The table mode enables you to export the following objects:

- Table data
- Table definitions
- Owner's table grants
- Table constraints
- Table triggers

The user mode enables you to export the same set of objects as in the table mode, as well as the following additional objects:

- Views
- Snapshots
- Snapshot logs
- Clusters
- Database links
- Sequences
- Private synonyms
- Stored procedures

Export Preparation

Prior to running the export utility, the following must be evaluated:

- Be sure there is sufficient storage space on the disk drive or tape for the export file. If there is not enough storage space, Oracle terminates the export and generates an error. You can use the table sizes in the source tables to estimate the storage requirements of the export file.
- Be sure that you have the `create session` system privilege on the Oracle database.

Executing the Export Utility

To use the export utility, type `exp` at the command line to start the export utility.

Oracle allows three different ways to use the export utility:

- At the command line, issue the `exp` command with the name of the parameter file. The username and password of the source database must also be supplied. This method is the preferred one. The following example illustrates this method:

```
exp username/password parfile=filename
```

- At the command line, issue the `exp` command followed by the parameters that control how export runs. The following is an example of this method:

```
exp username/password tables=(emp,master_dept) grants=y
```

- At the command line, issue the `exp` command with the username and password. Oracle begins an interactive session that prompts you for the necessary parameters needed to run the export utility. If you omit the username and password on the command line, Oracle prompts you for this information. The following is an example of this method:

```
exp username/password
```

Export Parameters

The following are the parameters that can be used with the export utility:

buffer	The size in bytes of the buffer used to fetch rows of data. Use the following equation to calculate the correct buffer size: `buffer size = rows_in_array * maximum_row_size.`
file	This is the name of the output file created by the export utility. The default is `expdat.dmp`.
grants	This is a Y or N flag to indicate whether to export grants. The default is Y.
indexes	This is a Y or N flag to indicate whether to export indexes. The default is Y.
rows	This is a Y or N flag to indicate whether to export rows of data from a table. The default is Y.
constraints	This is a Y or N flag to indicate whether to export constraints. The default is Y.
compress	This is a Y or N flag to indicate whether to compress table data into one extent during an import. The default is Y.
full	This is a Y or N flag to indicate a full database export. The default is N.
owner	This is a list of usernames whose objects will be exported. The default is undefined.
tables	This is a list of table names to export. The default is undefined.
recordlength	This defines the length in bytes of the output file. The default is defined by the operating system.
inctype	This defines the type of increment. The valid values are `complete`, `cumulative`, and `incremental`. The default value is none.
parfile	This specifies the name of the parameter file. There is no default value for this parameter.
log	This specifies the filename of the log file. The default is not to create a log file.
statistics	This indicates the type of database optimizer statistics that will be generated. The valid options are `estimate`, `compute`, and `none`. The default is none.
consistent	This is a Y or N flag to indicate whether a read-consistent view is created for the database. This parameter is very useful when other applications are updating the database during the export. The default value is No.

During an interactive export session, Oracle prompts you for a subset of parameters to be used. The following parameters are prompted for during an interactive session: username, password, buffer, export file, export mode, grants, table data, compress, schemas to export, and tables to export. All other parameters assume their default values.

To minimize the time and space required to execute an export, you should follow these rules:

- Export only those tables that are needed.
- Export tables together that need to remain consistent. All other tables should be exported in a second pass of the export utility.

Export Examples

The following is an example of the export being initiated by using the interactive method. In this example the table MASTER_DEPT is being exported into the external file mast_dept.dmp. All default values are being used in this example.

```
Connected to: Corporate instance PRODUCTION

> EXP

Export: Release 7.0.16 - Production on Fri Jun 23 1995

Copyright (c) Oracle Corporation 1979, 1992.
All rights reserved.

Username: user_01
Password: ........

Connected to: ORACLE7 Server Release 7.0.16 - Production
With procedural, distributed, and Parallel Server options
PL/SQL Release 2.0.18.1.0 - Production

Enter array fetch buffer size: 4096 > 4096
Export file: DISK_1:[USER_01]EXPDAT.DMP > MAST_DEPT.DMP
(2)U(sers), or (3)T(ables): (2)U > T
Export table data (yes/no): yes > YES
Compress extents (yes/no): yes > YES

About to export specified tables ...
Table to be exported: (RETURN to quit) > MASTER_DEPT

exporting table       MASTER_DEPT     76 rows exported

Table to be exported: (RETURN to quit) >

Export terminated successfully without warnings.
>EXIT
```

The parameters issued in this example could just as well have been placed in a parameter file or on the command line. In either case, the output would be the same. The following statement is the export command line equivalent to the previous interactive session:

```
> EXP USER_01/password FILE=MAST_DEPT.DMP TABLES=MASTER_DEPT
```

Complete, Cumulative, and Incremental Exports

To improve export performance, complete, cumulative, and incremental exports can be performed.

Complete exports are equivalent to a full database export except that they also update the tables used to track incremental and cumulative exports. The complete export is used to establish the base export for the incremental and cumulative exports.

The cumulative export backs up tables that have changed since the last cumulative or complete export.

The incremental export backs up only tables that have changed since the last incremental, cumulative, or complete export.

Using the cumulative and incremental exports benefits the Oracle server by reducing the export processing time and space requirements of a full or complete export.

Export Sequences

During an export and import cycle, if transactions continue to be processed, sequence numbers can be skipped. It is advised that sequence numbers not be accessed during any `export` or `import` operation.

The exported value of a sequence is the next sequence number (after any cached values). Sequence numbers that have been cached but not used are lost when the sequence is imported. Sequence numbers can be skipped only when the sequence is cached and in use. When a cache of sequence numbers has been allocated, they are available for use in the current database only.

Export Online Help

Oracle provides online help. Enter `exp help=y` at the command line to see the export help screen.

Import

The import utility can read only files that were created by the export utility. Import reads export files into an Oracle database. For example, if you exported your table's objects and data into a file named emp_exp.dmp, import would read this file, rebuild the database objects, and load the data.

When you import database objects, you need the appropriate system privileges to create the objects. For example, you need the `create table` and `insert table` system privileges to create a table and load it with data during an import process. Additionally, you need the `create session` system privilege.

You can import an export file that you did not create if you have the `imp_full_database` role.

Importing Table Objects

The import utility imports the table objects from the export file in the following order:

1. Table definitions—Tables are created first.
2. Table data—Data is loaded into the newly created tables.
3. Table indexes—Indexes are built after the data is loaded.
4. Integrated constraints and triggers—Finally, triggers are imported and constraints are enabled.

This order of table object loading is important. This particular loading order prevents data from being rejected and prevents redundant triggers from firing twice on the same data.

Importing Grants

To import the privileges that a user has extended to others, the import utility user must be empowered to grant these privileges. The following items detail the conditions that must be satisfied for the authorizations to be valid on the target database.

- For object privileges to take effect, the object must exist in the user's schema, or the user must have the privileges along with the with grant option.
- For system privileges to take effect, the user must have the privileges along with the with admin option.

Importing Objects into Other Schemas

Oracle requires that you have the IMP_FULL_DATABASE role enabled to import objects into another user's schema.

Snapshots

Four different objects make up a snapshot. They are the master table, the optional snapshot log, the master table trigger, and the snapshot itself. All four of these are exported and imported according to the following guidelines:

- If the master table already exists, import data is recorded in the snapshot log. If not, the new master table is imported.
- Oracle imports all triggers after the master tables are created and loaded.
- After an import, the snapshot log is empty. Therefore, you must execute a full refresh before attempting a fast refresh.

Care must be taken not to allow too much time to elapse between the last refresh and the import of the snapshot. The exported copy of the snapshot can become out of date. One guideline to follow is to always execute a full refresh when the import is completed.

Stored Procedures, Functions, and Packages

When stored procedures, functions, and packages are imported, they retain their original time stamp. This functionality exists to prevent unnecessary recompilation of remote procedures that use these imported versions.

If the time stamp of the imported versions matches the time stamp of the database, the local dependent procedures are not marked for recompilation. If the time stamps are different, local dependent procedures are marked for recompilation. When a remote procedure or package calls one of these dependent procedures, the dependent procedure is recompiled and its time stamp is updated. This action triggers an error in the calling procedure.

Import Parameters

The following parameters can be used with the import utility:

buffer	This is the size in bytes of the buffer used to transfer rows of data. Use the following equation to calculate the correct buffer size: `buffer size = rows_in_array * maximum_row_size.`
file	This is the name of the output file created by the export utility that is to be imported. The default is `expdat.dmp`.
grants	This is a Y or N flag to indicate whether to import grants. The default is Y.
indexes	This is a Y or N flag to indicate whether to import indexes. The default is Y.
rows	This is a Y or N flag to indicate whether to import rows of data from a table. The default is Y.
full	This is a Y or N flag to indicate a full database import. The default value is N.
tables	This is a list of table names to import. The default is none.
recordlength	This defines the length in bytes of the output file. The default is defined by the operating system.
inctype	This defines the type of increment import. The valid values are `complete`, `cumulative`, and `incremental`. The default value is none.
parfile	This specifies the name of the parameter file. There is no default value for this parameter.
log	This specifies the filename of the log file. The default is not to create a log file.
destroy	This specifies whether the existing data files making up the database should be reused. The default is no. This default setting generates an error if the data file already exists when the tablespace is created.

commit	This is a flag indicating whether a commit should occur after each array of data is inserted. The default is N.
show	This is a flag to indicate whether to list the contents of the export file and import the table data, or not create any objects and not modify the database. The default value is No.

During an interactive import session, Oracle prompts you for a subset of parameters to be used. The following parameters are prompted for during an interactive session: `username`, `password`, `buffer`, `import file`, `show`, `grants`, `table data`, and `tables to import`. All other parameters assume their default values.

Executing the Import Utility

Like the export utility, Oracle allows three different ways to use the import utility:

- At the command line, issue the `imp` command with the name of the parameter file. The username and password of the destination database must also be supplied. This method is the preferred one. The following example illustrates this method:

  ```
  imp username/password parfile=filename
  ```

- At the command line, issue the `imp` command followed by the parameters that control how import runs. The following is an example of this method:

  ```
  imp username/password tables=(emp,master_dept) grants=y
  ```

- At the command line, issue the `imp` command with the username and password. Oracle begins an interactive session that prompts you for the necessary parameters needed to run the import utility. If you omit the username and password on the command line, Oracle prompts you for this information. An example of this method follows:

  ```
  imp username/password
  ```

Import Examples

The following is an example of an interactive import session. This import session is initiated by issuing the `imp` command with the username and password of the receiving database. The user accepts all default values.

```
> IMP user_01/password
Import: Release 7.0.16- Production on Fri Jun 23 1995
Copyright (c) Oracle Corporation 1979, 1992.
All rights reserved.


Connected to: ORACLE7 Server Release 7.0.16 - Production
With the procedural, distributed, and Parallel Server options
PL/SQL Release 2.0.18.1.0 - Production

Import file: DISK_1:[USER_01]EXPDAT.DMP >
Enter insert buffer size (minimum is 4096) 30720>
Export file created by EXPORT:V07.00.16
```

```
List contents of import file only (yes/no): no >
Ignore create error due to object existence (yes/no): yes >
Import grants (yes/no): yes >
Import table data (yes/no): yes >
Import entire export file (yes/no): yes >
. importing USER_01's objects into USER_02
. . importing table "MASTER_DEPT    18 rows imported
Import terminated successfully without warnings.
```

> **EXIT**

Import Online Help

Oracle provides online help. Enter imp help=y at the command line to see the import help screen.

Essential Summary

What The import and export utilities enable the user to transfer data from one database to another. This chapter covered the numerous parameters that can be used to give these utilities flexibility.

Why   There are many advantages to using the import and export utilities. These utilities enable you to archive and restore data and facilitate in migrating to different versions of Oracle and defragmenting the database.

How   This chapter reviewed the various ways to execute the import and export utilities: interactively, with parameter files, or with the command line. Finally, the parameters that control the import and export process were reviewed.

SQL*Loader

SQL*Loader is an Oracle tool that enables you to load data from external files into Oracle database tables. This chapter covers the various inputs to SQL*Loader, data-loading options, and output files from SQL*Loader.

What Is SQL*Loader?

What SQL*Loader is a tool for loading data from external data files into one or more Oracle tables. It can load data in a variety of data formats, perform filtering, load data into multiple tables, and create one logical record from one or more physical input records. SQL*Loader generates a detailed log file, a bad file that can contain rejected (due to incorrect data) input records, and a discard file to hold the records that you selectively don't load.

SQL*Loader is executed from the command line. To invoke SQL*Loader, you need an Oracle username with a password and the name of your control file.

Why Use SQL*Loader?

Why SQL*Loader enables you to load data from external files into your Oracle database quickly and accurately. Using SQL*Loader provides you with the following benefits:

- It automatically loads data from multiple data files of different datatypes into multiple Oracle tables. This saves you time by executing SQL*Loader once to handle all your data-loading needs.

- It filters data for you so that you can selectively load certain records. This enables you to load only the data that you need and helps to keep your database clear of unwanted data.

- It can generate unique sequence numbers automatically for specific columns. This optional feature enables you to build referential integrity into your database.

- It provides extensive error diagnostics on your data to assist you in correcting errors and reloading all records.

- SQL*Loader enables you to manipulate the input data with SQL functions before inserting the data into the database columns.

How to Use SQL*Loader

How You, as the programmer, initiate the loading of data by providing SQL*Loader with two pieces of information: the input data and the processing control file. The data that is to be loaded must exist, on disk or tape, at the time of the load. This input data is described to SQL*Loader by the control file.

The following is an outline of the steps used to load data via SQL*Loader. Each of these steps is covered in detail in the following sections.

1. Determine your input data source
2. Create the control file
3. Execute the loading process
4. Verify the results

Input Data

Your first required input to SQL*Loader is the data that is to be loaded. This input data to be loaded into an Oracle table can be provided from an external data file, as in Case 1, or be included in the control file, as shown in Case 2. No matter which approach you take, you can load data in various formats.

SQL*Loader accepts the following five datatypes. These datatypes identify the datatype of the fields being loaded, not the Oracle column datatype.

- `varchar`
- `date`

- integer external

- float external

- decimal external

- zoned

- double

- graphic

- raw

- vargraphic

- smallint

- byteint

You can load numeric data in binary or character format. Data in both formats can be in a fixed-length or variable-length format. In fixed-length records, the data fields have a fixed length and type and occur in the same position. This holds true for every record in the file. In variable-length records, each record is only as long as necessary. The length of the record and individual fields varies from record to record. These variable-length records usually end with some type of terminator. The operating system uses this terminator to determine the end of each record.

With SQL*Loader, you can create multiple logical records from one physical record as well as one logical record from several physical records. A *logical record* is usually thought of as a single row in the database. A *physical record* is a single record of input data. Sometimes, these two are the same. Normally, physical records are combined or concatenated to create one or more logical records. These physical records contain a field that indicates a record type and whether to concatenate the following record. Sometimes a fixed number of records makes up one logical record. Case 3 illustrates these concepts by creating one logical record from several physical records.

Control File

The control file is the second of the two required inputs to SQL*Loader. You create this file to instruct SQL*Loader on the following information:

- The location of the data that is to be loaded. This can be the name and location of an external data file or it can be the actual data itself.

- The mapping of input data to their corresponding Oracle table columns. This is where you define which input fields go to which Oracle tables and columns.

- The specifications for loading the data. You include logic to filter, format, or create data for specific table columns.

Some information is mandatory, such as the names of the tables to be loaded. However, some information is optional and might be included to assist you in manipulating the data. For example, you can include an option to filter the data in a particular way.

Control files should be written so that they are easy to understand and easy to write. One way to accomplish this is to write in a free format style of writing. Use blank lines as needed for clarity and ease of reading. Include comment lines to explain the control file and any complex logic. Feel free to continue command lines from one line to the next to assist in comprehension.

The syntax of a typical control file is as follows:

```
LOAD DATA
INFILE filename
INSERT
INTO TABLE table_name
(field_name1 POSITION(start:end) CHAR,
field_name2 POSITION(start:end) CHAR)
```

The following three case studies illustrate the various features of SQL*Loader and ways to set up the input data and control files. These examples are based on a typical company that has an Employee table and a Department table. The individual that has access to this database is Thomas, who has a password of Pacer. The numbers down the left side are not part of the control file; they correspond to the notes that follow the case study.

Case 1: Employee Data Load

Case 1 demonstrates the following features:

- Loading an external data file
- Loading multiple tables
- Using the sequence function to generate input data
- Using the insert and when clauses

```
1    -- Program Name: CASE1.CTL
     -- The following SQL*Loader program loads the EMP and
     -- DEPT Oracle Tables using the EMP_DEPT.DAT data file.
2    LOAD DATA
3    INFILE 'DISK1:EMP_DEPT.DAT'
4    INSERT
5    INTO TABLE EMP
6           (EMP_ID SEQUENCE (MAX,1),
7            F_NAME POSITION(01:35) CHAR,
             L_NAME POSITION(36:75) CHAR,
             EMP_NBR POSITION (76:85) CHAR,
8            START_DATE   SYSDATE)
9    INTO TABLE DEPT
     -- Only load records that have a DEPT
10   WHEN DEPT != ' '
             (EMP_NBR POSITION (76:85) CHAR,
              DEPT POSITION (86:95) INTEGER EXTERNAL)
```

Notes:

1. These two lines are comments. You should always give a detailed description of the purpose of the control file.

2. This line is mandatory at the beginning of every SQL*Loader control file.

3. This line gives the file specifications for the input data file. If an asterisk appears here, the input data is appended to the end of this control file.

4. By default, SQL*Loader assumes the insert option. With this option, the table that is to be loaded must be empty before any inserts can occur. You can also use the append or replace commands.

5. The into table statement is required to identify the name of the table that is to be loaded.

6. This line automatically generates a sequence number and loads that value into the emp_id column. This sequence function goes out and finds the current maximum value for emp_id and then increments it by 1 for the current record's insert.

7. These are the column names that are to be loaded. Note that they are enclosed in parentheses.

8. This line loads the current date into the start_date field.

9. A second table, DEPT, is loaded by using a second into table clause.

10. This loads data into the DEPT table only when dept is not equal to blanks.

Case 2: Employee Data Load

Case 2 demonstrates the following features:

- Loading data from the control file itself
- Loading data that is delimited
- Using the append clause

```
-- Program Name: CASE2.CTL
    -- The following SQL*Loader program appends the data in
    -- this control file to the EMP table.
1   LOAD DATA
2   INFILE *
3   APPEND
4   INTO TABLE EMP
5   FIELDS TERMINATED BY ',' OPTIONALLY ENCLOSED BY '"'
6   TRAILING NULLCOLS
7   (EMP_ID, F_NAME, L_NAME, EMP_NBR, DEPT)
8   BEGINDATA
9       1022,"JONATHAN","WILSON",1283,"23B"
        3397,"MATTHEW","ANDERSON",8210
        7817,"SARAH","BROWN",2391,"293"
```

Notes:

1. This line is mandatory at the beginning of every SQL*Loader control file.

2. This line gives the file specifications for the input data file. If an asterisk appears here, the input data is appended to the end of this control file.

3. append adds the input data to the existing table.

4. The into table statement is required to identify the name of the table that is to be loaded.

5. The input data fields are terminated by a comma, and some fields might also be enclosed by quotation marks.

6. The `training nullcols` clause causes SQL*Loader to treat any fields that are missing at the end of the record as null.

7. These are the columns that are to be loaded. Note that they are enclosed in parentheses.

8. This specifies that the following lines are the input data.

9. This is the data that is to be loaded.

Case 3: Employee Data Load

Case 3 demonstrates the following features:

- Combining multiple input records to form one logical record
- Using the `replace` clause

```
-- Program Name: CASE3.CTL
      -- This SQL*Loader program replaces the EMP table with
      -- enclosed in-stream data. This program creates one
      -- logical record from two physical input records.
      LOAD DATA
      INFILE *
1     REPLACE
2     CONTINUEIF THIS (1) = '*'
      INTO TABLE EMP
      FIELDS TERMINATED BY ',' OPTIONALLY ENCLOSED BY '"'
      (EMP_ID,F_NAME, L_NAME, EMP_NBR, DEPT)
      BEGINDATA
3        *988,"JACK","WILSON"
          1283,"23B"
         *1002,"THOMAS","ANDERSON",
          8210,"9S"
         *1192,"CATHERINE","WHITE",
          9001,"45A"
```

Notes:

1. This tells SQL*Loader to delete the contents of the table EMP and insert the new data.

2. This specifies that if an asterisk is found in column 1 of the current record, the next physical record following should be appended to it to form one logical record. This means that column 1 of the file should contain either an asterisk or any other non-data value.

3. This is the input data.

SQL Operators in SQL*Loader

A wide variety of SQL operators can be used in the SQL*Loader control file. Within a SQL string, you can use any SQL expression that is recognized by Oracle as valid for use in the `values` clause of an `insert` statement.

This SQL string appears after any other specification for a given column and is enclosed in quotation marks. The following are valid examples that can be used with a control file:

- `field1 DATE 'mm-dd-yyyy' "RTRIM(:field1)"`   The date mask is evaluated after the SQL string.

- `job_title POSITION (34:55) CHAR"UPPER(:job_title)"`   This converts the job_title field to uppercase.

SQL*Loader Execution

To invoke SQL*Loader for Case 1, you would type the following at the command line:

`>SQLLOAD Control=CASE1.CTL USERID=THOMAS/PACER`

This command executes the control file that was created in Case 1 and loads the EMP table. Additionally, you can optionally include arguments that override the default values and output filenames. For example, you could type

`>SQLLOAD Control=CASE1.CTL USERID=THOMAS/PACER  SKIP 50`

The addition of SKIP 50 on the command line instructs SQL*Loader to skip the first 50 records of the input file. Data loading would begin with the 51st record. The following list of arguments can be used on the command line:

LOG	Names the log file created by SQL*Loader to store information about the loading process
BAD	Names the bad file created by SQL*Loader to store the records that caused errors during loading
DISCARD	Names an optional discard file created by SQL*Loader to store records that are not inserted into the table and do not contain errors
DISCARDMAX	Specifies the number of discard records allowed before terminating the load
ERRORS	Specifies the number of insert errors allowed before terminating the load
SKIP	Specifies the number of logical records from the beginning of the file that should not be loaded
ROWS	Specifies the number of rows in the bind array

SQL*Loader Output Files

The typical SQL*Loader execution creates three output files:

- Log file
- Bad Record file
- Discard file

Log File

The log file contains a detailed summary of the data-load execution. The following listing shows the log file that was created when Case 1 was executed:

```
SQL*Loader: Release 7.1 - Production Database APR 21, 1995

Copyright (c) Oracle Corporation 1979, 1992.  All rights reserved.

Control File:   DISK1:CASE1.CTL
Data File:      DISK1:EMP_DEPT.DAT
Bad File:       DISK1:CASE1.BAD
Discard File:   none specified

 (Allow all discards)

Number to load: ALL
Number to skip: 0
Errors allowed: 50
Bind array:     64 rows, maximum of 65536 bytes
Continuation:   none specified
Path used:      Conventional

Table EMP, loaded from every logical record.
Insert option in effect for this table: REPLACE
TRAILING NULLCOLS option in effect

    Column Name          Position   Len  Term Encl Datatype
--------- ---------- ---- ---- ---- ----------------------
F_NAME                    1:35      36    ,        CHARACTER
L_NAME                   36:75      40    ,        CHARACTER
EMP_NBR                  76:85      10    ,        CHARACTER
START_DATE               SYSDATE          ,        DATE
EMP_ID                   SEQUENCE (1500,1)

Table EMP:
  58 Rows successfully loaded.
  0 Rows not loaded due to data errors.
  0 Rows not loaded because all WHEN clauses were failed.
  0 Rows not loaded because all fields were null.

Table DEPT, loaded from every logical record.
Insert option in effect for this table: REPLACE
TRAILING NULLCOLS option in effect

    Column Name          Position   Len  Term Encl Datatype
--------- ---------- ---- ---- ---- ----------------------
EMP_NBR                  76:85      10    ,        CHARACTER
DEPT                     86:95      10    ,        INTEGER

Table DEPT:
  58 Rows successfully loaded.
  0 Rows not loaded due to data errors.
  0 Rows not loaded because all WHEN clauses were failed.
  0 Rows not loaded because all fields were null.


Space allocated for bind array:      768 bytes(64 rows)
Space allocated for memory besides bind array:43308 bytes
```

```
Total logical records skipped:        0
Total logical records read:          58
Total logical records rejected:       0
Total logical records discarded:      0

Run began on Fri Apr 21 13:35:15 1995
Run ended on Fri Apr 21 13:35:20 1995
Elapsed time was:    00:00:04.56
CPU time was:        00:00:00.25
```

The header section of the log file contains the date of the run and the software version number. In Case 1, the date that SQL*Loader was executed was Friday, April 21, 1995. It loaded the data into the Oracle 7.1 database.

Following the header section of the log is the detailed information about the input and output files, table names, load conditions, and column information.

The final portion of the log file contains the table load and summary statistics. This lists the following:

- Number of rows loaded
- Number of rows that were not loaded and reasons why not
- Number of records skipped
- Number of records read
- Date and time of the load

Bad and Discard Files

The bad file contains records that are rejected, either by SQL*Loader or by the Oracle database. Records are rejected by SQL*Loader if the input format is invalid. Oracle rejects records if any item in the row is invalid—for example, if the key is not unique or a required field is null.

The bad file is written in the same format as the data file, so the rejected records can be reloaded with the same control file after the data is corrected.

The discard file is created only when specified or needed. This file contains records that were filtered out of the load because they did not match any of the record-selection criteria specified in the control file. These records do not necessarily have bad data—they just didn't satisfy the loading-data logic. Hence, any record that was inserted into a table does not appear in this file.

The discard file is written in the same format as the data file, so the discarded records can be reloaded with the same control file after the data is reviewed.

SQL*Loader Privileges

The following are the privileges required for conventional loading via the SQL*Loader utility:

- The insert system privilege is required on the table to be loaded.
- The delete system privilege is required on the table to be loaded when the replace option is used. This is necessary to empty out the existing table prior to the load.

Essential Summary

What   In this chapter you were introduced to SQL*Loader, an Oracle tool that enables you to load external data into Oracle tables quickly and accurately. SQL*Loader requires two inputs: input data and the control file.

Why   SQL*Loader gives you full control of your data-loading needs. It enables you to filter your input data so that you load only the data you require. Additionally, SQL*Loader performs error checking of the input data, formats your data as specified, and loads multiple tables simultaneously.

How   SQL*Loader is invoked at the command line with the input of a control file and input data. The control file gives SQL*Loader its flexibility and power when moving data from external data files to Oracle tables. Finally, the output files from SQL*Loader enable you to validate the results of your data-loading process.

SQL* DBA

What Is SQL*DBA?

What SQL*DBA is an Oracle utility that enables you to effectively and efficiently manage the operations of your Oracle database. SQL*DBA is operated in a command-line mode or in an interactive, menu-driven mode. This tool is primarily a tool for database administrators. Although developers and others may, on rare occasions, use this tool, usually you'll find that they do not have the necessary privileges to use SQL*DBA.

The menus provided in the interactive mode are all based on SQL commands. The SQL*DBA menu mode enables you to perform database operations without worrying about syntax because the menus take care of that. This chapter will focus on the command-line mode—which are the commands behind the menus.

Why Use SQL*DBA?

Why SQL*DBA makes managing your database easy by providing all the important commands at your fingertips. The following are some additional reasons as to why SQL*DBA should be used:

- To start and stop the database instance
- To create new users for the database
- To execute SQL and PL/SQL statements
- To monitor database performance statistics

How to Use SQL*DBA

How

The following sections review the various components of the SQL*DBA utility and how to use this tool. To enter SQL*DBA, issue the SQLDBA command at the host operating command line.

Interface

Oracle enables you to interact or interface with SQL*DBA using several different approaches. For example, you may request from Oracle that your session with SQL*DBA be in the menu-driven interactive mode (default mode). This default mode is defined as mode=screen in the SQL*DBA initialization parameter. With this interface, SQL*DBA functions can either be selected from menus or invoked by using commands in the command window.

You may also request an interactive line-mode session with SQL*DBA. With this interface, you type in all your commands and functions at a command line and the output is returned from SQL*DBA in text format. To enter this mode, enter the following command (You may also set the SQL*DBA initialization parameter equal to mode=line):

```
sqldba mode=line
```

SQL*DBA permits you to run a series of commands that have been previously stored in a file. This stored file of SQL commands is commonly known as a script file. To run a script file, issue the at (@) sign followed by the script filename at the command line. The following example illustrates:

- The use of the sqldba command being used at the operating-system command line
- Activation of the line-mode session
- Execution of the run_setup.sql script

```
> sqldba mode=line command="@run_setup.sql"
```

Line-Mode Interface

This section will discuss the SQL*DBA commands and how they are used in the line mode. Each of these commands may also be activated through the use of the menus.

You can enter any command from within SQL*DBA once you have connected to your database. You signal the end of a statement with either the slash (/) character or the semicolon (;) character. The following describes each of the individual SQL*DBA commands:

Archive Log

This command starts and stops archiving of online redo-log files, manually archives specified redo-log files, or displays information about redo-log files. The syntax for this command is:

```
archive log parameter
```

The valid parameters are:

- `list`—Displays the range of redo-log files to be archived, the current sequence number for the log-file group, and final destination for the archive
- `start`—Enables automatic archive
- `stop`—Disables the automatic archive
- `next`—Manually archives the next online redo-log file group that has been filled but not yet archived
- `all`—Manually archives all filled, but not yet archived, online log-file groups
- `to`—Specifies the destination filename

Connect

This command connects you to a database using the specified username. The syntax for this command is:

```
connect username/password instance/database
```

The username/password is any valid Oracle username and corresponding password. The instance/database is the current connect string for the desired database.

Describe

This command describes a table, stored procedure, or function. The syntax for this command is:

```
describe parameter
```

The parameters used with this command are:

- `table` tablename—Requests the specified table information be displayed
- `view` viewname—Requests the specified view information be displayed
- `procedure` procedurename—Requests the specified procedure information be displayed

Disconnect

This command disconnects the user from the database. The syntax for this command is:

```
disconnect
```

Execute

This command executes a one-line PL/SQL statement. The syntax for this command is:

```
execute PL/SQL statement
```

Exit

This command causes you to leave the current SQL*DBA session unconditionally. The command returns you to the host-operating-system prompt and commits the current transaction. The syntax for this command is:

```
exit
```

Host

This command executes an operating-system command without exiting SQL*DBA. The syntax for this command is:

```
host operating_system_command
```

You may alternatively just enter the command host. This will temporarily exit SQL*DBA so that you may enter your host commands directly to the host operating system.

Print

This command prints the value of a variable defined with the variable command. The syntax for this command is:

```
print variable_name
```

This command only displays variables defined in the current SQL*DBA session. Also, the set charwidth and the set numwidth commands may be used to alter the format of the output information.

Recover

The recover command performs media recovery on one or more tablespaces, database files, or the entire database. The syntax for this command is:

```
recover parameter
```

The parameters that may be used with the command are:

- database—Specifies that you want to recover the entire database. You may optionally include the until time clause to specify a time-based recovery.
- tablespace tablespace_name—Specifies the tablespace that is to be recovered.
- datafile filename—Specifies the name of the datafile to be recovered.

Remark

This command is used to create a comment in a script file. This comment is ignored by SQL*DBA and by Oracle. The syntax for this command is:

```
remark text
```

Set

The set command is used to establish or change characteristics of the current SQL*DBA session. The syntax for this command is:

```
set parameter
```

The parameters that may be included with this command are:

- arraysize integer—Sets the number of rows fetched at a time from the database.
- autorecovery on/off—Enables or disables the automatic recovery processes.
- charwidth integer—Sets the column display width for character data.
- compatibility v6/v7—Sets the compatibility mode to either V6 or V7.
- datewidth integer—Sets the column display width for date data.
- echo on/off—Enables or disables the echoing of commands entered from the command line.
- fetchrows integer—Limits the number of rows returned by a query.
- history integer—Determines the size of SQL*DBA's command-history buffer. This directly determines the number of commands that can be recalled, altered, and reissued.
- instance – Changes the default instance for your SQL*DBA session.
- lines integer—Specifies the number of lines of output that can be stored in SQL*DBA's output window.
- logsource pathname—Specifies the location from which archive logs are retrieved during recovery.
- longwidth integer—Sets the column display width for long data.
- maxdata integer—Sets the maximum data size.
- numwidth integer—Sets the column display width for number data.
- retries integer—Sets the number of tries that will be attempted with the startup command.
- spool filename/off—Defines the name of the file that will be used to capture all future SQL*DBA output data.
- stoponerror on/off—If enabled with the on statement, then processing is stopped if an error is detected during processing. This is disabled when the off statement is used.

- term page/nopage—page causes one page of output to be displayed at a time in the SQL*DBA output window. The nopage clause causes all output to be displayed.
- termout on/off—Enables or disables terminal output for SQL commands.
- timing on/off—Enables or disables the display of parse, execute, and fetch times.

Show

This command displays the current settings of any of the parameters established by the SQL*DBA set command. The syntax for this command is:

```
show parameter
```

Shutdown

This command shuts down a running Oracle instance. The syntax for this command is:

```
shutdown parameter
```

The following are the parameters that are permitted with this command:

- abort—Proceeds with the shutdown in the fastest way possible. This will shut down the instance but will not wait for transactions to complete. This command will close or dismount the database.
- immediate—Does not wait for current call to complete and will close and dismount the database.
- normal—This will wait for all calls to complete, and will shut down the instance in the normal way.

Spool

This command causes all output to be echoed to a specified file. The command syntax is:

```
spool filename/off
```

The filename may be any valid filename. The off clause disables the spool process.

Startup

This command will start up an Oracle instance. The syntax for this command is:

```
startup parameter
```

The following are the valid parameters allowed with this command:

- exclusive—Signifies that the database can only be mounted and opened by the current instance.
- force—Will start the instance. If there is an instance currently running, this will shut down the current instance with the abort option prior to restarting the instance.
- mount—Mounts the database but does not open it.

Variable

This command declares a bind variable for use in the current session. A bind variable is a variable that must be replaced with a valid value in order for the SQL statement to execute successfully. The syntax for this command is:

```
variable name type
```

The name parameter is the name of the bind variable that is to be declared. The type is the datatype for the declared bind variable.

Reserved Words

Appendix D, "SQL*DBA Reserved Words," contains a complete list of the SQL*DBA reserved words.

Menu Mode Interface

In addition to the line mode, SQL*DBA offers a menu-based interface. This mode is the default mode. Because this mode is very intuitive in the way it works, I will only briefly discuss the main points of this mode.

Figure 29.1 displays the SQL*DBA interface screen. The screen is broken into three components:

- The menu bar is across the top of the screen. This bar provides quick access to the underlying menus.
- The middle portion of the window is the output display area. This is where SQL*DBA displays the results of your command.
- The bottom portion of the window is where you can manually type in your SQL or PL/SQL commands.

Figure 29.1.
*The SQL*DBA
interface window.*

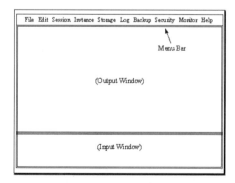

SQL*DBA has a series of pull-down menus that you access from the menu bar. Each menu pulls down to display a list of operations that are named after the SQL command or operation that they execute. For example, the Session menu has an option named "Connect." This option is equivalent to the SQL connect command.

Part VII

The following is a brief overview of each of the SQL*DBA pull-down menus.

The *file* menu contains the following items:

- ■ SQL Script—Lets you enter a filename for the script you want to run
- ■ Spool On—Enables spooling
- ■ Spool Off—Disables spooling
- ■ Quit—Exits SQL*DBA utility

The *edit* menu contains the following items:

- ■ Cut—Removes selected text from the screen and places it in the clipboard
- ■ Copy—Copies selected text to the clipboard
- ■ Paste—Pastes from the clipboard to the current cursor location
- ■ Clear—Erases the selected text
- ■ Previous Command—Copies the previous command from the command-history buffer to the input window
- ■ Next Command—Copies the next command from the command-history buffer to the input window

The *session* menu contains the following items:

- ■ Connect—Connects to a database
- ■ Disconnect—Disconnects from a database
- ■ Enter System Command—Runs a single system command from within SQL*DBA
- ■ Go to System—Causes you to temporarily leave SQL*DBA in order to execute a series of operating-system commands
- ■ Set Serverout On—Enables output to the SQL*DBA screen from stored procedures and functions
- ■ Set Serverout Off—Disables output to the SQL*DBA screen from stored procedures and functions

The database *instance* menu contains the following items:

- ■ Start Up—Starts up a database
- ■ Shut Down—Shuts down a database
- ■ Mount Database—Mounts a database
- ■ Open Database—Opens a mounted database
- ■ Force Checkpoint—Checkpoints all instances
- ■ Force Log Switch—Forces a log switch from the current active redo log to the next group
- ■ Configure Dispatcher—Specifies the number of dispatcher processes

- `Configure Shared Server`—Specifies the number of shared-server processes
- `Prevent Connection`—Denies a connection from happening
- `Allow Connection`—Permits a connection to the database
- `Kill Session`—Kills a user session
- `Recover In-Doubt Transactions`—Recovers any in-doubt transaction (reserved for distributed databases only)

The *storage* menu contains the following items:

- `Tablespace`—Allows for the creation of a tablespace and specifying its intial storage parameters, data files, and online/offline status.
- `Rollback Segment`—Allows for the creation and dropping of rollback segments. This menu also allows the setting of the online/offline parameters.

The *log* menu contains the following items:

- `Add Group`—Adds a new online redo-log group
- `Drop Group`—Drops an online redo-log group
- `Add Member`—Adds a new redo file to a redo-log group
- `Rename Member`—Renames a redo-log file in a redo-log group
- `Drop Member`—Drops a redo-log file from a redo-log group
- `Enable Thread`—Enables a specified thread of redo-log files
- `Disable Thread`—Disables a specified thread of redo-log files
- `Start Archiving`—Starts automatic archiving of redo logs
- `Stop Archiving`—Stops automatic archiving of redo logs
- `Begin Manual Archive`—Performs a manual archive of one or more redo logs
- `List Archive Status`—Displays redo-log information

The *backup* menu contains the following items:

- `Begin Online Tablespace Backup`—Marks a tablespace for backup purposes
- `End Online Tablespace Backup`—Informs the server that the backup of the tablespace has been completed
- `Recover Database`—Performs media recovery on the entire database
- `Recover Tablespace`—Performs media recovery on tablespace
- `Recover Data File`—Performs media recovery on data files

The *security* menu contains the following items:

- `Create User`—Creates a user definition
- `Alter User`—Alters a user definition
- `Drop User`—Drops a user definition

- Create Role—Defines an abstract group of users so that you can grant and revoke privileges on this group
- Alter Role—Changes the authentication method for the rule
- Drop Role—Drops a role
- Create Profile—Creates a profile
- Alter Profile—Modifies a profile
- Drop Profile—Drops a resource-limited profile
- Alter Resource Cost—Specifies a formula for calculating the total cost of resources used in a session
- Grant—Grants system privileges and roles to a user or role
- Revoke—Revokes system privileges from a user or a role

The *monitor* menu enables you to dynamically monitor and manage the resources of the Oracle server.

Essential Summary

What SQL*DBA is an Oracle utility that enables you to easily manage all aspects of your database. SQL*DBA uses a menu-driven interface to make this database process easier to accomplish.

Why SQL*DBA enables you to quickly monitor all aspects of your database. Included, you can execute an of the required database commands through SQL*DBA.

How In this chapter, you learned about the menus and submenus that drive SQL*DBA. Also, in the Input window, you may directly enter SQL and PL/SQL commands to meet your needs.

PART VIII

Database Security

Managing Database Users

What Does Managing Database Users Mean?

What The primary purpose of database security is to establish the correct level of security for the different types of database users. This security defines the level of database access for each user. Generally speaking, you have three types of users who require three different levels of access to the database. These users are database administrators, application developers, and end users.

Each Oracle database has a list of valid users. These are users who can connect to the database. All users have a set of privileges created for them defining the type of user they are. A privilege is the authority to access a database object in some prescribed manner. For example, an end user could have the privileges to select data from some of the database tables but be unable to create or drop any of the database objects.

For most institutions, database security is based on the sensitivity of the data. If the data is not sensitive, the various types of users can have a more relaxed level of access. Conversely, if the data is highly sensitive, such as that in many military computers, a tight control of users and user access should be established.

Why Manage Database Users?

Why

An organization must establish a database security policy that defines, among other things, the appropriate levels of database access for the different types of users. Once this policy is defined, you can then manage database users appropriately. For example, it might be perfectly acceptable to have very little user security in a training computer that has students learning about computer programming. In this case you want to encourage the students to try various commands. Alternately, you would want very tight security around a bank's computers.

Another area that falls into the realm of managing database users is licensing. For your Oracle server, you have a license that states how many concurrent users are allowed to connect to the database. Through the management of users and their access, you can make sure that your facility complies with the license agreement.

How to Manage Database Users

How

Oracle provides many tools to help manage database users. Included in the process of database management are the authentication of users, creating and managing users, monitoring users, and managing resource limits. This chapter discusses these topics in detail.

Authentication of Users

Oracle enables validation of users through two different methods. The first method is authentication by the Oracle database. Oracle requires each user to supply a username and password when attempting to connect to the database. Oracle authenticates the user using its own internal data files. Be sure that when creating users, you specify the identified by clause.

The second method of authentication is by the operating system. With this method, Oracle uses information about the user that is maintained by the operating system to authenticate users. This provides the user the following benefits:

■ The user can connect to the database easily without having to provide a username and password. For example, a user can connect directly to the database by using the SQL*Plus command.

■ Control of user authorization lies with the operating system rather than with Oracle.

■ Audit trails are established in both the operating system and Oracle.

If you are running a multithreaded server, you cannot have the operating system authenticate users as they attempt to connect. This restriction is the default due to the risk of a remote user impersonating another operating system user over a network connection. To change the default to enable remote access on a multithreaded server, change the initialization parameter to True.

Creating Users

You can create a new database user by using the Create User dialog box in SQL*DBA or the SQL command `create user`.

When you create a new user, you also have to specify the following information:

- Username—An identifier that is unique with respect to all other usernames and roles.
- Default segment tablespace—Identifies the tablespace for objects that the user creates. By default it is the system tablespace.
- Temporary segment tablespaces—Identifies the tablespace for the user's temporary segments. By default it is the system tablespace.
- Tablespace quotas—Enables the user to allocate space in the tablespace, and optionally establishes a quota in integer bytes.
- Profile—Assigns a named profile to the user. The profile limits the amount of database resources the user can access. By default, the profile is set to the default profile. A user automatically assumes the default profile if he or she is not explicitly assigned a profile. This default profile is established by the database administrator and contains the parameters that define default limits on all database resources.

The following example creates the new database user user_01:

```
create user user_01
identified by D82KLW9
default tablespace ts_101
temporary tablespace ts_temp
quota 5m on ts_101
quota 5m on ts_temp
quota 3m on system
profile clerk;
```

The `identified by` clause establishes the user's password. The `identified externally` clause can replace the `identified by` clause if you want the operating system to perform the user authentication. A newly created user cannot connect to the database until he or she is granted the `connect` system privilege.

To change a user's password, issue the `alter user` command as shown in the following example. This example establishes the new password as 2JAW3HZ for the user tom_01's account:

```
alter user tom_01
identified by 2JAW3HZ;
```

Managing Users and Resources

Each database user has a security domain established that contains defined limits on the amount of various system resources available to that user. Resource limits are a vital part of managing users and the database. Without such controls, there could be unchecked consumption of system resources, which would adversely affect all users of the database.

System resource limits are managed with user profiles. A profile is a named set of resource limits that can be assigned to a user. These resources can generally be established at the session and call levels.

A session is created every time a database user connects to the database. This session requires a certain amount of CPU time and memory on the host computer. If a session-level resource limit is exceeded, the current statement is rolled back and an error message is returned to the user. Once this occurs, all previous statements in the current transaction are intact, and the user is limited to the commit and rollback commands. The user can also simply disconnect from the session at this point. If the user attempts any other operation, Oracle generates an error.

During the processing of SQL commands, several calls are made as part of the statement's execution. If a call-level resource limit is exceeded, the processing of the current statement is halted and rolled back. Oracle also returns an error message to the user. All previous statements of the current transaction remain intact, and the user's session remains connected.

The database administrator has the option to globally enable or disable profiles. That is, the DBA has the capability to make specific resource limits apply to all users.

To create a profile, issue the create profile SQL command or use the Create Profile dialog box in SQL*DBA. Oracle requires you to possess the create profile system privilege to create profiles. In the profile creation, you explicitly set the following resource limits:

sessions_per_user	Limits the number of concurrent sessions for the user.
cpu_per_session	Limits the CPU time for a session. This value is expressed in hundredths of seconds.
cpu_per_call	Limits the CPU time for a call. This is expressed in hundredths of seconds.
connect_time	Limits the total elapsed connect time of a session.
idle_time	Defines the maximum amount of continuous inactive time span.
logical_read_per_session	Limits the number of data blocks read in a session.
logical_reads_per_call	Limits the number of data blocks read for a call to process a SQL statement.
private_sga	Limits the amount of private space a session can reserve in the system global area. This limit applies only if you are using a multithreaded server.

composite_limit   Limits the total resource cost per session. This is a composite of the following resources: `cpu_per_session`, `connect_time`, `logical_reads_per_session`, and `private_sga`. Use the SQL `alter resource cost` command to define the costs associated with these resources.

For each resource defined in the `create profile` command, you can include the `unlimited` and the `default` keywords. The `unlimited` keyword indicates that a user assigned this profile can use an unlimited amount of this resource. The `default` keyword indicates that the user of this specific resource is subject to the limit of the resource specified in the default profile.

Oracle automatically creates the default profile. By default, this profile initially defines unlimited resources. The DBA can alter the limits of the default profile with the `alter profile` command. Any user who is not explicitly assigned a profile is subject to the resource limit defined in the default profile.

The following statement creates the profile named "clerk." This statement explicitly defines only four resources. All others assume their resource limits as defined by the default profile.

```
create profile clerk limit
sessions_per_user 1
connect_time 560
cpu_per_call unlimited
idle_time 15;
```

The `alter profile` statement redefines the specified resource to the supplied value. For example, the following statement alters the profile clerk, reestablishes the `sessions_per_user` to three, and establishes an explicit resource limit on the `logical_reads_per_call`. All other resource limits remain unchanged.

```
alter profile clerk limit
sessions_per_user 3
logical_reads_per_call 100;
```

Once a profile has been created, assign it to a user with the SQL `create user` or `alter user` commands. You can also use the SQL*DBA Create User or Alter User dialog boxes. You cannot assign profiles to roles or other profiles. Also, only one profile can be assigned to a user at a time.

The following example assigns the profile clerk to the user tom_01. This new profile takes effect in the next session.

```
alter user tom_01
profile clerk;
```

To drop a profile, issue the `drop profile` command with the `cascade` clause.

Dropping Users

Dropping a user removes that user and associated schema from the data dictionary and all schema objects contained in the user's schema. To drop all the user's objects, specify the cascade clause in the drop user command. If you specify the cascade option, Oracle automatically drops any referential integrity constraints on the tables in other schemas that refer to primary and unique keys on the dropped tables.

You might occasionally need the dropped user's schema to remain intact to support others' operations. In this case, simply revoke the user's access to the database by removing the create session system privilege. The SQL*DBA screen shown in Figure 30.1 drops the user tom_01 and all his schema objects from the database. You can also use the drop user SQL command.

Figure 30.1.
*SQL*DBA Drop User
screen.*

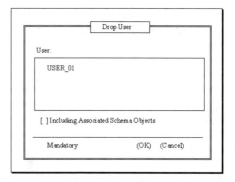

For a user to be dropped, the user cannot have any active processes or be connected to the database. The person performing the dropping activity must have the drop user system privilege.

Data Dictionary Views for Managing Users

The following information is stored in the data dictionary for every user and profile:

- List of users in the database
- Each user's default tablespace for tables, clusters, and indexes
- Memory usage for each current session
- Each user's tablespace for temporary segments
- Space quotas for each user
- Each user's assigned profile and resource limits
- The cost assigned to each applicable system resource

The following data dictionary views are available for obtaining information about users and profiles:

all_users	Information about all users of the database. Information includes the name of the user, user_id, and the date the user_id was created.
user_users	Information about the current users of the database. Information includes the name of the user, user_id, and tablespaces used by the user.
dba_users	Information about all the users of the database. Information includes the name of the user, user_id, and tablespaces used by the user.
user_ts_quotas	Information about the user's tablespace quotas.
dba_ts_quotas	Information about tablespace quotas for all users.
user_resource_limits	Displays the resource limits for the current user.
dba_profiles	Information about the resource limits assigned to each profile.
resource_cost	Displays the cost for each resource.

The following example selects information from the dba_users view to obtain the profile of a specific user:

```
select username, profile from dba_users
where user_name like 'OPS$TOM%';
```

Sample output:

```
USERNAME PROFILE
-------- -------
OPS$TOM_01 CLERK
```

Licensing

Oracle helps you comply with your site-licensing agreement with Oracle. You have a license that defines the number of concurrent connects that are enabled. You might also have a license by named users. In either case, you need to know what your concurrent limits are.

Once the database limit is reached, only those users with the restricted_session system privilege can connect to the database. When this user connects, a message is sent to the alert file and to the screen stating that the maximum number of concurrent users has been reached.

Three initialization parameters are defined to help keep you honest. They are as follows:

license_max_sessions	Defines the maximum number of concurrent sessions.
license_sessions_warning	Set this value to some number less than the license_max_sessions parameter. This is used to give you advanced warning that you are approaching your maximum limit of concurrent sessions.
license_max_users	Defines the maximum permitted number of users concurrently connected.

Oracle provides the v$license data dictionary view. The following display information is contained in this view:

```
select sessions_max s_max,
sessions_warning s_warn,
sessions_current s_curr,
sessions_highwater s_high,
users_max u_max
from v$license;
```

Sample output:

```
S_MAX  S_WARN  S_CURR  S_HIGH  U_MAX
-----  ------  ------  ------  -----
200    180     78      113     300
```

Essential Summary

What In this chapter, you learned what is meant by managing users as well as how to accomplish this task. Included in the management of database users is the authentication of users and the creation and assignment of a user to a database profile.

Why Managing database users and resources is critical to prevent unwanted consumption of too many system resources. This consumption can cause disruption of database services for all users of the database.

How DBAs use profiles and authentication techniques to manage users' access to the database and the consumption of resources of the system once they are connected to the database.

Roles

What Are Roles?

What Roles are named groups of related privileges that are granted to individual users and other roles. Roles are created to manage the privileges for a database application or to manage the privileges for a user group.

An application role is granted all the necessary privileges to run an application. This role is typically granted to specific application users and to other roles. An application can have multiple roles. You will have a role established for each type of user of the application. For example, in a grocery store you might have one role for the cashier and a different role for the store manager.

User roles are created for a group of users with the same privilege requirements. Individual privilege administration is simplified and better managed when privileges are granted to user roles, which are then granted to individual users.

Figure 31.1 illustrates a simplistic use of a role. The system privileges select and insert on any table are granted to the role clerk. The security administrator has in turn granted this role to three different users so that they can run different applications.

Figure 31.1.
Common use of a role.

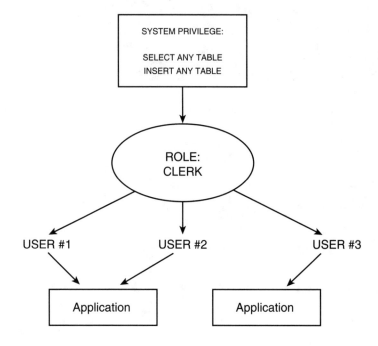

Why Use Roles?

Roles have a certain set of properties that promote an easier management of database privileges. These properties are as follows:

- Simplistic privilege management. This is obtained because privileges are granted to roles and the role in turn is granted to users. You do not have to grant all the privileges to all users—just grant the role.

- Individual dynamic privilege management. When the privileges of a role are modified, these changes are automatically granted to the users that have been granted this role.

- Application-specific security. Applications can query the data dictionary to enable or disable a role automatically when the user attempts to execute the application via a given username. This allows applications to enable roles with the correct password.

How to Use Roles

Roles are a named group of privileges that one Oracle user can grant to another Oracle user or role. This chapter reviews the steps to create, alter, enable, disable, and drop roles.

Creating Roles

Roles are created with the SQL create role command or with the Create Role dialog box in SQL*DBA. The following SQL statement creates the role named clerk:

```
create role clerk
identified by Y8DS20J;
```

Figure 31.2 shows the Create Role dialog box from SQL*DBA. This dialog box performs the same actions as the preceding SQL statement.

Figure 31.2.
*The SQL*DBA Create Role dialog box.*

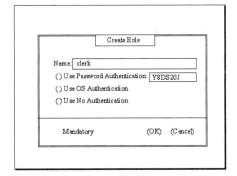

The identified by clause establishes a password that is used when enabling the role. Alternately, you can use the identified externally clause to have the host operating system verify the user and enable the role. The not identified clause can be used to indicate that the role does not need to be verified when it is enabled.

At times you might want the host operating system to authenticate roles. This is useful only when the operating system can dynamically link operating system privileges with applications. For example, when a user starts up an application, the operating-system grants an operating-system privilege to the user. The granted operating-system privilege corresponds to the role associated with the application. At this point the application can enable the Oracle role. This enabled role is revoked when the application terminates.

If you are running a multithreaded server, you cannot have the operating system authenticate users as they attempt to connect. This restriction is the default because of the risk of a remote user impersonating another operating-system user over a network connection. To change the default to enable remote access on a multithreaded server, change the initialization parameter to True.

The name you provide for the role must be unique among other usernames and roles in the database. Roles are not contained in the schema of any user.

When a role is created, it has no privileges associated with it. At this point, it is a meaningless role. You must grant privileges or other roles to the new role. The SQL `grant` command is used to assign privileges and roles to the new role. Granting privileges is covered in more detail later in this chapter.

To create a role, you must have the `create role` system privilege. Also, when you create a role, you are granted the role `with admin option`. The admin option enables you to perform these operations:

- Grant this new role to another user or role
- Revoke the role from another user or role
- Alter the role to change the authorization needed to access it
- Drop the role

System-Defined Roles

Oracle provides five predefined roles with the Oracle server. You can grant and revoke privileges and roles to these predefined roles just as you can to any role you define.

The following is a list of the Oracle predefined roles and their granted privileges:

- Connect—`alter session`, `create cluster`, `create database link`, `create sequence`, `create session`, `create synonym`, `create table`, and `create view`
- Resource—`create cluster`, `create procedure`, `create sequence`, `create table`, and `create trigger`
- DBA—All system privileges with the admin option
- Exp_full_database—`select any table`, `back up_any_table`, `insert`, `delete`, and `update` on the tables SYS.INCVID, SYS.INCFIL, and SYS.INCEXP
- Imp_full_database—`become user`, `writedown` (only with Trusted Oracle server)

Altering Roles

You can change the authorization method for a role by using the SQL `alter role` command or the SQL*DBA Alter Role dialog box. You can specifically alter the following items:

- The password required to enable the role.
- Whether you want the role to be verified when it is enabled. If so, define whether you want Oracle or the operating system to perform the role verification.

The following role establishes a new password and defines that the operating system is to perform the role verification:

```
alter role clerk identified by JL10C3Q
```

To alter a role, you must have the `alter any role` system privilege or have been granted the role with admin option.

Changing a User's Role

A database user can have multiple default roles granted to him. For example, an application developer can be granted the role of a developer and also the role for the application he is developing.

To set or alter the user's default roles, use the SQL `alter user` command or the SQL*DBA Alter User dialog box. The following is the SQL command to grant by default all the roles granted to the user except for the DBA role:

```
alter user tom_01
default role all except dba;
```

Any changes to the user's default role take effect the next time the user connects to the database.

Dropping Roles

To drop a role from the database, use the Drop Role dialog box in SQL*DBA or issue the `drop role` SQL command. The security domains of all users and roles granted a dropped role are immediately updated to reflect the absence of the dropped role's privileges. Dropping a role removes the role from the user's default role list. The following statement drops the role clerk from the database:

```
drop role clerk;
```

Granting Roles

Roles can be granted to users, to other roles, and to Public. Public represents all users of the system. Use the SQL `grant` command or the Grant System Privilege/Role dialog box in SQL*DBA.

The next statement grants the role manager to the user NT9K3BH with the admin option:

```
grant manager to NT9K3BH with admin option;
```

A system role can be granted with the admin option. This option enables users to do the following:

- Grant or revoke the role to or from any user or role in the database
- Grant the role with admin option to other users and roles
- Alter or drop the role

The creator of a role is automatically granted the role with admin option. Implicit in this command is the ability for the user to grant the role to other users. Any user with the `grant any role` system privilege can grant any role in a database.

All grants of roles to users, other roles, and Public are observed only when a current user session issues a `set role` statement to reenable the role after the grant. Also the revoke takes effect when a new user session is created after the grant is executed.

Revoking Roles

Roles can be revoked using either the Revoke System Privilege/Role dialog box in SQL*DBA or the SQL command revoke. The following example revokes the role clerk from the user tom_01:

```
revoke clerk from tom_01;
```

You cannot selectively revoke the admin option of a role. To remove the admin option, you must revoke the role and then regrant the role without the admin option.

Any user with the admin option can revoke the role from any other user or role. A user cannot revoke a role from himself. Also, any user with the grant any role can revoke any and all roles.

All revokes of roles from users, other roles, and Public are observed only when a current user session issues a set role statement to reenable the role after the revoke. The revoke also takes effect when a new user session is created after the revoke is executed.

The Public User Group

Every Oracle database has a user group known as Public. Public represents all database users and is accessible to all of them. Therefore, any role granted to the user group Public is accessible to every database user. Roles should be granted to the user Public only if everyone in the database requires the role.

Operating System Grants and Revokes

You can have the operating system administer roles instead of the security administrator explicitly handling the roles. The operating system can grant roles to users at connect time. These roles are then administered by the operating system and passed to Oracle when the user establishes a session.

Security administration is centralized with this approach to role management. This is because you have both the operating system and the database security functions pulled together in one place.

To operate a database so that it uses the operating system to manage each user's roles when a session is created, set the os_roles initialization parameter to True and restart the instance. Now when a user initiates a new session with the database, Oracle initializes the user's security domain using the database roles identified by the operating system.

The user's operating system account has operating system identifiers that indicate which database roles are available for the user. Also, the identifiers indicate the user's default roles and which roles have the admin option. Whether you are using UNIX, VMS, or another operating system, the role specification at the operating system level follows the following format:

```
ora_<id>_<role>[_[d][a]]
```

The identifiers have the following meanings:

id   Can mean different things to different operating systems. For example, the id is the instance identifier on a VMS machine but represents the machine type on a MVS machine.

role   The name of the role being granted.

d   An optional character indicating that this role is to be a default role of the user.

a   An optional character indicating that the role is to be granted with the admin option.

Following are some examples of operating-system identifiers:

```
ora_accounting_clerk
ora_systems_developer a;
```

If the operating system is managing roles, any previous grants of roles to users issued with the SQL grant command do not apply. These roles still appear in the data dictionary but are not active. Only those roles granted by the operating system apply to the user. For all this to occur, the os_roles initialization parameter must be set to True.

Listing Role Information

The Oracle server comes with some predefined views. The following data dictionary views provide information about roles and the users they are granted to:

DBA_roles   A list of all roles that exist in the database

user_role_privs   A list of roles granted to the user

DBA_role_privs   Descriptions of roles granted to users and to roles

role_role_privs   Information about roles granted to other roles

role_sys_privs   Information about system privileges granted to roles

role_tab_privs   Information about table privileges granted to roles

session_roles   A list of roles that the user currently has enabled

The following examples query these dictionary views to obtain view information. The first example gives information about each user and his or her granted roles:

```
select * from dba_role_privs;
```

Sample output:

```
GRANTEE    GRANTED ROLE    ADMIN_OPTION    DEFAULT_ROLE
- - - - - - - - - - - - - - - - - - - - - - - - -    - - - - - - - - - -
Jackie     Pharmacist      Y               Y
Loretta    Administration  Y               N
William    Engineer        N               N
```

This next example uses the DBA_ROLES table to display whether certain roles are password-protected:

```
select * from dba_roles;
```

Sample output:

```
ROLE            PASSWORD
------------------------------
CLERK           NO
ADMINISTRATION  YES
DBA             NO
```

Essential Summary

What In this chapter, you learned that roles are collections of privileges that can be granted to specific users or to other roles.

Why Roles provide an easy and manageable means of administering system privileges. Grouping privileges together in a role and then granting that role to users and other roles promotes a flexible and simplistic privilege management system.

How Roles are designed to meet the needs of groups of users. Once designed, roles are created and granted to users and other roles.

Privileges

What Is a Privilege?

What A privilege is a permission to execute an action or to access another user's object. In Oracle, you cannot perform any action without having the privilege to do so. The following are a few examples of privileges:

- The right to access the database
- The right to select data from another user's tables
- The right to execute another user's stored procedures
- The right to create new users

Privileges are granted to users so that these users can perform the actions necessary to accomplish a task. Privileges can be granted to a user explicitly or granted to a role. Care should be exercised to grant only those privileges needed.

There are two categories of privileges: system and object privileges. System privileges enable the user to perform an action on a type of object, whereas object privileges give the user permission to perform the action on a specific object.

Why Use Privileges?

Why

Privileges are one of the most fundamental controls of database security. You cannot perform any action in the database unless you have the privilege or permission to accomplish the action.

Privileges enable the database administrator to assign the appropriate levels of security to the database objects and to the users.

How to Use Privileges

How

Privileges are provided by the Oracle server as part of its internal security schema. Users are granted privileges to perform a task. Likewise, privileges can be revoked from a user. This chapter discusses the various system and object privileges and how to administer them to users.

System Privileges

A system privilege is the right or permission to execute a particular database action on a particular type of object. For example, the right to create tablespace is a system privilege. There are over 80 distinct system privileges.

Because system privileges are very powerful, they should be granted to trusted users with discretion.

The following are the Oracle system privileges. Oracle has named these privileges after the actions they permit.

Analyze (any table, index, or cluster):

- `analyze any`

Audit (any schema object in the database):

- `audit any`
- `audit system`

Cluster:

- `create cluster`
- `create any cluster`
- `alter any cluster`
- `drop any cluster`

Database:

- `alter database`

Database Link:

- ■ create database link

Index:

- ■ create any index
- ■ alter any index
- ■ drop any index

Privilege:

- ■ grant any privilege

Procedure:

- ■ create procedure
- ■ create any procedure
- ■ alter any procedure
- ■ drop any procedure
- ■ execute any procedure

Profile:

- ■ create profile
- ■ alter profile
- ■ drop profile
- ■ alter resource cost

Public Database Link:

- ■ create public database link
- ■ drop public database link

Public Synonym:

- ■ create public synonym
- ■ drop public synonym

Role:

- ■ create role
- ■ alter any role
- ■ drop any role
- ■ grant any role

Rollback Segment:

- create rollback segment
- alter rollback segment
- drop rollback segment

Sequence:

- create sequence
- create any sequence
- alter any sequence
- drop any sequence
- select any sequence

Session:

- create session
- alter session
- restrict session

Snapshot:

- create snapshot
- create any snapshot
- alter any snapshot
- drop any snapshot

Synonym:

- create synonym
- create any synonym
- drop any synonym

System:

- alter system

Table:

- create table
- create any table
- alter any table
- back up any table
- drop any table
- lock any table
- comment any table

- select any table
- insert any table
- update any table
- delete any table

Tablespace:

- create tablespace
- alter tablespace
- manage tablespace
- drop tablespace
- unlimited tablespace

Transaction:

- force transaction
- force any transaction

Trigger:

- create trigger
- create any trigger
- alter any trigger
- drop any trigger

User:

- create user
- become user
- alter user
- drop user

View:

- create view
- create any view
- drop any view

Granting System Privileges

System privileges can be granted to users and roles using either the grant SQL command or the SQL*DBA Grant System Privilege/Role dialog box. The following statement grants system privileges to the user J9SK72D and to the role finance:

```
grant create session to J9SK72D, finance;
```

System privileges cannot be granted along with object privileges and roles in the same grant command.

To grant system privileges, you must have the admin option for the system privilege being granted or possess the grant any privilege system privilege.

Revoking System Privileges

System privileges can be revoked using either the revoke SQL command or the SQL*DBA Revoke System Privilege/Role dialog box. Figure 32.1 shows system privileges being revoked from the user ROBERT_C using SQL*DBA.

```
revoke all from robert_c
```

To revoke a system privilege, the user must have the admin option for the system privilege being revoked.

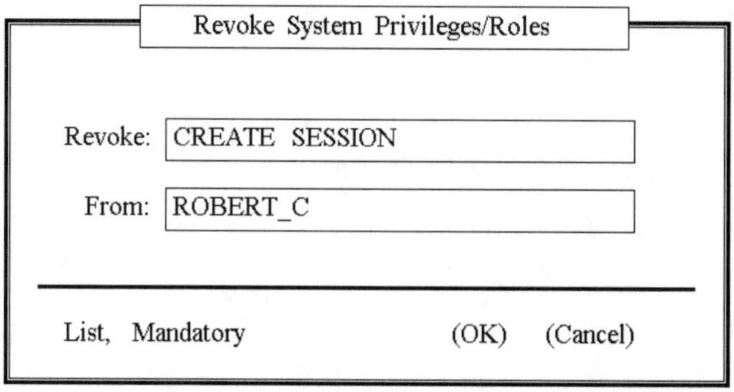

Figure 32.1.
Revoking a system
privilege through
*SQL*DBA.*

Sometimes a revoke causes a cascading effect. For example, cascading effects can be seen when privileges relating to data manipulation commands are revoked. If a user has the select any table system privilege revoked, and that user has created any functions, all functions contained in that user's schema must be reauthorized before they can be executed again. There are no cascading effects from a revoke on any data definition language commands.

All revokes of roles to users, other roles, and Public are observed only when a current user session issues a set role statement to reenable the role after the revoke. The revoke also takes effect when a new user session is created after the revoke is executed.

Object Privileges

An object privilege is permission to perform an action on a specific object, such as a table, package, or view. Some database objects don't have an associated object privilege. For example, the following objects don't have object privileges: triggers, clusters, indexes, and database links. Different objects have different object privileges.

Following are the available object privileges and their associated objects:

Alter:

- Tables
- Sequences

Delete:

- Tables
- Views

Execute:

- Procedures (stand-alone and subprograms)

Index:

- Tables

Insert:

- Tables
- Views

Reference:

- Tables

Select:

- Tables
- Views
- Sequences

Update:

- Tables
- Views

Granting Object Privileges

Object privileges can be granted to users and roles using the grant SQL command. The following statement grants object privileges to the user J9SK72D and to the role finance:

```
grant select,alter table to J9SK72D, finance;
```

To grant object privileges, you must own the object specified or have been granted the object privileges with the grant option. System privileges cannot be granted along with object privileges and roles in the same grant command.

Revoking Object Privileges

Object privileges can be revoked using the `revoke` SQL command. The following statement illustrates object privileges being revoked:

```
revoke update on mst_parts
from tom_01;
```

You cannot explicitly revoke column-specific privileges. Instead, the grantor must first revoke the object privileges for all columns of a table or view, and then selectively regrant the column-specific privileges that should remain.

Revoking object privileges usually causes a cascading effect. For example, a procedure or function becomes invalid if in that procedure or function a DML statement is used on an object where the privileges were revoked.

Public User Group

Every Oracle database has a user group known as Public. Public represents all database users and is accessible to all of them. Therefore, any privilege granted to the user group Public is accessible to every database user. Privileges should be granted to the user Public only if everyone in the database requires the privilege.

Listing Privilege Information

The Oracle server comes with some predefined views. The following data dictionary views provide information about privileges and the user they are granted to:

- `all_col_privs`—Displays grants on columns for which the user Public is the grantee
- `user_col_privs`—Displays grants on columns for which the user is the owner, grantor, or grantee
- `dba_col_privs`—Displays all grants on columns in the database
- `dba_sys_privs`—Description of system privileges granted to users and roles
- `all_col_privs_made`—Displays grants on columns for which the user is owner or grantor
- `all_col_privs_recd`—Displays grants on columns for which the user or Public is the grantee
- `all_tab_privs`—Displays grants on objects for which the user or Public is the grantee
- `all_tab_privs_made`—Displays user grants and grants on user's objects
- `all_tab_privs_recd`—Displays grants on objects for which the user or Public is the grantee
- `user_role_privs`—Displays roles granted to the user
- `user_sys_privs`—Displays system privileges granted to the user
- `column_privileges`—Displays grants on columns for which the user is the grantor, grantee, or owner, or Public is the grantee

- session_privs—Displays privileges that are currently available to the user

The following examples query these dictionary views to obtain privilege information. The first example provides information about each privilege grantee:

```
select * from dba_sys_privs;
```

Sample output:

```
GRANTEE PRIVILEGE ADM
-----------------------------------------
SYS_ADMIN ALTER PROFILE YES
SYS_ADMIN ALTER USER YES
SYS_ADMIN CREATE USER YES
SYS_ADMIN CREATE SESSION YES
CLERK CREATE SESSION NO
CATHERINE CREATE SESSION NO
```

This next example uses the SESSION_PRIVS table to display system privileges currently granted to the user:

```
select * from sys_privs;
```

Sample output:

```
PRIVILEGE
-------------------
CREATE SESSION
AUDIT ANY
```

Essential Summary

A privilege is the permission or right to execute a particular type of SQL statement or to access another user's objects. There are two types of privileges: system and object.

What

In this chapter, you learned that privileges are one of the most fundamental security controls in Oracle. Through privileges, you control the user's access to the database objects and the data within.

Why

Privileges are explicitly granted to users and to roles. Once granted, the user can perform the action the privilege has the right to perform.

How

Auditing the Database

What Does Auditing the Database Mean?

What Auditing is the process of monitoring the actions of a selected database user. Auditing is generally performed on three types of database activities:

- Statements—SQL statements are audited with respect to the type of statement only, not specific objects. This type of audit can be applied to individual users or to all users of the database.

- Objects—Selective auditing of a specific statement on a specific schema object. This type of auditing is very specific because it audits only a specific statement on a specific object. Object auditing applies to all users of the database.

- Privileges—Selective auditing of the use of system privileges that perform corresponding actions. This audits only the target privilege. Privilege auditing can be applied to individual users or to all users of the database.

Auditing records information such as the operation that was audited, the user performing the operation, the date and time of the operation, and an indication of the success or failure of the operation. This information is stored in audit records that are stored in either an Oracle audit-trail table or an operating-system audit file.

Why Audit the Database?

Auditing is performed for a variety of reasons, including the following:

- To collect data and statistics about database resources and activities. This might include collecting data about the number of logical I/Os per day or the number of concurrent users on the system. This information can then be used to fine-tune the database, as well as improve performance of the server in general.
- To monitor questionable activities and suspicious users. For example, you would want to audit objects and users to identify who is deleting data from a production table.

How to Audit the Database

Auditing is a vital activity of any database. The following sections provide information on the different methods of auditing.

Considerations when Auditing

You can perform your auditing by using the Oracle database audit facility or by using the operating-system audit facility. Either way, the audit process collects and stores audit records. The advantage of using the operating-system audit facility is that it enables you to consolidate all your audit data from multiple sources, including Oracle and other applications. This single source of audit information allows for efficient evaluation of the data.

If Oracle performs the auditing, the audit-trail data is stored in the data dictionary. Afterwards, you can use any of the audit data-dictionary views to examine the data. You can also use any of the other Oracle tools, such as Data Browser or Oracle Reports, to view and print the audit-trail data.

It is advisable to use restraint when auditing. More audited events means more overhead burden placed on the Oracle server. Hence, if a lot of auditing is occurring, performance begins to be degraded. You should always have a clear reason for auditing and avoid any unnecessary auditing.

Audit only those statements or objects required to accomplish your auditing strategy. This helps minimize unwanted audit-trail information and keeps the auditing overhead to a minimum.

If you are auditing to detect questionable activities or suspicious users, start your audits at a high level. That is, audit options should be set more general at first. Take and evaluate this general auditing information. From this data, determine the correct specific audits necessary. This helps avoid unnecessary specific audits.

Statement Versus Object Versus Privilege Auditing

Statement auditing is the auditing of specific related groups of statements. For example, the audit table audits all `create table` and `drop table` commands. Another example would be if the audit table audits all `select from table/view/snapshot` statements regardless of the table, view, or snapshot.

Statement audits are generally broad in scope and audit the activities of all users or a select group of users.

Privilege auditing is the auditing of the selected system privileges and the statements associated with them. For example, auditing the `create user` system privilege audits all user's statements that require this privilege to be executed.

If similar statement and privilege audits are enabled, only a single audit record is created. For example, if the privilege `audit` is enabled for `create table` and the statement `audit` is enabled for `create table`, only one audit-trail record is created. Individually, they would each create their own record.

Object auditing is the selective auditing of specific data-manipulation language statements and the grant and revoke statements for specific schema objects. You can audit statements that reference tables, views, packages, functions, sequences, and stand-alone procedures. Object auditing is always set for all users of the database.

Configuring the Audit

Configuring your audit defines exactly what information is contained in the audit-trail file. No matter how you configure the audit, the following pieces of information are always captured by the audit:

- The username of the person who executed the audited statement
- Action code that indicates the audited statement executed by the user
- Object or objects referenced in the audited statement
- Date and time that the audited statement was executed

Oracle enables you to define your audit according to three types of audit options:

- Statement—Audits based on the type of SQL statement
- Privilege—Audits a particular system privilege
- Object—Audits specific statements on specific objects

Statement Audit Options

The following lists the statement audit options that you can include in the `audit` and `noaudit` SQL statements. The left column lists the audit option and the right column lists the SQL statements that are audited when the `audit` option is enabled:

alter system	alter system
cluster	create cluster, alter cluster, truncate cluster, drop cluster
database link	create database link, drop database link
index	create index, alter index, drop index
not exists	All SQL statements that return an Oracle error because the specified structure or object does not exist
procedure	create/replace function, create/replace procedure, create/replace package/body, create/replace function, drop procedure, drop package, drop function
public database link	create public database link, drop public database link
public synonym	create public synonym, drop public synonym
role	create role, alter role, drop role, set role
rollback segment	create rollback segment, alter rollback segment, drop rollback segment
sequence	create sequence, drop sequence
session	connect
synonym	create synonym, drop synonym
system audit	audit, noaudit
system grant	grant/to, revoke/from
table	create table, truncate table, drop table
tablespace	create tablespace, drop tablespace, alter tablespace
trigger	create trigger, alter trigger with enable/disable, alter table with enable/disable/drop
user	create user, alter user, drop user
view	create/replace view, drop view

For example, to specify an audit of all connect activity for the user clerk_01, issue the following:

```
audit session
by clerk_01;
```

Oracle provides several keywords that you can use in the audit and noaudit statements that capture several of these options simultaneously. The following list shows the keyword, sometimes known as the audit option shortcut, and the audit options that are encapsulated in the keyword:

connect	Session option
resource	Incorporates the following options: alter system, cluster, database link, procedure, rollback segment, sequence, synonym, table, tablespace, and view
dba	Includes system audit, public database link, public synonym, role, system, grant, and user options
all	Incorporates all audit options listed previously

For example, the next two sets of statements are equivalent. The first example uses the appropriate audit options and the second statement uses the equivalent audit option shortcut. Both examples produce the same output.

Example 1: Explicitly stating audit option

```
audit system audit, public database link, public synonym, role, system, grant,user
by clerk_01;
```

Example 2: Audit option defined with shortcut option

```
audit dba by clerk_01
```

A few final audit options are not covered by the individual or shortcut options listed previously. These are as follows:

alter sequence	Audits the alter sequence statement
alter table	Audits the alter table statement
comment table	Audits the comment on object statement
delete table	Audits the delete table statement
execute procedure	Audits the calls to procedures and functions
grant procedure	Audits the grant/revoke privileges on procedure statements
grant sequence	Audits the grant/revoke privileges on sequence statements
grant table	Audits the grant/revoke privileges on table statements
insert table	Audits the insert into statement
lock table	Audits the lock table/view statement
select sequence	Audits all references to sequences
select table	Audits the select...from statement
update table	Audits the update table/view statement

Object Audit Options

The following is a list of the object audit options you can use. The audit option is listed in the left column and the SQL statement that it audits is in the right column.

```
alter               alter object

audit               audit object

comment             comment object

delete              delete from object

execute             execute object

grant               grant privilege on object

index               create index on table object

insert              insert into object

lock                lock object

rename              rename object

select              select from object

update              update object
```

The object audit option also supports the all option. This option can be used to specify all the individual audit options listed previously.

Privilege Audit Options

The privilege audit options match exactly the system privileges they audit. For example, to audit the system privilege alter user, the statement would be as follows:

```
audit alter user
by access;
```

Enabling and Disabling the Audit

The SQL audit command specifies which audit options are to be enabled. For example, the following example specifies to audit only the successful role statements:

```
audit role
whenever successful;
```

This statement simply sets up the auditing; it does not actually generate or store audit records. Database auditing is enabled and disabled by the audit_trail initialization parameter in the database's parameter file. The audit_trail parameter can have any of the following values:

- db—Enables database auditing and directs all audit records to the database audit trail
- os—Enables database auditing and directs all audit records to the operating system audit trail
- none—Disables auditing

With the audit SQL command, you can include four parameters:

- by session—Causes the audit to write a single record for all SQL statements of the same type issued in the same session

- `by access`—Causes Oracle to write one record for each audited statement
- `whenever successful`—Chooses auditing only for SQL statements that complete successfully
- `whenever not successful`—Chooses auditing only for SQL statements that fail or result in errors

Audit-Trail Views

The Oracle data dictionary contains a single table to hold the audit-trail information. To assist you in examining audit-trail information, Oracle provides the following views to help you in viewing this information:

- `stmt_audit_option_map`—Description table for auditing option type code
- `audit_actions`—Description table for audit-trail action type code
- `all_def_audit_opts`—Default object-auditing options that are applied when objects are created
- `dba_stmt_audit_opts`—Describes current system auditing options across the system and by user
- `dba_priv_audit_opts`—Privilege-auditing options
- `dba_obj_audit_opts`—Audit options for all tables and views
- `user_obj_audit_opts`—Auditing options for the user's own tables and views
- `user_audit_trail`—Audit-trail entries relevant to the user
- `user_audit_session`—All audit-trail records concerning connections and disconnections for the user
- `user_audit_statement`—Audit-trail entries for the following statements that were issued by the user: `grant`, `revoke`, `audit`, `noaudit`, and `alter system`
- `user_audit_object`—Audit-trail records for statements concerning objects

The following statement displays information about all privileged audit options that are currently set:

```
select * from dba_priv_audit_opts;
```

Sample output:

```
USER_NAME AUDIT_OPTON SUCCESS FAILURE
- - - - - - - - - - - - - - - - - - - - - - - - - - - - - - - - - - - - - - - -
 ALTER USER BY SESSION BY SESSION
USER_01 DROP TABLE BY SESSION BY ACCESS
USER_01 CREATE TABLE BY SESSION BY SESSION
```

These views are created when you run the `cataudit.sql` script. Do not run this script if you don't want the audit-trail views created.

Audit-Trail Management

When auditing is enabled, Oracle generates audit information that is stored in the audit-trail table named SYS.AUD$. This table can become quite large if many audits are being performed. When auditing is enabled, the audit trail grows according to the following information:

- The number of audit options turned on
- The frequency of execution of the audited statements

If the audit-trail table becomes full, audited statements cannot be successfully executed until the audit-trail table is purged. This happens because the audited statements cannot insert audit information into the audit table. Also, warning messages are sent out to all users who issue audited statements indicating that the audit-trail table is full.

The audit-trail table growth can be controlled if these guidelines are followed:

- Turn on only the absolutely required audit options. Do not generate unneeded or unwarranted audit information.
- Enable and disable database auditing as needed.
- Limit object auditing, because this tends to generate more audit information than statement auditing. This can be accomplished by limiting those who possess the `audit any` system privilege.

To purge the audit trail of all records, issue the following:

```
delete from sys.aud$;
```

You can selectively delete records with the `where` clause. For example, to delete the audit records that belong to the table MST_PARTS, issue the following:

```
delete from sys,aud$
where obj$name = 'mst_parts';
```

To delete records from the audit-trail table, Oracle requires that you meet one of the following qualifications:

- Have the `delete any table` system privilege
- Be the user, `sys`
- Have been granted, by `sys`, `delete` system privileges on the SYS$AUD table

Auditing with Triggers

You can use Oracle triggers to provide supplemental auditing information. Triggers can be used to provide similar information to that provided by the audit system but in much more detail. When deciding to use the internal audit facility or triggers to capture audit data, consider the following advantages of the internal facility over the use of triggers:

- Oracle audit facility options cover DDL and DML statements, whereas the trigger can cover DML statements only

- Oracle stores the audit information in one centralized table
- Using the audit options is simpler and less prone to human error
- Auditing can monitor the statements that change the audit options
- Triggers cannot audit by `session`

When using triggers to generate additional auditing information, you should use the `after` triggers. By using the `after` triggers, you avoid unnecessary auditing of statements that fail due to integrity constraints. Whether you are using the `after row` or `after statement` trigger, your trigger should supply a reason or audit code to explain why the trigger is being fired.

Essential Summary

Auditing the database is the process of monitoring database-user activities. Normally you audit specific types of SQL statements or specific object activities. Either way, auditing generates audit-trail information for your evaluation.

What

Auditing is performed to monitor general database activities or to monitor the activities of specific database users. Information gained by auditing can be used to manage the database better, ensure licensing compliance, or watch questionable or suspicious activities.

Why

In this chapter, you learned about the various types of auditing and the numerous options associated with each type. The auditing process is enabled and disabled for the database through the auditing initialization parameter.

How

Backup and Recovery

What Are Backup and Recovery?

What Performing a backup is simply the act of making a copy of the database that can be used to rebuild the database during recovery operations. Backups are generally categorized as physical backups and logical backups. A physical backup is a backup where the actual physical databases are backed up to a different physical location. Typically, operating systems perform this type of backup. A logical backup is a backup where SQL or SQL*DBA is used to extract the database data into external nondatabase files. These files are then stored away in a safe location.

Databases may be backed up completely or partially. Normally you will perform a backup of the entire database on a scheduled recurring basis. For example, you may wish to make a copy of the entire database every Sunday evening. Then during the week, you may do partial, or incremental, backups to capture only the changes that occurred to the database since the last full backup. Also, a partial database backup can be made to capture a particular portion of a database.

Recovery processes vary depending on the type and severity of the failure and which parts of the database are affected. If no data is affected, it can be as simple as restarting the instance. However, if data is lost, additional recovery steps must be taken to recover the lost data from the backup files.

Why Use Backup and Recovery?

Why

Backing up your Oracle database is the only insurance you have against hardware or software failure that causes loss of vital database files. Although backing up the database does not prevent media failures, it certainly protects the data that can be used for immediate recovery.

Recovery is vital to restore lost data to its original state so that normal database operations can return as quickly as possible. Recovery helps reduce downtime to the users and minimizes inconvenience to business operations.

How to Use Backup and Recovery

How

Oracle provides several different approaches to perform database backup and recovery activities. This chapter presents information on the steps necessary to back up and recover your database.

Backup and Recovery Structures

Recovery processes vary depending on the type of failure that has occurred, the structures that are affected, and the desired recovery process. The most simple recovery is the restart of the instance. This can be accomplished if no data has been lost or damaged. However, many database failures are the result of more serious causes that result in data loss. The following are some definitions you must understand to accomplish adequate backup and recovery processes of an Oracle database:

- Process failure—A failure in a user, server, or background process. An example of this type of failure is an abnormal disconnect from the server.
- Network failure—A failure in any of the network components.
- Instance failure—An instance failure as a result of a hardware failure or an operating system problem.
- Media failure—A failure due to a failed read/write attempt.
- Redo log—This records all changes made in an Oracle database.
- Rollback segment—Stores changed values or old values of data changed by the current transaction.

Database Backups

Creating a backup process builds insurance for yourself against future database disasters. This is a necessary activity that every database administrator must insist upon. The following sections review the database backup process.

Guidelines for Backups

Here is a set of guidelines to follow when backing up an Oracle database:

- Be prepared. A vital part of creating a database is planning for and implementing appropriate backup procedures. If this task is not done now, database recovery in the event of a database loss would be impossible.

- Test the backup. Test the backup and recovery procedures in a test environment before and after you move the database to a productive environment. Perform the initial testing prior to the database going into production for the first time. Perform testing on a regular basis to ensure that your archives and recovery process work.

- Perform backups regularly. Perform frequent backups to ensure a successful recovery process. Scheduled full and partial backups are critical to every backup plan. The frequency of backups and the types of backups depend on the number of changes the database incurs. More database changes and a high usage rate indicate more frequent backups.

- Protect the database during restructuring. Perform database backups immediately before and after any significant database modification. Significant modifications include creating or dropping tablespaces, adding or renaming data files, and adding or renaming redo logs.

- Back up tablespaces. Sometimes one particular tablespace or data file is used more frequently than others. To provide adequate protection for isolated tablespaces and files, back them up frequently.

- Retain backups. Every database backup and recovery plan includes the retention time for backed up files. The two generally used approaches to retention time are point-in-time and previous copies. If you want to recover to a point in time, such as the beginning of the month, you need to retain the backup copy from the first of the month. The other approach is simply to keep two or more backups to the previous backup.

- Protect the distributed database. All databases participating in the distributed database need to be part of the same backup plan. Backups must be performed at the same time if the database is operating in the noarchivelog mode. If the archivelog mode is enabled, backups do not have to be synchronized.

Types of Backups

Oracle provides two types of backups. They are the full and the partial backup. The full backup occurs on the operating system files that contain all the data files, online redo log files, parameter files, and the control file that constitute the Oracle database.

Full database backups are taken after the database is shut down cleanly and all associated files are closed. Full backups must be used when recovering a database which was running in the noarchive mode.

A partial backup is a backup that is not as comprehensive as a full backup. This backup can be taken when the database is open and running with archivelog mode enabled. Examples of partial backups are as follows:

- Complete backup of all the data files of an individual tablespace. Individual data files or groups of data files can be backed up independently of the other data files, online redo logs, and control files for a database. A data file can be backed up while the file is online or offline.

- Backup of a single data file. Individual data files can be individually backed up independently of other data files, redo logs, and control files.

- Backup of a control file. Control files should be backed up whenever the database structure changes.

Another technique you can use to back up and recover data is to use the Oracle utilities Export and Import. These utilities transport data to and from operating system files. Refer to Chapter 27, "Import and Export," for additional information about these utilities.

Backup Modes

The Oracle database can operate two different modes with respect to backup and recovery. These are the archivelog and the noarchivelog modes.

Archivelog mode ensures that a full and complete backup to the moment of a database failure is possible. This is achieved by archiving the online redo logs to a different tape or disk drive. The online redo log is a set of operating system files that records all changes made to any database buffer, including data, index, and rollback segments, whether or not the changes are committed. The redo log protects changes made to database buffers in memory that have not been written to the data files.

The archivelog mode enables you to do complete and point-in-time recoveries using either online or offline backups. For customers running critical applications where loss of data is not acceptable, this is Oracle's recommended mode.

A database that is running in the archivelog mode can recover the database from a backup and then roll forward to the point where the failure occurred. This provides a complete recovery.

Running in the noarchivelog mode does not archive the online redo log. This type of backup protects you against an instance failure but not a media failure. Only the most recent changes made to the database can be recovered.

Performing Backups

Before any backup is performed, create a list of the files to be backed up. The view v$datafile contains a list of the data files of a database. The view v$logfile contains a listing of the online redo log file. To obtain a list of the current control files of a database, issue the following command in SQL*DBA:

```
show parameter control_file
```

Full Backup Process

Following are the steps necessary to perform a full backup:

1. Shut down the database with normal priority. The database cannot be backed up if the instance is aborted or stopped because of a failure.

2. Perform a backup of all files used by the database. Use a backup utility (like SQL*DBA) or operating system commands to make copies of all the appropriate files.

3. Restart the database.

The files that result from the full backup are consistent with each other. That is, they all correspond to the same point in time. If a database recovery is necessary, the files can be used to recover to a specific point in time. After this recovery, additional steps can be taken to roll forward to the point in time of the failure.

Partial Backup Process

To perform an online tablespace or online data file backup, perform the following steps:

1. Identify the data files by using the dba_data_files view. The following statement displays the corresponding data files for the tablespace users_01:

   ```
   select tablespace_name, file_name from sys.dba_data_files where
   ➡tablespace_name = 'users_01';
   ```

   Sample output:

   ```
   TABLESPACE NAME FILE_NAME
   ---------------------------------------
   USERS_01 DF_US_01
   USERS_01 DF_US_02
   ```

2. Mark the beginning of the online tablespace. This is accomplished by using the alter tablespace command with the begin clause or using the SQL*DBA Begin Online Tablespace Backup dialog box, as shown in Figure 34.1.

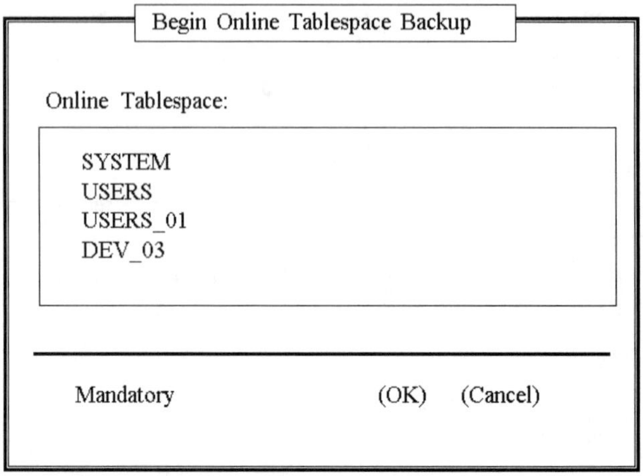

Figure 34.1.
*Marking the beginning
of a tablespace via
SQL*DBA.*

```
                    ┌──────────────────────────────────┐
                    │  Begin Online Tablespace Backup  │
┌───────────────────┴──────────────────────────────────┴──────────────┐
│                                                                      │
│  Online  Tablespace:                                                 │
│  ┌────────────────────────────────────────────────────────────────┐ │
│  │  SYSTEM                                                          │ │
│  │  USERS                                                           │ │
│  │  USERS_01                                                        │ │
│  │  DEV_03                                                          │ │
│  │                                                                  │ │
│  └────────────────────────────────────────────────────────────────┘ │
│  ─────────────────────────────────────────────────────────────────  │
│      Mandatory                        (OK)      (Cancel)             │
│                                                                      │
└──────────────────────────────────────────────────────────────────────┘
```

3. Back up the online data file using the SQL*DBA host command or the operating system backup commands.

4. Mark the end of the online tablespace backup. Use the alter tablespace command with the end backup clause or use the SQL*DBA End Online Tablespace Backup dialog box.

To back up an online tablespace, you must have the manage tablespace system privilege.

To back up an offline tablespace, execute the following steps:

1. Identify the data files by using the dba_data_files view. The following statement displays the corresponding data files for the tablespace users_01:

```
select tablespace_name, file_name
from dba_data_files
where tablespace_name = 'users_01';
```

Sample output:

```
TABLESPACE_NAME          FILE_NAME
----------------          ----------
users_01                 ts_users_01_1
users_01                 ts_users_01_02
```

2. Take the tablespace offline using normal priority.

3. Back up the data file using the SQL*DBA host command or the operating system backup commands.

To back up control files, issue the alter database command with the backup control file parameter. An example of the cf_user_01 control file backup command follows. The reuse parameter is used because the backup file already exists. This causes Oracle to overwrite the control file.

```
alter database backup controlfile cf_user_01 reuse;
```

Database Recovery

In case of database failure, it is critical to recover the database as quickly as possible. The following sections review the recovery process.

Guidelines for Recovery

Following are some guidelines to follow when recovering a database:

- Test the recovery procedures. Your backup and recovery procedures must be tested before the database goes into production. By testing the backup and recovery procedures, you eliminate problems with the process before an actual recovery is necessary.
- Determine the correct recovery method. If the database is running in the noarchivelog mode, a full database recovery is required. If archivelog mode is enabled, several recovery options are possible.

Buffers, Redo Logs, and Rollback Segments

Oracle's internal buffers write to the system global area only when necessary. Because of the algorithm used by Oracle to write to the SGA, data files might contain some data blocks modified by uncommitted transactions and some data blocks missing changes from committed transactions. If there is an instance failure at this moment in time, the redo log might contain some modified data blocks that do not exist in the data files. Additionally, the redo log might contain some uncommitted changes. To solve this problem during recovery, simply roll forward the redo log and roll back using the rollback segment.

To roll forward a redo log, issue the `alter database` command. The following example rolls forward the redo log named arch0021:

```
alter database

recover logfile 'tape_3:arch0021.arc';
```

To roll back the uncommitted transactions that were just applied during the previous example, issue the `rollback` SQL command.

The redo log uses a set of operating system files that record all changes made to the database buffer, including indexes, data, and rollback segments, whether the changes are committed or uncommitted. The first step in recovering a database is to roll forward (or reapply) all of the changes recorded in the redo log to the data files.

When you reapply the redo logs, this creates corresponding rollback segments. The rollback segments are used to undo the effects of uncommitted changes applied previously by the rolling forward phase.

Performing Recovery

The following sections discuss the full and partial recovery processes.

Full Recovery

A full recovery is required if the database has been operating in the noarchivelog mode. The following steps describe the full recovery process:

1. Shut the database down using the shutdown command with the abort clause or use the SQL*DBA Abort Instance option of the Shutdown menu.
2. Restore all data files, online redo log files, control files, and the parameter file of the database.
3. Edit the restored parameter file to reflect the location of the new disk, if applicable.
4. Start the instance using the restored and edited parameter file.
5. Mount the database.
6. Record the relocation of the restored data files and online redo log files.
7. Reopen the database.

Partial Recovery

During certain database recoveries, partial file recovery can be required. Use the v$recover_file file to display the files that need to be recovered. The following statement generates the information necessary to recover individual files:

```
select file#, online, error
from v$recover_file;
```

Sample output:

```
FILE# ONLINE ERROR
-----------------------
0102 online file not found
0118 online
0129 offline offline normal
```

Instance Recovery

The instance recovery process recovers the database to its transaction-consistent state just prior to instance failure. Instance recovery consists of the following:

- Rolling forward the redo log to recover data not yet stored in the data files. This is accomplished with the alter database command with the recover clause.
- Rolling back uncommitted transactions as specified by the rollback segments. The rollback SQL command will rollback the uncommitted transactions.
- Releasing all resource locks such as DDL table locks. Locks remain in place until a transaction is committed or rolled back.
- Resolving two-phase commits from pending distributed transactions. The two-phase commit guarantees that a transaction is valid at all nodes of a distributed database when either a commit or rollback is executed.

Recovery from Media Failure

Two different modes are available to recover a database from media failure. The modes are dictated by which archiving mode the database is using:

- If noarchivelog mode is enabled, the recovery of a database is accomplished by a restoration of the most recent full backup
- If archivelog mode is enabled, the process to recover a database can be an actual database recovery procedure

Recovery from any media failure always recovers the entire database to a transaction-consistent state prior to the media failure. Different types of complete media recovery are available depending on the files that are damaged and the availability of the database that requires recovery.

Following are the types of full media recovery processes available to recover all lost data and changes:

- Closed database recovery. Closed database recovery can proceed while the database is mounted but closed to all users. Normally you use this type of recovery when the database doesn't have to be open, and when files are damaged that make up all or part of the system tablespace or active rollback segment tablespace.
- Open database offline tablespace recovery. This recovery can proceed while a database is open. Undamaged tablespaces are online and available for use while the damaged tablespaces are offline. This type of recovery normally is used when the undamaged tablespaces need to be available to the users or when the system tablespace is intact and operational.
- Open database offline tablespace individual data file recovery. This recovery can proceed while a database is open. Undamaged tablespaces are online and available for use while the damaged tablespace is offline and specific damaged data files are being recovered. This recovery type is normally used when the undamaged tablespaces need to be available to the users or when the system tablespace is intact and operational. The individual data files are recovered by SQL*DBA to expedite recovery.
- Complete media recovery using a backup of the control file. Complete media recovery can proceed without loss of data even if all control files are damaged by disk failure. The control file is recovered by the reset log at database opening.

Complete media recovery follows these three general steps:

1. Restoration of backup data files
2. Rolling forward with the redo log
3. Rolling back using the rollback segment

Incomplete Media Recovery

There might be a situation when you do not want to fully recover the database. In certain circumstances, the recovery process is closely watched so the database administrator can cancel the recovery at a certain point. This cancel-based recovery is usually done when the necessary data files and logs for full recovery are not available.

Another time that incomplete recovery is warranted is when you would like to recover up to a point in time. For example, a user accidentally truncates a table. At that moment, he notices the time on his watch. The database administrator can recover up to that point in time just prior to the accidental table truncation.

Recovery from User Errors

Oracle provides a means to recover data that might have been lost due to a serious user error. The following are the general steps necessary to completely recover data from a user error:

1. Back up the existing, intact database.
2. Leave the existing database intact and reconstruct a temporary copy of the database up to the user error using time-based recovery.
3. Export the lost data from the reconstructed, temporary copy of the database.
4. Import the lost data into the permanent database.
5. Delete the temporary copy of the database.

Essential Summary

What   Backup is the act of taking a partial or complete copy of the database files and data. Recovery is the process of re-creating the database by using the files created from the backup process.

Why   Backup and recovery are vital processes that the database administrator must go through to completely protect the database against loss of any type.

How   In this chapter, you learned about fully and partially backing up the database. You also read about the different types of database recovery. The entire backup and recovery process is a formal process that must be planned, created, and tested.

PART IX

Server Messages and Codes

Understanding Server Messages and Codes

What Are Server Messages and Codes?

What Server messages and codes are generated by the Oracle server when you run any Oracle program. These messages and codes provide information about the state of the server or the results of a process. For example, messages are generated when a process completes normally as well as when the process completes abnormally.

Server messages and codes are composed of two components. The server code has a prefix which defines the Oracle product that generated the message. The code also contains a unique numeric identifier. The message is a descriptive text that briefly describes the event that caused the message to be generated.

Why Use Server Messages and Codes?

Why

Server messages and codes are generated by the server for your benefit. They tell you when an unexpected event occurs as well as when processes terminate normally. In both cases, you can use these codes to debug your programs, fine-tune your applications, and confirm the success of a program's execution.

These messages and codes provide direct and quick feedback on unanticipated problems. Without these messages and codes, you would have to manually research each and every problem, which is a very time-consuming and painful process.

How to Use Server Messages and Codes

How

Messages and codes are generated either by the Oracle server or, under some circumstances, by the user program. Understanding how to read and use the messages and codes is vital to successful application development and database administration.

Message and Code Format

Every message generated by the Oracle server has a predefined format. The format of each message includes an error message code and a descriptive text. Each message code has a prefix that defines which program issued the error message. Following is a list of the prefix codes you might encounter. These prefix codes indicate which program generated the error:

- BRW—Data Browser
- DBA—SQL*DBA
- EXP—Export Utility
- FRM—SQL*Forms
- IMP—Import Utility
- INS—Install
- LCC—Parameter file error
- ORA—Generic Oracle Server error
- PCC—Precompiler message
- PLS—PL/SQL message
- REP—Oracle Reports
- RTL—Precompiler runtime message
- SQL*Loader—SQL*Loader message

Message and Code Variables

In some messages, Oracle uses variables to represent object names, numbers, and character strings to make the message more meaningful. This will help you in finding and fixing the error. For example, the following message would not be as meaningful if the variable (50) were not present. Without the variable, you would have to do additional research to discover what the maximum allowable number of processes is.

```
ORA-0020: maximum number of processes (50) exceeded
```

The following message example shows the use of the server supplying the name of the missing file:

```
IMP-00002: failed to open mst_part.exp for read
```

Message and Code Stacks

On many occasions, Oracle displays a series of messages that is commonly known as a message stack. These messages are related and refer to the same error. The following example illustrates a stack. This stack was generated when the PL/SQL program part_parser abnormally stopped processing at line 14.

```
ORA-6502: PL/SQL: numeric or value error
ORA-6512: at "Part_Parser", line 14
ORA-6512: at line 14
```

Message and Code Ranges

Oracle has grouped the message codes into specific ranges. Each group of message codes indicates the type of event that caused Oracle to generate the message. Following are the groupings of the message codes. Some platform-specific ranges have been omitted. Please refer to the appropriate manual for an explanation of these messages.

- 00000–00099—Oracle Server

  These messages are generated by the Oracle server.

- 00100–00150—Multi_Threaded Server

  These messages are generated by the multi-threaded server.

- 00151–00159—Oracle * XA

- 00200–00249—Control Files

  These messages relate to control files.

- 00250–00299—Archiving and Recovery

  These messages are generated when archiving or recovery of the database is in progress.

- 00300–00379—Redo Log Files

  These messages are generated when the redo log files are being accessed.

- 00400–00420—Oracle Compatibility

  These messages are generated when two different versions of Oracle communicate.

- 00436–00437—Oracle Licensing

  These messages are generated when the installed Oracle product discovers a discrepancy in licensing codes.

- 00440–00485—Background Processes

  These messages are generated when background processes of the Oracle server are started or shut down.

- 00486–00569—Interrupt Handlers

- 00570–00599—SQL * Connect Opening and Reading Files

- 00600–00639—Oracle Exceptions

  These messages are generated when an internal exception is generated within Oracle.

- 00700–00709—Data Dictionary Cache

  These messages are generated when the data dictionary cache is accessed.

- 00900–00999—SQL Parsing

  These messages are generated when SQL statements are parsed by the Oracle server. Most of these messages indicate incorrect SQL syntax in your statement.

- 01000–01099—User Program Interface

  These messages are generated when using a UPI (such as Oracle precompilers and SQL*Forms) on the Oracle server.

- 01100–01250—Oracle Files

- 01400–01489—SQL Execution

  These messages are generated during SQL execution.

- 01500–01699—Oracle Commands

  These messages are generated when entering Oracle commands.

- 01700–01799—SQL Parsing

- 01800–01899—The Date Function

- 01900–02039—SQL Parsing

- 02040–02099—Distributed Transactions

- 02100–02139—Precompiler Runtime

- 02140–02299—SQL Parsing

- 02351–02375—SQL*Loader in direct path mode

- 02376–02399—Oracle Resources

  These messages are generated when resources within the Oracle server are altered.

- 02400–02419—Explain Plan

  These messages are generated when using the SQL Explain Plan command.

- 02420–02429—Schema

  These messages are generated when commands are used that alter schemas or schema objects.

- 02430–02449—Constraint Enabling and Disabling

  These messages are generated when commands are used that affect constraints on a table.

- 03276–03289—Extent Allocation

  These messages are generated during extent allocation.

- 03290–03295—Truncate Command

  These commands are generated when the truncate command is used.

- 03500–03699

  These commands refer to Macintosh-specific errors. Refer to the appropriate Apple manual for these messages.

- 04000–04109—Command Parameters

  These messages are generated when inconsistent values are used in a command.

- 04020–04029—Library Object Locks

  These messages are generated when a library object is locked and cannot be accessed.

- 04030–04039—System Memory

  These messages are generated by an Oracle server when the operating system cannot allocate sufficient memory during an Oracle session.

- 04040–04069—Stored Procedures

  These messages are generated when stored procedures are accessed.

- 04070–04099—Triggers

  These messages are generated when triggers are accessed.

- 06000–06429—SQL*Net

- 06500–06599—PL/SQL

  These messages are generated when Oracle detects a problem with PL/SQL. Usually ORA and PLS prefixed messages accompany this message. The accompanying messages provide additional information about the problem.

- 06600–06699—SQL*Net

- 08000–08174—Accessing Data

  These messages are generated when Oracle is accessing data or database objects.

- 08175–08190—Discrete Transactions

  These messages are generated when a discrete transaction is attempted.

- 12000–12014—Table Snapshots

  These messages are generated when a table snapshot is accessed.

- 12300–12499—Trusted Oracle

  These messages are generated while using the trusted Oracle server.

- 19999–20000—Stored Procedures

- 20000–20999—User Defined

  These messages are defined by the user.

- 23300–24299—DBMS PL/SQL Packages

Trace Files

A trace file is created for every instance that is started and every user process and background process that encounters an unexpected event. When an event occurs, the process dumps information about the error to its trace file. Some of the information written to the trace file is intended for the database administrator and other information is intended for the Oracle World-wide Customer Support Center.

The trace file can contain dumps of the system global area, process global area, supervisor stack, and registers. Some of this information can also be used to fine-tune an application or an instance.

The trace file's name is created by Oracle and includes the instance name, process name, and the Oracle process number. The file extension is trc.

The database administrator initializes the parameters background_dump_dest and user_dump_dest to define the exact location of the trace file. Because the trace file can contain a dump of information, it might need to be formatted prior to being used to diagnose problems. The utility dumpfmt can be used to format the trace file.

The parameter max_dump_file_size determines the maximum size the trace file is allowed to grow to. This limit is set as a number of operating system blocks.

Alert Files

One special kind of trace file is the alert file. The alert file is a chronological log of messages, codes, and errors that includes the following:

- All internal errors, block corruption errors, and deadlock errors
- Administrative operation statements such as create SQL statements
- Several messages and errors relating to the functions of shared server and dispatcher processes
- Errors during the automatic refresh of a snapshot
- The values of all initialization parameters when the database and instance are started

When an internal error occurs, the message is sent to the alert file as well as to the user's terminal screen. Additionally, the locations and names of the trace files can be included in the alert file.

The name of the alert file is operating system specific. Please refer to your installation guide for your local alert file naming conventions. The location of the alert file is defined in the `background_dump_dest` parameter.

The alert file also records activities such as backups and archiving online redo log files.

To control the size of the alert file, you must manually delete it when it is no longer needed. Until it is deleted, Oracle continues to write to it. You can delete this file when the instance is running. You don't have to shut down the instance to delete it.

Internal Errors

Oracle continuously performs self-diagnostics to detect internal errors. When an internal error is detected by the Oracle server, the following message is generated:

```
ORA-00600: internal error code. arguments [] [] [] [] [] []
```

This message can contain up to six arguments that indicate the origin and attributes of the error. The first argument is the internal error number. The remaining arguments are various numbers, strings, and names. Empty brackets are ignored.

This specific message is displayed to the user and is also written to the alert file. In addition to the message, Oracle supplies information about the event causing the message to the alert file.

When this message is received, you should contact the Oracle Worldwide Customer Support Center.

User-Defined Errors

Oracle permits the user to create and generate error messages in PL/SQL. The messages that are returned to the client application have a user-specific error code number and message. The client application has error trapping logic set up in the PL/SQL code to handle these user-specific errors.

User-specific error messages are returned using the `raise_application_error` procedure:

```
raise_application_error(error_number,'error text')
```

The `error_number` must be in the range of 20000 to 20999, and the error text must no be longer than 2000 characters.

This procedure terminates procedure execution, rolls back any changes made by the procedure, and returns the user-specified error number and text.

Message and Code Definitions

Each of the following messages listed includes the following:

- Error code
- Error message

- Probable cause of the message
- When appropriate, possible corrective action

The following is a list of the more common messages and codes received by developers, users, and database administrators. For a complete list, please refer to your Oracle Messages and Codes manual.

00000–00099—Oracle Server

`ORA-00000 normal, successful completion`

Cause: An operation or process ended normally and encountered no usual events.

Corrective Action: This is an information message alerting you to the fact that processing has completed normally. No additional user actions are required.

`ORA-00001 unique constraint (table.column) violated`

Cause: An update insert attempted to insert a duplicate key.

Corrective Action: Either remove the constraint on the column or do not insert the key.

`ORA-00018 maximum number of sessions exceeded`

Cause: An attempt was made to exceed the maximum allowable sessions as defined by the sessions variable. No new sessions can be started at this time.

Corrective Action: Either increase the value of the session parameter or wait until other sessions terminate.

`ORA-00020 maximum number of processes (number) exceeded`

Cause: An attempt was made to exceed the maximum allowable processes as defined by the process parameter. No new processes can be started at this time.

Corrective Action: Either increase the value of the process parameter or wait until other processes terminate.

`ORA-00024 logins from more than one process not allowed in single-process mode`

Cause: An attempt was made to log in more than once from different processes after Oracle had been started in single-process mode.

Corrective Action: Log off from the previous process, then log in from another process. Alternately, restart Oracle in multi-process mode.

`ORA-00051 time-out occurred while waiting for resource`

Cause: Usually generated when an instance terminates abnormally.

Corrective Action: Check for a nonrecovered instance and restart it.

`ORA-00055 maximum number of DML locks exceeded`

Cause: An operation requested a resource that was not available. The number of DML locks is defined in the `DML_Locks` parameter.

Corrective Action: Either increase the value of the `DML_Locks` parameter or wait until other locks are released.

00100–00150—Multi_Threaded Server

`ORA-00100 idle public server terminating`

Cause: There are too many idle shared servers waiting on the common dispatcher request queue.

Corrective Action: No user action is required as the Oracle server will automatically terminate the 'extra' shared servers.

`ORA-00106 cannot startup/shutdown database when connected to a dispatcher`

Cause: An attempt was made to start up or shut down an instance while connected to a shared server process via a dispatcher.

Corrective Action: Reconnect to the database using a dedicated server.

00200–00249—Control Files

`ORA-00200 cannot create control file 'name'`

Cause: There is insufficient disk space or there is a filename conflict.

Corrective Action: Ensure there is sufficient disk space and there are no conflicts with the filename. Try action again.

`ORA-00202 control file 'name'`

Cause: This message is in a message stack.

Corrective Action: Refer to the other messages in the stack for additional actions.

`ORA-00205 message in identifying control file 'name'`

Cause: Server unable to locate the control file.

Corrective Action: Either ensure correct control filename is used or create a new control file using a different name in the initialization parameter file.

00250–00299—Archiving and Recovery

`ORA-00250 archiver not started`

Cause: An attempt was made to stop automatic archiving, but the archiver process was not running.

Corrective Action: This is an informational message indicating the user issued the wrong command. No additional user action is required.

`ORA-00251 archiving/media recovery requires OS DBA or OPER privileges`

Cause: An attempt was made to perform archiving or media recovery without having the DBA or OPER privileges.

Corrective Action: Obtain necessary privileges.

00400–00420—Oracle Compatibility

```
ORA-00402 database changes by release 'rel' cannot be used by release 'rel'
```

Cause: Changes have been made to the database that require a newer software release.

Corrective Action: Use a version of the software that can understand the changes or relax the compatibility requirements in the initialization parameter file.

00436–00437—Oracle Licensing

```
ORA-00437 Oracle feature is not licensed. Contact Oracle Corporation for
assistance.
```

Cause: This installed Oracle product is not licensed to run on this CPU.

Corrective Action: Confirm Oracle is installed correctly. Contact Oracle Worldwide Customer Support Center for assistance.

00440–00485—Background Processes

```
ORA-00445 background process 'num' did not start
```

Cause: The specified process did not start.

Corrective Action: Check any accompanying messages, confirm executable image is in correct location, read the background trace file for additional information.

```
ORA-00448 normal completion of background process
```

Cause: The background process completed normally.

Corrective Action: This is an information message alerting you to the fact that background processing has completed normally. No additional user actions are required.

00600–00639—Oracle Exceptions

```
ORA-00600 internal message code, arguments [num],[?],...
```

Cause: This is a catchall internal message for Oracle programming exceptions.

Corrective Action: Contact the Oracle Worldwide Customer Support Center for assistance.

00700–00709—Data Dictionary Cache

```
ORA-00703 maximum number of dictionary cache instance locks exceeded
```

Cause: An operation requested a resource that was unavailable.

Corrective Action: Try operation again in a few minutes when other locks might be released. If the problem continues, contact the Oracle Worldwide Customer Support Center for assistance.

00900–00999—SQL Parsing

`ORA-00900 invalid SQL statement`

Cause: The SQL statement entered has invalid syntax.

Corrective Action: Correct the syntax.

`ORA-00901 invalid create statement`

Cause: The `create` statement contained an invalid option.

Corrective Action: Correct the syntax.

`ORA-00902 invalid datatype`

Cause: An invalid datatype was used in a `create` or `alter table` statement.

Corrective Action: Correct the syntax.

`ORA-00903 invalid table name`

Cause: A table or cluster name is invalid or does not exist.

Corrective Action: Check the spelling of the name.

`ORA-00904 invalid column name`

Cause: The column name is invalid or missing.

Corrective Action: Check the spelling or enter the correct name.

`ORA-00905 missing keyword`

Cause: A required keyword is missing.

Corrective Action: Correct the syntax.

`ORA-00913 too many values`

Cause: The statement entered contains too many values.

Corrective Action: Check the number of required values with the number in the statement.

`ORA-00919 invalid function`

Cause: The syntax of the entry was not recognized as a function.

Corrective Action: Check the syntax.

`ORA-00920 invalid relational operator`

Cause: A search condition was attempted with an invalid or missing relational operator.

Corrective Action: Include the proper relational operator.

ORA-00942 table or view does not exist

Cause: The table or view in the entered statement does not exist, or a synonym was used and not allowed here, or a view was referenced where a table name is required.

Corrective Action: Check the spelling of the table or view. Be sure that a view is not present where a table is expected.

01000–01099—User Program Interface

ORA-01000 maximum open cursors exceeded

Cause: A client program attempted to open too many cursors as defined in the open_cursor initialization parameter.

Corrective Action: Modify client program to use fewer cursors, or increase the value of the open_cursor parameter.

ORA-01012 not logged on

Cause: A client program attempted an Oracle call without being logged on to the server.

Corrective Action: Log on to Oracle with the OLON or OLOGON call before issuing any Oracle calls.

ORA-01017 invalid username/password; logon denied

Cause: An attempt was made to log on to the Oracle server with an invalid username or password.

Corrective Action: Enter a valid username and password in the correct format.

ORA-01031 insufficient privileges

Cause: An attempt was made by the user to perform an operation that the user didn't have the necessary privileges for.

Corrective Action: Obtain the necessary privileges and perform the operation again.

ORA-01075 currently logged on

Cause: An attempt was made to log on while already logged on.

Corrective Action: Alter application to prevent multiple logon attempts.

01400–01489—SQL Execution

ORA-01400 primary key or mandatory (not null) column is missing or null during insert.

Cause: A value was not specified for a mandatory column during an `insert` or `update` operation.

Corrective Action: Supply a value for every mandatory column and retry the operation.

ORA-01408 such column list already indexed

Cause: A `create index` was attempted on a column that is already indexed.

Corrective Action: Do not attempt to re-index the column.

ORA-01416 two tables cannot be out-joined to each other

Cause: Two tables in a `join` operation specified an outer join with respect to each other.

Corrective Action: Remove the outer join specification (+) from one of the tables in the statement.

ORA-01417 a table can be outer-joined to at most one other table

Cause: A table in a `join` operation specified an outer join to more than one table.

Corrective Action: Specify only one outer join and retry the operation.

ORA-01418 specified index does not exist

Cause: An attempt was made to perform an operation on an index that does not exist.

Corrective Action: Specify the current name of the existing index in your statement.

01500–01699—Oracle Commands

ORA-01506 missing or illegal database name

Cause: No database name was provided in the `alter database` statement, or the initialization parameter db_name was not specified.

Corrective Action: Provide the correct database name in your statement or correct the value for the initialization parameter, then attempt the operation again.

ORA-01507 database not mounted

Cause: An `alter database` command specified a database name, but the database was not mounted.

Corrective Action: Use the `mount` clause in your `alter database` command.

ORA-01534 rollback segment 'name' doesn't exist

Cause: The rollback segment could not be found by the name supplied in your statement.

Corrective Action: Correct syntax and spelling of the statement and retry your operation. You can also specify a different rollback segment.

ORA-01535 rollback segment 'name' already exists

Cause: The specified rollback segment already exists.

Corrective Action: Correct the syntax or spelling, or specify a different rollback segment name.

02420–02429—Schema

ORA-02425 create table failed

Cause: A create table statement failed in the create schema statement.

Corrective Action: This message is accompanied by several other messages. Refer to the accompanying messages for more information on the cause of the problem.

02430–02449—Constraint Enabling and Disabling

ORA-02430 cannot enable constraint 'name' - no such constraint

Cause: The named constraint does not exist for this table.

Corrective Action: Make sure that a constraint exists before trying to enable it.

ORA-02432 cannot enable primary key - primary key not defined for table

Cause: An attempt was made to enable a primary key that is not defined for the table.

Corrective Action: Add a primary key constraint on the table.

ORA-02434 cannot enable unique key - unique key not defined for table

Cause: An attempt was made to enable a unique key that is not defined for the table.

Corrective Action: Add a unique key constraint on the table.

03290–03295—Truncate Command

ORA-03290 invalid truncate command - missing cluster or table keyword

Cause: An invalid object specification was given for the truncate command.

Corrective Action: Check the syntax and spelling of the command and retry the operation.

04000–04109—Command Parameters

ORA-04000 the sum of pctused and pctfree cannot exceed 100

Cause: The sum of pctused and pctfree for a specified cluster or table exceeds 100.

Corrective Action: Specify values for pctused and pctfree whose sum does not exceed 100.

04030–04039—System Memory

ORA-04031 out of shared memory when trying to allocate 'num' bytes 'str'

Cause: More shared memory is needed than was allocated in the SGA.

Corrective Action: Reduce the use of shared memory or increase the allocated memory.

04040–04069—Stored Procedures

ORA-04041 package specification must be created first before creating package body.

Cause: An attempt was made to create a package body prior to creating the package specification.

Corrective Action: Create the package specification first, then create the package body.

ORA-04042 procedure, function, package, or package body does not exist

Cause: An attempt was made to access a procedure, function, package, or package body that does not exist.

Corrective Action: Ensure the name specified is correct.

04070–04099—Triggers

ORA-04070 invalid trigger name

Cause: An invalid trigger name was specified.

Corrective Action: Verify trigger name in the statement and check to make sure the trigger name is not a reserved word.

06500–06599—PL/SQL

ORA-06502 PL/SQL:Numeric or value error

Cause: An arithmetic, numeric, string, conversion, or constraint error occurred.

Corrective Action: Change the data, how it is manipulated, or how it is declared so that the values do not violate constraints.

ORA-06503 PL/SQL:Function returned without value

Cause: A call to a PL/SQL function completed, but no return statement was executed.

Corrective Action: Modify the PL/SQL function to include a return statement.

ORA-06511 PL/SQL:Cursor already open

Cause: An attempt was made to open a cursor that was already open.

Corrective Action: Close the cursor before attempting to reopen the cursor.

08000–08174—Accessing Data

ORA-08001 maximum number of sequences exceed per session

Cause: An operation was attempted that requested a resource that was not available. The maximum number of user sequences per session was met. This limit is specified by the initialization parameter dc_sequences.

Corrective Action: Wait a few minutes and try again. If the problem persists, increase the value of the dc_sequences parameter.

ORA-08002 name.currval is not yet defined in this session

Cause: currval was selected before the sequence nextval was referenced.

Corrective Action: Select nextval from the sequence prior to referencing currval.

ORA-08006 specified row no longer exists

Cause: The row has been deleted by another user since the operation began.

Corrective Action: This is an informational message indicating that the desired row is already deleted. No additional action is required by the user.

ORA-08103 object no longer exists

Cause: The object has been deleted by another user since the operation began.

Corrective Action: Remove the reference to the object.

12000–12014—Table Snapshots

ORA-12003 snapshot 'name' does not exist

Cause: An attempt was made to reference a snapshot that does not exist.

Corrective Action: Check the name of the snapshot and retry the operation.

ORA-12004 refresh fast cannot be used

Cause: There is no snapshot log for the master table.

Corrective Action: Create a snapshot log on the master table and retry operation.

Essential Summary

What In this chapter, you learned that Oracle generates information messages and codes when performing an operation in the Oracle server. These codes contain a prefix indicating which program the error originated from.

Why Messages and codes are generated when something unexpected happens as well as when operations terminate normally. Use these messages and codes to debug and fine-tune your applications and databases.

How Oracle automatically generates the server messages and codes. Under some circumstances, the user application can generate a user-specified message and code.

Handling Runtime Exceptions in PL/SQL

What Is a Runtime Exception?

What A runtime exception is an error or warning that is generated either from the Oracle server or from the user's application. These errors can arise from hardware or network failures, application logic errors, data integrity errors, and many other sources. Errors are caused by abnormal conditions that prevent PL/SQL execution from continuing processing.

Exceptions arise from the Oracle environment or from the user's application. An example of an exception from the Oracle environment might be `insufficient privileges to`.... Your application can be designed to anticipate and look for certain conditions that warrant an exception. For example, a bank would have its applications set up to prevent someone from overdrawing their bank account. This type of exception is a user-defined exception.

Why Handle Runtime Exceptions?

Why

Typically, when an error occurs, processing of the PL/SQL block terminates. Hence, your application stops processing and the task at hand goes unfinished. With exception handling, when an error is detected, control is passed to the exception-handling portion of your program, and processing completes normally.

Applications should always anticipate errors and provide application logic to handle them so processing can continue. Handling errors also provides valuable information in debugging applications and bullet-proofing applications against future errors.

If you don't provide a means to handle exceptions, your program must check for execution errors after each statement, as the following example shows:

```
select ....
if error-- check for error associated with select statement
then....
insert ....
if error-- check for error associated with insert statement
then...
update ....
if error-- check for error associated with update statement
then...
```

As you can see, this increases the processing overhead because you have to explicitly check for errors after each statement. There is always a risk that you might overlook a statement and not check for errors, thereby leaving open the potential for an abnormal termination of your application.

With exception handling incorporated into your application, the preceding statement would be transformed to look like this:

```
begin
select ....
insert ....
update ....
exception
-- check for errors
end
```

This way of handling errors removes all the added processing required for explicitly handling errors. Also, readability of the program is improved.

How to Handle Runtime Exceptions

How

PL/SQL provides several ways to handle system and user-defined exceptions. The following sections review these techniques.

Exception-Handling Structures

PL/SQL enables the user to anticipate and trap for certain runtime errors. These errors are known as exceptions and, if not handled in the PL/SQL block, would cause the program to terminate under abnormal conditions. Exceptions can be internally defined by Oracle or the user.

There are three types of exceptions:

- Predefined Oracle errors
- Undefined Oracle errors
- User-defined errors

Predefined Oracle Errors

When an exception is raised, normal processing stops and control is passed to the exception-handling portion of your program. If the exception handling does not trap for the error, control passes to the host environment.

To build the exception-handling portion of your program, start the block of code with the keyword `exception`. The following example shows the typical syntax of an exception-handling PL/SQL block:

```
exception
when exception 1 then
statement(s)
when exception 2 then
statement(s)
```

The Oracle server defines several errors with standard names. Although every Oracle error has a number, they must be referenced by name. PL/SQL has predefined some common Oracle errors and exceptions. Some of these predefined exception names are listed here:

- `no_data_found`—Single row select returned no data.
- `too_many_rows`—Single row select returned more than one row.
- `invalid_cursor`—Illegal cursor operation was attempted.
- `value_error`—Arithmetic, conversion, truncation, or constraint error occurred.
- `invalid_number`—Conversion of a number to character string failed.
- `zero_divide`—Attempted to divide by zero.
- `dup_val_on_index`—Attempted to insert a duplicate value into a column that has a unique index.
- `cursor_already_open`—Attempted to open a cursor that was previously opened.
- `not_logged_on`—A database call was made without being logged on to Oracle.
- `too_many_rows`—A `select into` statement returned more than one row.
- `transaction_backed_out`—Usually raised when a remote portion of a transaction is rolled back.

- login_denied—Login to Oracle failed because of invalid username and password.
- program_error—Raised if PL/SQL encounters an internal problem.
- storage_error—Raised if PL/SQL runs out of memory or if memory is corrupted.
- timeout_on_resource—Timeout occurred while Oracle was waiting on a resource.
- others—This is a catch-all. If the error was not trapped in the previous exception traps, it is trapped by this statement.

Oracle declares predefined exceptions globally in the package standard. Therefore, you do not need to declare them yourself.

The following example illustrates a PL/SQL exception-handling block:

```
exception -- Exceptions block beginning
when no_data_found then -- first exceptions trap
eof := true;
commit;
when others then -- second exceptions trap .
rollback;
commit;
end; -- end of exceptions handling
```

Undefined Oracle Errors

As seen earlier, the others exception is used as a catchall error. others is normally used when the exact nature of the exception isn't important or when the exception is unnamed.

One other way to handle an unnamed error is with the pragma exception_init compiler directive. This directive simply transfers information to the compiler. The pragma statement tells the compiler to associate an exception name with an Oracle error number. This enables you to refer to any internal exception by name and to write a specific handler for it.

The declaration of the pragma exception_init statement must appear in the declarative portion of the PL/SQL block, package, or subprogram. The following is the syntax for this declaration:

```
pragma exception_init (exception_name, error_number);
```

The exception name is a previously declared execution. The pragma declaration must appear somewhere after the exception declaration. The following example shows the exception and pragma declarations and the exception-handling block for the exception:

```
insufficient_funds exception;
pragma exception_init (insufficient _funds, -2019);
begin
exception
when insufficient_funds then
rollback;
end;
```

User-Defined Errors

Users can explicitly raise an exception with the raise command. The raise exception procedure should be used only when Oracle does not raise its own exception or when processing is undesirable or impossible to complete.

Steps for trapping a user-defined error include the following:

■ Declare the name for the user exception within the declaration section of the block

■ Raise the exception explicitly within the executable portion of the block using the raise command

■ Reference the declared exception with an error-handling routine

The following example illustrates the use of the user-defined exception:

```
declare
invalid_fam_code exception; -- user-defined exception
part_fam_code varchar2(2);
begin
if part_fam_code not in ('AU','UC','BG') then -- error trap
raise invalid_fam_code; -- raise user defined exception
end if;
exception -- handle user defined exception
when invalid_fam_code then
rollback;
end;
```

Exceptions can be raised in declarations when declarations and initializations are done incorrectly. When this happens, the exception handler must reside in the enclosing block. This is called exception propagation. The following sections provide more detail on this topic.

Continuing Processing After an Exception

Exception handlers let you handle errors that normally would be fatal to your application. However, the exception handlers described so far in this chapter create a logic processing problem. Look at the following PL/SQL block:

```
declare
invalid_fam_code exception; -- user-defined exception
part_fam_code varchar2(2);
begin
if part_fam_code not in ('AU','UC','BG') then -- error trap
raise invalid_fam_code; -- raise user defined exception
end if;
insert....
update....
exception -- handle user define exception
when invalid_fam_code then
rollback;
end;
```

When the invalid_fam_code exception occurs, process control is transferred to the handler. The insert and update commands are never executed in this scenario. This could pose a problem for your application. To get around the problem of code being bypassed due to an exception, embed the exception handler in its own sub-block, as shown in the following example:

```
declare
invalid_fam_code exception; -- user-defined exception
part_fam_code varchar2(2);
begin
begin -- sub-block begin
if part_fam_code not in ('AU','UC','BG') then -- error trap
exception -- handle user define exception
when invalid_fam_code then
rollback;
end if;
end; -- sub-block end
insert...
update...
end;
```

In this example, the exception `invalid_fam_code` is handled locally in its own sub-block. This enables `insert`, `update`, and any other following statements to be executed.

Retrying a Transaction After an Exception

At times you might want to retry a transaction after some exceptions. For example, say you are creating new identification numbers for new parts coming out of the factory. You attempt to create a new part number and receive a message stating that that particular part number already exists. What would you do? Normally, you would create a different part number and retry the task. The following example follows this same scenario. You would not want to cease transaction processing when you get a duplicate part number message. Fortunately, you know enough about the cause of the problem to add corrective logic to your program:

```
declare
max_count integer;
part_number integer := 1;
begin
/* determine number of new parts today and loop */
/* for that amount */
select count(*) into max_count from new_parts;
for I in 1..max_count loop
begin -- create a sub-block
savepoint top_loop; -- establish rollback point
part_number :=part_number+1; -- create new part number
insert into inventory value (part_number);
commit;
exit;
exception
when dup_val_on_index then
part_number :=part_number+1; -- create a newer part number
rollback to top_loop; -- force us to top of loop
end; -- end sub-block
end loop; -- end loop
end; -- end block
```

Reraising an Exception

Sometimes you might want to handle an exception locally and pass the exception to an enclosed block. For example, the following statement raises the exception out_of_stock in the sub-block and passes the exception handling to the enclosed block:

```
declare
out_of_stock exception; -- declare exception
-- beginning of sub-block to check qty of order
begin
if qty_ordered > qty_on_hand then
raise out_of_stock; -- raise the exception
end if;
exception
-- for exception indicated that order_qty is invalid
when out_of_stock then
raise; -- reraise the current exception
end;
-- end of sub-block
exception
-- handle the exception differently than earlier.
when out_of_stock then
end;
```

Exception Scope Rules

Following are a few guidelines to be aware of with regard to the scope of an exception declaration:

- An exception cannot be declared twice in the same block, but you can declare the same exception in two different blocks.
- Exceptions are local to the block where they were declared and global to all of their sub-blocks. Enclosing blocks cannot reference exceptions that were declared in any of their sub-blocks.
- Global declarations can be redeclared at the local sub-block level. If this occurs, the local declaration takes precedence over the global declaration.

Propagating Exceptions

When an error is encountered, PL/SQL looks in the current block for the appropriate exception handler. If no handler is present, PL/SQL propagates the error to the enclosing block. PL/SQL searches the enclosing block for the correct error handler. If no handler is found there, the error is continually propagated to the enclosing blocks until a handler is found. This process can continue until the host environment receives and handles the error. For example, if SQL*Plus receives an unhandled error from a PL/SQL block, SQL*Plus's way of handling the error is to display the error code and message on the user's terminal.

SQLCODE and SQLERRM

In the exception-handling part of your program, use the functions SQLCODE and SQLERRM to obtain information about the most recent exception. This is especially useful when the exception is trapped with the when others clause. The when others clause is used to trap unanticipated or unknown exceptions.

The SQLCODE function returns the error code for the exception. SQLERRM returns the corresponding error message.

Following are the valid values for the SQLCODE function:

0	Indicates that no exception has been raised
1	Indicates that a user-defined exception has been raised
+1403	Indicates that a no_data_found exception has been raised
−###	The remaining negative values correspond to the actual error codes as defined in the *Oracle Server Messages and Codes Manual*

The following example traps the error code and message of the offending exception and stores it in a table for access later:

```
declare
error_code number;
error_msg varchar2(250);
begin
exception
when others then
error_code := SQLCODE;
error_msg := SQLERRM;
insert into user_exceptions_table (error_message)
values (to_char(error_code) || ': ' || error_msg);
commit;
end;
```

You can now perform a select on the user_exceptions_table to view the exception error code and message.

You cannot use SQLCODE and SQLERRM directly in a SQL statement. Instead, you must assign their values to local variables, then use these variables in the SQL statement.

If PL/SQL cannot find an exception handler for an error, it turns the exception over to the host environment for handling.

Essential Summary

Exceptions are unwanted errors that arise from many different sources, including hardware and network failures, application logic problems, and data issues. Exceptions are defined and generated either by the Oracle environment or by the user.

Exceptions should be handled in your application to prevent the unwanted termination of your application processes. Handling exceptions in PL/SQL blocks provides the added benefit of reducing the processing overhead required to individually check each block statement.

Why

This chapter reviewed the techniques to trap for defined and undefined Oracle errors as well as for user-defined exceptions. You learned the various formats and procedures available to trap unwanted exceptions efficiently and effectively.

How

PART X

Tuning Oracle Applications

Tuning SQL Statements

What Does Tuning SQL Statements Mean?

What Tuning SQL statements refers to a series of steps you take to make your final SQL statements efficient during their execution. Tuning begins at the planning stage of any project or code development effort and continues through to the ongoing support of the finished, implemented project.

During the planning stages of any development effort, decisions that affect code performance must be made correctly. For example, consider how your code or application will be integrated with other applications. Items like data and file sharing need to be considered now during planning rather than during the code implementation stage. Another consideration during the planning of any project is the number of users that will use the application. What are the memory requirements of the application?

During analysis and design, tuning considerations include data modeling and program design. Again, keep performance in the front of your thoughts during these stages. During the construction of your project, optimization and specific tuning tasks should be accomplished. This is the area that this chapter focuses on: the tuning of your individual SQL statements. Chapter 38, "Tuning Applications," addresses tuning in a broader scope.

Why Tune SQL Statements?

Tuning is performed for the following reasons:

- To improve the performance of Oracle database applications
- To improve the performance of specific SQL statements
- To improve memory allocations within Oracle
- To reduce user contention and disk I/O

Tuning is also performed in hopes of reducing current costs or projected future expenses. For example, tuning your application might help you avoid buying additional computer hardware. If you reduce an application's memory requirements, you won't have to buy additional memory. Also, better performance directly relates to better throughput for your organization. This makes users more productive.

How to Tune SQL Statements

The following sections review the various techniques for tuning your SQL statements. During your tuning efforts, you will be using several of these methods either independently of each other or a combination of each. You may find that tuning is a repetitive process where you tune a little, examine the results, tune some more, examine, and so on.

Tuning New SQL Statements

When planning to write new SQL statements, consider using the following methods to optimize your code: indexes, clusters, hash clusters, and hints.

Using Indexes

Indexes improve the performance of queries that select a small portion (2 to 4 percent) of a table. When creating an index, consider these guiding points:

- Index columns that are frequently referenced in a where clause.
- Index columns that are used frequently to join tables in SQL statements.
- Select columns for indexes if the values of the rows vary greatly. Also, the number of distinct values should be fairly large. A column whose values are either Yes or No is not a good candidate for an index.

- Do not index columns where the values of the rows change frequently. Indexing here would slow down the update and insert processes.
- Do not index columns of a where clause if the where clause also references functions.
- Use indexes on columns that make up foreign keys of referential integrity constraints.
- Consider using composite indexes made up of two or more columns. Usually, if two separate columns have poor selectivity, a few distinct values can be combined to provide great selectivity.

When considering the use of composite indexes, the following points should be taken into account:

- Use a composite index on columns that are used together in where clauses.
- If several queries select the same set of columns based on specific values of one or more column values, create a composite index on these columns.
- Order the columns according to their selectivity in the create index statement. The columns with the highest selectivity should appear first, followed by the columns with the lower selectivity rates.

Avoiding Indexes

There might be times when you don't want Oracle to take advantage of indexing and would rather have Oracle use full table scans. If your statements create a possible access path that includes an indexed access path, you can arrange for the optimizer to do a full table scan through the following method:

Make the indexed access path unavailable to the optimizer. You can suppress the use of the index by concatenating a null (or +0 for numeric columns) to the index character column. This concatenation does not change the meaning of a where clause and returns the exact same result set as it would without the concatenation. An example is shown here:

```
select *
from employee
where emp_dept ||''= 'ABCDEFG';
```

If you evaluate the execution path of the preceding statement, the access path indicates a full table scan. Before the concatenation, an indexed access path was planned. Again, this explicit use of a full table scan makes sense, for example, if 75 percent of the values in the emp_dept column are the same value.

Using Clusters

Clusters, as you recall from Chapter 2, "Logical Database Storage Structures," are schema objects where tables that have common columns are physically stored together. Clusters can help the performance of your application. Look at the following guidelines when considering the use of clusters:

- Use clustered tables that are often accessed in join statements. Do not cluster the tables if the joins are infrequently used.

- Do not cluster tables if full table scans are performed on only one of the clustered tables.

- Do not cluster tables if the data in the clustered tables exceeds more than two Oracle data blocks in size.

Using Hash Clusters

Hash clustering is very similar to clustering except that the retrieval of rows for a hash cluster is according to a hash function.

A hash function is used by Oracle to generate a distribution on numeric values, called hash values, which are based on a specific cluster key value. To find a specific row in a hash cluster, Oracle applies the hash function to the row's cluster key value resulting in a hash value that corresponds to a data block in the cluster. This data block is then accessed normally by Oracle.

The following guidelines should be used when considering the use of hash clustering:

- Use hash clusters for tables that are frequently accessed by where clauses that contain equality conditions that use the same columns or combination of columns

- Use hash clusters if you can determine how much space is required to hold all the rows of a cluster key value

- Do not use hash clustering if you are running low on database storage

- Do not use hash clustering if a table is continuously growing and it is impractical for you to create a new, larger hash cluster

- Do not use hash clusters if full table scans are normal and you feel you must allocate a great deal of extra space to the hash cluster in anticipation of future table growth

- Do not use hash clusters if the hash cluster key values are frequently modified

With clustering and hash clustering, you need to weigh the benefits and drawbacks of using these tuning techniques. You should experiment with using clusters and hash clusters to see the improvements gained by your application. Finding the right use of clusters will truly improve the performance of your application.

Using Hints

In Chapter 41, "The Optimizer," the Oracle optimizer utility is discussed in detail. The optimizer is responsible for creating possible execution paths for the statement block being processed. In addition, the optimizer selects the best execution path to use. There are times that you can make a better determination of what the best execution path should be. Your knowledge of the data and how the application is used puts you in a better position than the optimizer for selecting execution paths. Most of the time, you and the optimizer will come to the same conclusion regarding the best execution path, but there will be times where your suggested path is better than Oracle's.

Hints are used to impose your execution path selection into the processing of your statement block. Hints are not database directives, but rather suggestions to the optimizer. You can use hints to specify the following:

- The optimization approach for a SQL statement
- The goal of the cost-based approach for a SQL statement
- The access path for a table
- The join order for a `join` statement
- The join operation in a `join` statement

Hints apply only locally to the block in which they appear. Oracle recognizes hints only when using the cost-based approach. If you include any hint (except the rule hint) in a statement block, the optimizer automatically uses the cost-based approach. If you specify a hint incorrectly, Oracle ignores the hint and does not return an error message. This is because the hints are placed inside the comment indicator.

The syntax for a hint is

```
SQL statement /*+ hint */ SQL statement continuation
```

or

```
SQL statement —+ hint SQL statement continuation
```

As you can see, you place hints as comments inside your SQL statement blocks. Following are the hints you can use and their descriptions:

`all_rows`	Optimize SQL for best throughput.

	`select /*+all_rows*/`
	`from employee`
	`where emp_id like '29058%';`

`and_equal`	Use index merging on a specified table.
`cluster`	Use a cluster scan on a specified table.
`cost`	Use cost-based optimizer.
`first_row`	Optimize SQL for best response times.
	This hint causes the optimizer to make these choices:

- Use an index scan, if available, over a full table scan.
- If an index scan is available, the nested-loop join is used before the sort-merge join.
- If an index scan is available by an `order by` clause, the optimizer always chooses it to avoid a sort operation.

- This hint is ignored for delete and update statements that contain any of the following clauses: group by, for update, distinct, or set operators. These statements cannot be optimized for best response time because all rows must be retrieved for these statements.

```
select /*+first_row*/ f_name, l_name,
➥emp_no
from employee
where dept_no = '23C'
```

full	Use a full table scan on a specified table.
hash	Use a hash search on a specified table.
index	Use a specified index scan on a specified table.
index_asc	Use a specified index scan, in ascending order, on a specified table.
index_desc	Use a specified index scan, in descending order, on a specified table.
ordered	Use the from clause join sequence. If you omit the ordered clause in your join statement, Oracle determines the order of the columns.
rowid	Use the rowid access method.
rule	Use rule-based optimization. This also forces the optimizer to ignore any other hints that appear in this statement block.
user_merge	Use sort-merge join techniques on a specified table.
use_nl	Use nested-loop join techniques on a specified table.

Tuning Existing SQL Statements

Tuning existing SQL statements is similar to tuning new SQL statements. The difference lies in your approach to the situation. For one thing, with existing SQL you have actual working code, so you can monitor, tune, and evaluate any improvements.

The TKPROF Utility

The TKPROF utility is used to translate the trace file to a readable format. The trace file contains the following information for each SQL statement executed:

- Parse, fetch, and execution counts
- CPU and elapsed time

- Physical and logical times
- Number of rows processed
- Misses on the library cache

To use the TKPROF utility, you must first execute your code while the SQL trace facility is enabled. The sql_trace initialization parameter is set to TRUE for the trace facility to be enabled. Once the code is completed, run the TKPROF utility. The syntax for running this utility is

```
tkprof infile outfile
```

The infile is the input file containing the statistics produced by the SQL trace facility. The output file is where TKPROF writes its output.

The following example uses the SQL trace file st_user_01.trc as the input file to the TKPROF utility. The output file is st_user_01.prf:

```
tkprof st_user_01.trc st_user01.prf
```

Sample output file:

```
count = number of times OCI procedure was executed
CPU = CPU time in seconds executing
elapsed = elapsed time in seconds executing
disk = number of physical reads on buffers from disk
query = number of buffers gotten from consistent read
current = number of buffers gotten in current mode
rows = number of rows processed by the fetch/execute call
************************************************************
select * employee where dept_no = '23C'
call    count CPU  elapsed disk query current rows
-------- ----- ---- ------- ---- ----- ------- ----
Parse   1     0.01 0.18    0    0     0       0
Execute 1     0.00 0.03    0    0     0       0
Fetch   1     0.04 0.06    0    58    2       18
Misses in library cache during parse: 1
Parsing user id: 29
```

From the results of the TKPROF utility, you can determine which SQL statements take the most time to process. Concentrate your tuning activities on these statements.

You can also include sort, print, and explain clauses in the TKPROF command line. The sort clause sorts the traced SQL statements in descending order based on the specified sort option.

The print clause lists only the specified number of SQL statements into the output file. You might want to use this to limit the amount of output to the worst-performing statements. Sometimes this file gets rather large.

The explain clause is used to direct TKPROF to issue the explain plan command. The output of the plan is displayed immediately after the TKPROF statistics are printed.

The following guidelines can help you in using the statistics generated from the TKPROF utility:

- If the number of logical I/Os is much greater than the number of rows returned, consider making an index available to the statement.
- If the number of fetches performed is equal to the number of rows retrieved, consider using the array interface.
- If the statement is parsed as often as it is executed, library cache could improve performance.
- If the number of physical I/Os is close to the number of logical I/Os, a larger database buffer cache could improve performance.

Discrete Transactions

You can improve the performance of your short, nondistributed SQL statement by using the `begin_discrete_transaction` procedure. This procedure streamlines transaction processing so short transactions can execute more quickly.

Use this discrete procedure if your transactions fall into one of these categories:

- Modifies only a few database blocks
- Seldom changes an individual database block more than once per transaction
- Does not modify data likely to be requested by long-running queries
- Does not need to see the new value of the data after modifying the data
- Does not modify tables containing any long values

Discrete transactions have the following characteristics:

- All changes made to any data is deferred until the transaction commits
- Redo information is generated but is stored in a separate location in memory
- Undo information is not generated
- The transaction cannot see its own changes
- Rows can be locked using a `select/for update` statement for the duration of the discrete transaction
- Any errors encountered during a `discrete transaction` cause the `discrete_transaction_failed` exception to be raised

The following example illustrates the use of the discrete transaction procedure:

```
declare -- beginning of a normal procedure
begin
begin_discrete_transaction; - begin the discrete procedure
exit; - end the discrete transaction
exception
when discrete_transaction_failed
then
rollback;
end; - end of exceptions
end; - end of procedure
```

Statistics from SQL*DBA

You can use the monitor facility in SQL*DBA to display the following SQL tuning statistics. The general syntax for the monitor command is:

```
monitor keyword
```

For example, to monitor the number of disk sorts, your command would look like:

```
monitor sorts(disk);
```

- `cluster key scans`—The number of full table scans or clustered tables performed by fetching rows using the cluster key
- `cluster key scan block gets`—The number of blocks read while performing full table scans or clustered tables using the cluster key
- `table fetch by rowid`—The number of logical rows fetched from a table
- `table fetch continued row`—The number of additional physical fetches required to access broken rows
- `table scan rows gotten`—The number of rows fetched during a full table scan
- `table scan blocks gotten`—The number of logical block reads during a full table scan
- `table scans (long tables)`—The number of long table scans
- `table scans (short tables)`—The number of full table scans of short tables
- `parse count`—The number of SQL statements parsed
- `parse time CPU`—The amount of CPU time spent parsing SQL statements
- `parse time elapsed`—The amount of elapsed time spent parsing SQL statements
- `sorts (disk)`—The number of disk sorts
- `sorts (rows)`—The number of rows sorted
- `sorts (memory)`—The number of in-memory sorts

Essential Summary

SQL tuning is the process of making your SQL statements more efficient. Oracle provides several methods for accomplishing this task. **What**

You want to tune your SQL statements to improve overall performance and to try to reduce future expenses related to buying additional memory or disk drives. **Why**

This chapter reviewed several methods you can use to tune your application. Normally, you use several of these methods in an iterative fashion to truly optimize your SQL statements. **How**

Tuning Applications

What Does Tuning Applications Mean?

What Tuning your application involves tuning the individual lines of code, the interfaces with the Oracle server, and the environment in which the application runs.

This chapter discusses the tuning of your application's cursors, precompiler programs, arrays, server memory allocations, server I/O contentions, and multi-threaded server contentions.

Why Tune Applications?

Why Tuning is performed with the ultimate goal of improving the performance of Oracle applications, SQL statements, and PL/SQL blocks.

Better performance equates to improved throughput for an organization. This can translate directly into dollars saved. For example, if the bottleneck in an organization is the inability to process orders quickly, their revenue is tied to orders. If these orders were processed quickly, due to some application tuning, their revenue could benefit.

How to Tune Applications

Tuning applications begins with a good application design and efficient SQL statements. Chapter 37, "Tuning SQL Statements," discusses the tuning of SQL statements. This chapter discusses the methods and considerations when tuning the application as well as the Oracle environment in which it runs.

Tuning PL/SQL

The following sections discuss specific tuning techniques for different aspects of the Oracle RDMS.

Cursors

PL/SQL supports two kinds of cursors: explicit and implicit. Explicit cursors are defined and managed by the application developer using the declare, open, fetch, and close statements. The statement is parsed when the cursor is first opened. Closing the cursor does not discard the parsed statement.

Implicit cursors are opened by PL/SQL when performing operations such as insert, update, or delete. When the operation finishes, the cursor closes automatically.

Understanding how PL/SQL uses implicit cursors is very important. Let's use an example to illustrate PL/SQL's behavior with cursors. The following simple statement has the adjoining TKPROF output file associated with it:

```
select * from employee where emp_no = '11'
```

Sample TKPROF output file:

call	count	cpu	elap	phys	cr	cur	rows
Parse	1	0	0	0	0	0	
Execute	1	0	0	1	0	2	1
Fetch	2	0	0	1	2	0	1

Notice that two fetches were executed. This is because PL/SQL issues an extra fetch to ensure that the select statement returns only one row of data. Let's perform the same statement with an explicitly declared cursor:

```
declare
emp varchar2(50);
cursor c_1 is
select * from employee
```

```
where emp_no = '11';
begin
open c_1;
fetch c_1 into emp;
close c_1;
end;
```

Sample TKPROF output file:

```
call     count   cpu   elap   phys   cr   cur rows
-------------------------------------------------
Parse    1       0     0      0      0    0
Execute  1       0     0      0      0    2    0
Fetch    1       0     0      0      1    0    1
```

Notice that this time only one fetch was executed because Oracle knew the explicit cursor would return only one row.

Calls to the Database

Even though PL/SQL is a powerful and flexible tool, there are certain activities the Oracle server can perform better. For example, you should use the Oracle server to enforce data integrity rather than the PL/SQL block. The server can enforce these constraints more efficiently than PL/SQL can.

You can also reduce the number of database calls by creating stored procedures to encapsulate activities common to several applications. Using a stored procedure requires only one network call. Using a PL/SQL block within an application can require several network transmissions. Stored procedures are stored in compiled form in the data dictionary and therefore need not be compiled each time they are called.

You should use database triggers to perform a specified action when an operation is performed on a table. This is because triggers are stored and executed on the server.

Following are some guidelines to help you determine where you should place your procedural code.

You should place your procedural code in the application in the following situations:

- You validate a value from an input field
- You are performing actions that are specific to one and only one application
- You need to customize error-handling routines

You should place your procedural code in the server in the following situations:

- The code updates several tables in the transaction
- Several applications share the procedural code
- The code is used to ensure referential integrity constraints
- The code specifies some action to occur upon an update, insert, or delete of a table

Sequences

Oracle provides a very fast and efficient sequence generator that is typically used to generate unique sequential numbers in an application. These unique numbers provide values for unique keys and other unique fields. Sequence generation also eliminates serialization.

Oracle enables you to preload a range of these sequenced numbers into the cache. Sequence numbers can be accessed more quickly in the cache than they can be read from disk. The following example creates a sequence named part_id where 50 of these sequential numbers will be kept in the cache:

```
create sequence part_id
increment by 1
cache 50;
```

Precompilers

In many client-server applications, your client application is written in a 3GL language such as C. SQL statements are likely to be embedded in this C program. A number of factors can cause poor performance with a precompiler program, including the following:

- Extensive database calls between a client program and Oracle. This is especially true if the call is going over a network.

- Inefficient SQL statements that do not take advantage of database resources such as indexes.

- Unnecessary reparsing and rebinding of embedded SQL statements.

Oracle precompiler programs can explicitly open cursors and use them as named resources throughout the execution of the program. Each application can open numerous cursors. The application should manage these cursors and close them when necessary to conserve system memory. The following precompiler options assist in this management of cursors:

- maxopencursors—This specifies the maximum number of open cursors the precompiler tries to keep cached. If there are no free cache entries available, the precompiler dynamically creates a temporary cache entry. Setting this cursor option low can potentially cause expensive dynamic allocations and deallocations of cache entries. If this is set too high, execution is fast but uses too much memory.

- hold_cursor—Specifies whether the link between the program cursor and the cursor cache should be maintained. You want to maintain this link as long as possible to make subsequent statement executions faster.

- release_cursor—Specifies whether the link between a cache entry and a context area should be maintained. These links are maintained in the program global area.

One final note on precompilers is that you should try to use PL/SQL code in the applications rather than SQL code (if possible). This forces the application to take advantage of the block nature of PL/SQL. Embedded blocks are sent over the network in their entirety to the Oracle server. This is in contrast to each individual SQL statement being sent over the network.

Arrays

Implement array processing whenever possible. Array processing can improve performance by reducing the number of calls from your application to Oracle. To pass a SQL statement to Oracle, the application must make a function call. These function calls incur overhead that can reduce performance. For example, with array processing your application can make a single call to execute a SQL statement 100 times. Without array processing, your application must call Oracle 100 times, once for each execution.

Some typical types of applications that can usually benefit from arrays include the following:

- Any batch-oriented system that processes large numbers of rows where high performance is mandated
- Any application that performs inserts and updates of many records at a time
- Client/server applications that move large volumes of data over the network
- Any SQL statement that must process more than one record

In many Oracle tools, array processing is used automatically. For example, array processing is used automatically in SQL*Plus, SQL*Forms, and SQL*Loader.

In SQL*Plus you can control the size of the array. That is the number of rows returned by a process. The default size of the array is 20. You can increase the size of the array with the set arraysize command. The following command sets the array size to 200:

```
set arraysize 200
```

Use array interfaces to achieve larger performance gains over row-at-a-time processing when an embedded SQL application stores and manipulates more than one row of information. Significant performance improvement can be gained from the reduction in messaging overhead that you incurred in the processing of every embedded SQL statement.

Network speed is, in many cases, the prime determinant of application performance. Therefore, use array interfaces whenever possible. As the number of array elements increases, array interface efficiency increases.

Tuning Memory Allocation

So far in this chapter, you have seen that many items can adversely affect the memory of the system. Proper allocation of memory resources can greatly improve overall server performance. Specifically, the following enhancements occur when memory is managed appropriately:

- Cache performance is improved
- Parsing of SQL and PL/SQL blocks is reduced
- Paging and swapping is reduced

Tuning memory allocation involves the following steps:

1. Tune the operating system. This involves reducing the paging and swapping that occurs, fitting the system global area into main memory rather than virtual or expanded memory, and allocating enough memory for users and their processes.

2. Tune private SQL and PL/SQL areas. Identify unnecessary parse calls or at least reduce the number if you can. The TKPROF utility can help you identify the number of parse calls.

3. Tune the shared pool. Start off by evaluating the number of misses listed in the v$librarycache table. Misses indicate the number of library cache misses on execution steps. The ratio of misses to the number of executed steps should be lower than 1 percent. If it is higher, try to get the number of misses down by adding more memory to the library cache and by writing identical SQL statements.

   The following two SQL statements do not share the same statement in the shared pool (notice the capital letter E in the second example):

   ```
   select * from emp;

   select * from Emp;
   ```

   Try to be consistent in your writing of SQL statements so that they can use the same shared pool. The following statements are parsed only once and hence share a spot in the pool:

   ```
   select * from emp;

   select * from emp;
   ```

4. Tune the buffer cache. To determine your buffer cache hit ratio, perform a select on the v$sysstat table to obtain the buffer's database block gets, the consistent gets, and the number of physical reads. The database block and consistent gets represent the number of requests for data. Perform the following to get the buffer hit ratio:

   ```
   hit ratio = 1-(physical reads/(database block gets + consistent gets))
   ```

   If this ratio is lower than 75 percent, you are getting too many misses. You will want to increase the number of buffers in your cache to improve performance.

Tuning I/O

Application performance is always hindered while memory is waiting on a disk read or write operation. Tuning I/O can help performance. Three general steps should be taken to reduce I/O overhead:

1. Reduce the disk contention

2. Allocate appropriate space for data blocks

3. Avoid dynamic space allocations

The first step in reducing disk contention is to learn your current disk I/O levels. The v$datafile table provides information on physical reads and writes for that particular database file. If you are running over 40 accesses (reads + writes) per second, that disk is over-utilized, and data contention is very likely. Simply move one or two of the data files to a less-used disk drive.

Data block size determination is greatly affected by the frequency of data block chaining and migrating that occurs. Chaining is the act of splitting a row of data into two pieces and physically storing them separately. Migrating is when Oracle moves a row of data from one block to another block, looking for a block with enough space to store it. If one cannot be found, chaining occurs.

If a database object, such as a table, grows larger than the size of the space allocated for it, Oracle dynamically allocates an additional segment to the object. This dynamic space allocation reduces memory and slows server performance. To avoid this dynamic allocation, allocate enough space when the object is created, or monitor the objects and manually make adjustments to the space as needed.

Tuning Contention

Contention occurs when multiple processes try to access the same resource simultaneously. The following areas tend to cause the most significant levels of contention:

- Rollback segments
- MTS servers

Rollback Segment Contention

Rollback segments have a problem with contention if the number of access waits is greater than 1 percent of the total number of database accesses. The following statement displays the number of waits for the database:

```
select class, count
from v$waitstat;
```

Sample output:

```
CLASS COUNT
---------------------------
system undo header 5392
system undo block 923
undo header 3012
undo block 911
```

`system undo header` represents the number of access waits for a buffer containing the header block of the system rollback segment.

`system undo block` represents the number of access waits for the buffer containing blocks other than header blocks of the system rollback segment.

`undo header` represents the number of access waits for the buffer containing header blocks of rollback segments other than the system rollback segment.

`undo block` represents the number of access waits for buffers containing blocks other than header blocks, or rollback segments other than the system rollback segment.

There is a contention problem if the number of waits in any class is greater than 1 percent of the total number of accesses. The total number of accesses can be obtained by summing the value column in the v$sysstat table. If the value is greater than 1 percent, you should create additional rollback segments.

MTS Server Contention

If a multi-threaded server dispatcher is busy more than 50 percent of the time, a new dispatcher should be added. Refer to Chapter 39, "MTSs, Locks, and Links," for additional information on MTS dispatchers. To determine the usage rate of a dispatcher, query the v$dispatcher table. This query returns the total busy rate for each protocol. For example:

```
select network,busy
from v$dispatcher;
```

Sample output:

```
NETWORK BUSY
- - - - - - - - - - - - - - -
decnet .019233
tcpip .007261
```

Contention for shared server processes can cause additional wait times during program execution. First you need to determine the average wait time to acquire a shared server process. The following command generates this number:

```
select (wait/totalq) "Average Wait Time"
from v$queue
where type = 'COMMON';
```

Sample output:

```
AVERAGE WAIT TIME
- - - - - - - - - - - - - - -
.08722
```

In the previous statement, wait represents the total waiting time for all requests that have ever been in the MTS queue. totalq represents the total number of requests that have ever been in the queue. The output of .08722 means that the average waiting time for a shared process server is .087 seconds.

Now determine the number of shared servers. The following statement supplies this number:

```
select count(*) "NBR OF SHARED SERVERS"
from v$shared-servers
where status !='QUIT';
```

Sample output:

```
NBR OF SHARED SERVERS
- - - - - - - - - - - - - - - - - - -
  18
```

The most important aspect of shared servers is knowing the maximum number of shared servers allowed by the server. By default it is 20. This is defined in the mts_max_server initialization parameter.

Because Oracle automatically adds new shared servers as they are needed, you don't gain much by explicitly adding new servers. But you can watch to see if you have maxed out the number of servers allowed. If so, you can modify the shared server initialization parameter to a bigger number.

Essential Summary

This chapter reviewed the concepts necessary to fine-tune your PL/SQL code to include cursors, array, and precompiler programs. The Oracle environment can also be tuned to reduce various types of contentions.

What

You learned that there are many benefits to tuning the Oracle application, including a performance improvement for all users.

Why

You tune various aspects of the Oracle application. For example, you can tune PL/SQL, server memory allocations and I/O levels, and precompiler programs. Each is tuned in its own unique way.

How

MTSs, Locks, and Links

What Are MTSs, Locks, and Links?

What MTSs, locks, and links are a variety of topics important to understand how to become more successful in using the Oracle database.

MTS stands for *Multi-Threaded Server*. It is Oracle's way of using its own resources more effectively and efficiently to improve database performance.

Locks are another Oracle mechanism that ensures data integrity, data concurrency, and data consistency.

Links provide a means to connect locally or remotely to another database. This is a vital mechanism for today's distributed databases.

Why Use MTSs, Locks, and Links?

Why

A multi-threaded server enables many user processes to share a smaller number of server processes, minimizing the number of server processes and maximizing the utilization of available system resources.

The multi-user database uses a form of data locking to solve problems associated with data concurrency, integrity, and consistency.

Database links are used to facilitate connections between the individual databases of a distributed database. These links define the path from one database to another database.

How to Use the Multi-Threaded Server (MTS)

How

The multi-threaded server enables many user processes to share a small number of server processes. Without the MTS configuration, each user process would require its own server process. This dedicated server process would remain active for the duration of the server connection. This tends to be inefficient because many of these server processes are idle or under-utilized. With the MTS server, many user processes connect to a dispatcher process. This dispatcher routes client requests to the next available shared server process. This sharing of server processes reduces system overhead; therefore, the number of user processes supported is increased.

Figure 39.1 illustrates a comparison of an MTS configured server and a non-MTS configured server.

Figure 39.1.
Comparison of MTS and non-MTS configured servers.

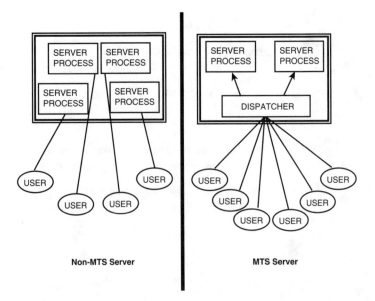

MTS Components

To use shared server processes, a user process must connect to the Oracle server through SQL*Net, even if the user process is on the same machine as the Oracle instance. Also, if a user process requests a dedicated server process, the server creates an individual dedicated server process.

In an MTS environment, shared server processes and dedicated server processes provide the same service except that the shared server process is not associated with any single user process. The shared server process serves any number of different user processes.

Oracle dynamically sets the number of shared server processes based on the number of user requests that are waiting for a shared server process. The maximum number of shared server processes is defined in the mts_max_server initialization parameter.

The dispatcher is the traffic cop of the MTS server. The dispatcher receives requests for server processes from user processes. The dispatcher processes the user requests on a first-in-first-out basis. Once the dispatcher completes the requested database action (for example, updating a table), it sends a response back to the user process.

In a multi-threaded server configuration, you cannot perform the following actions while attached to a dispatcher process:

- Starting or shutting down an instance
- Performing media recovery

MTS Setup

Following are the general steps necessary to set up and start an MTS configured server. Please refer to your Server Administrator's manual for more complete information on the MTS server.

1. Set initialization parameters.
2. Start the instance.
3. Allocate additional space for shared servers.
4. Establish a listener address. This is the port the network connects into.
5. Establish names for the dispatchers.
6. Establish the maximum number of dispatchers and shared server processes by defining their respective initialization parameters.
7. Establish the minimum number of dispatchers and shared server processes with the alter system command.

The SQL*DBA Configure Multi-Threaded Dispatcher dialog box (shown in Figure 39.2) establishes the number of dispatchers and the protocol used in the MTS configuration.

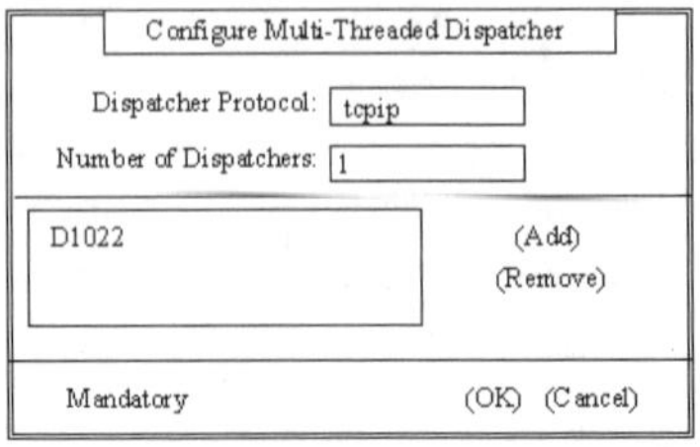

Figure 39.2.
SQL*DBA MTS
dispatcher configuration.

```
┌─────────────────────────────────────────────┐
│      Configure Multi-Threaded Dispatcher     │
├─────────────────────────────────────────────┤
│  Dispatcher Protocol: [ tcpip        ]        │
│  Number of Dispatchers: [ 1 ]                 │
│  ┌───────────────────────┐    (Add)          │
│  │ D1022                 │    (Remove)        │
│  │                       │                    │
│  └───────────────────────┘                    │
├─────────────────────────────────────────────┤
│    Mandatory              (OK)  (Cancel)      │
└─────────────────────────────────────────────┘
```

How to Use Locks

Locks are mechanisms used to prevent destructive interaction between users accessing the same resource. For example, you don't want one process attempting a table insert while a different process is simultaneously attempting to drop the same table. Databases with multiple users use some form of locks to solve the problems associated with data concurrency, integrity, and consistency.

Oracle locking is completely automatic and requires no user action. Implicit locks occur for all SQL statements so that the database user never needs to explicitly administer locks. Oracle's default locking mechanisms lock data at the lowest level of restrictiveness to guarantee data integrity yet allow the highest degree of data concurrency.

Levels of Locks

In general, two levels of locks can be used in a multi-user database:

- Exclusive locks—This lock prohibits the sharing of the associated resource. The first transaction that acquires the lock on a resource is the only transaction that can alter the resource until the exclusive lock is released.

- Share locks—This lock enables the associated resource to be shared (depending on the operations involved). Several transactions can acquire share locks on the same resource. This type of lock provides a higher degree of data concurrency than exclusive locks.

On occasion, a deadlock occurs when two or more users try to acquire an object that is already exclusively locked. This deadlock typically happens when the different users are waiting for a lock to be released. An Oracle error (ORA-00060) is generated for deadlocks.

One of the main reasons that locks are used is to increase the amount of data concurrency, as seen here:

- Readers of data do not wait for writers of the same data blocks

- Writers of data do not wait for readers of the same data blocks

- Writers wait for other writers only if they attempt to update the same rows at the same time

All locks acquired by a transaction are held intact for the duration of that transaction. All locks established in a transaction are released when the transaction is either committed or rolled back.

Lock Types

Oracle locks fall into one of the following types of locks:

- Data locks
- Dictionary locks
- Internal locks
- Distributed locks
- Parallel cache locks
- Manual locks

The following sections discuss each of the types of locks.

Data Locks

The data lock, sometimes known as the DML lock, is used to protect table data and ensure data integrity. Data locks prevent destructive interference by multiple users. Data locks can acquire locks at two different levels: rows and tables.

A row lock is acquired on an individual row on behalf of a transaction when the row is modified by any of the following commands: insert, update, delete, or select with the for update clause.

A row is always locked exclusively so that other users cannot modify the row until the holding transaction rolls back or commits. These locks are automatically acquired by Oracle. When a row lock is acquired, a corresponding table lock is issued to protect the table against destructive DDL commands.

A table lock is acquired when a table is modified by any of the following DML statements: insert, update, delete, or select with the for update clause.

Row locks can be held in the following modes:

- Row share—This mode indicates that a transaction is holding a lock and intends to update the table. This mode offers the highest degree of concurrency for a table.
- Row exclusive—This indicates that the transaction holding the lock has completed updates.
- Share table—This lock is automatically acquired by the lock table command. This lock permits queries, locks specific rows with the select/for update command, or executes the lock table/in share command.
- Share row exclusive—This lock is the same as the share table except that only one transaction can acquire the lock.

- Exclusive table—This is the most restrictive of all locks. Only one transaction can acquire the full table lock at a time.

Dictionary Locks

Dictionary locks, or data definition (DDL) locks, protect the schema objects from change during a transaction. This lock is automatically acquired by Oracle when a DDL statement requires it.

Exclusive DDL locks provide exclusive locks for a resource to prevent destructive actions by another DDL statement. The shared DDL lock allows data concurrency for similar DDL statements.

A SQL statement that is in the shared pool holds a parsed lock for each object referenced by the SQL statement. This parsed lock is acquired so that the associated shared SQL area can be invalidated if a referenced object is altered or dropped.

Internal Locks

Internal locks protect the internal components of the database and memory. These components are inaccessible by end users.

Dictionary cache locks are created when a data dictionary entry or modification is being made. These locks guarantee that statements being parsed do not see inconsistent object definitions.

File and log management locks protect a variety of files. For example, one lock protects and coordinates the use and archive of the redo log. Another lock protects the control file so that only one process can change the file at a time.

Distributed Locks

Distributed locks are created to ensure that data and other resources remain consistent across multiple instances. These locks are created automatically by Oracle and held by the instance, not the transaction.

Parallel Cache Locks

The parallel cache lock is a distributed lock that protects one or more data blocks in the buffer area.

Manual Locks

Manual locks are permitted in the Oracle server. Although most locks are created automatically, you can override these Oracle locks. Manual locks are created at the transaction and the system levels. The following statements enable you to override Oracle's default locking mechanism:

- `lock table`

- select...for update
- set transaction...for read only

System-level lock overrides are created by altering the initialization parameter's serialization and row locking.

Caution should be used when overriding the default locking mechanism. You must ensure that data concurrency is acceptable, data integrity is guaranteed, and deadlocks are handled appropriately, or they are not possible.

Monitoring Locks

SQL*DBA provides a lock monitor to view the currently established locks. (See Figure 39.3.) The combination of Session ID and Serial Number uniquely identifies the individual user session. The values for Mode Held and Mode Requested have the following meanings:

1	null
2	row share, share update
3	row exclusive
4	share
5	share row exclusive
6	exclusive

Figure 39.3.
*The SQL*DBA Lock Monitor dialog box.*

Oracle Lock Monitor

Username Filter:

Username	Session ID	Serial Number	Lock Type	Resource ID 1	Resource ID 2	Mode Held	Mode Requested

(Restart)   (Hide)   (Quit)

You need the alter system privilege to establish these minimum, maximum, and initial values.

How to Use Links

A database link defines the path from one database to another database. These links are effectively transparent to users of a distributed database. The following statement creates a database link in the local database:

```
create public database link node_01.corp.dist;
```

Once a link is created, users can access data in the database by using the global object names. For example, to query tables in the schema user_03 on the remote database, issue the following:

```
select * from user_03.parts@node_01.corp.dist;
```

When a SQL statement includes a reference to a global object name, Oracle attempts to locate a database link that matches the database name specified in the global object name. The global object name is followed by the at sign (@). If a local database link is found, a connection is attempted. If the link is not found locally, no connection is established and the SQL statement is not executed.

There are three types of database links:

- Private—This link is created for a specific user. This link can be used only by the designated user.
- Public—This link is created for the special user group named Public. All users of the database have access to the link.
- Network—This link is created and managed by a network domain service. A network database link can be used when any user of any database in the network specifies a global object name in a SQL statement.

If a database link is no longer required, you can remove it from the database with the drop database link command. The following is an example of a link being dropped:

```
drop database link user_03.parts@node_01.corp.dist;
```

Essential Summary

In this chapter, you learned about several useful Oracle mechanisms. The MTS is an internal tool that controls the processing of user processes. Locks are automatically enabled on many of the DML and DDL statements. Finally, database links are road maps or paths between databases.

You also learned in this chapter that the MTS is provided to improve server performance; locks are in place to protect data integrity and improve concurrency; and links enable distributed database connections.

How

The MTS is an internal Oracle facility that you can configure to your requirements. Links are established to satisfy a need for individuals to connect across a distributed database. Locks are implicitly enabled by Oracle.

Distributed Databases and Processes

What Are Distributed Databases and Processes?

What Distributed databases and processes come in many different flavors and styles. Generally speaking, a distributed database is a collection of databases that appears to the end user as a single database. Each individual database is its own entity with its own database management system. The data on several different computers can be accessed simultaneously and modified using a network.

Why Use Distributed Databases and Processes?

Why Each node, or database, of a distributed database is administered separately and independently of the others, as though each database was a non-networked database. Each database is maintained independently of the other databases. Each database has its own security system and backup/recovery plan and procedures. Although the databases work together much of the time, they are distinct and separate repositories of data. Some of the reasons for using distributed databases are as follows:

- The nodes of the distributed system can mirror the organization of the company. For example, an international insurance company that has offices in New York and London operates with a distributed architecture. Each of the two sites typically processes their own claims, new policies, and modifications to existing policies. This is all done locally. At a predefined time interval, usually nightly or weekly, one office transmits summary data to the parent office.
- Having local control and administrative responsibilities makes the local domain more manageable. It would be a rather large task to be a database administrator for an internationally distributed architecture.
- Having independence provides a level of insurance against computer failures at other nodes. You are protected from each other's failures.

How to Use Distributed Databases and Processes

How This chapter discusses the definitions of the various pieces of the distributed database and how they are used.

Distributed Architecture

A distributed architecture, as shown in Figure 40.1, consists of multiple databases that physically reside on different computers and applications that access data on each of these computers via their local client workstation.

Following are some terms and concepts used when discussing a distributed architecture:

client—A client is an application that requests information from the server. The client can be another mainframe system or a PC.

distributed query—Retrieves information from more than one node.

distributed transaction—A transaction that includes one or more statements that update data on two or more distinct nodes of a distributed database.

distributed update—Modifies data on two or more nodes.

network—The network is the hardware and software that tie each component of the distributed database together.

node—A node represents each computer in the network. A node can be a client, server, or both.

remote query—This is a query that selects information from one or more remote tables that reside on the same remote node.

remote transaction—A transaction that contains one or more remote statements, all of which reference one remote node.

remote update—An update that modifies data in one or more tables that all reside on the same remote node.

schema object—A schema object, like a table, is accessible from all nodes that form a distributed database. Therefore, the distributed database must provide a naming scheme so that objects throughout can be uniquely identified and referenced.

server—A server is the software managing a database. For example, you might have an Oracle server that is a database managed by the Oracle software.

Figure 40.1.
A distributed architec-ture map.

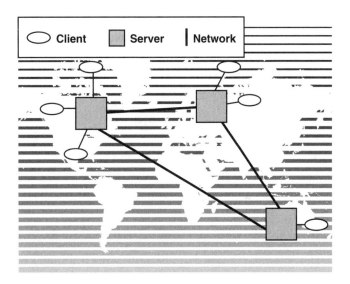

Distributed Databases

Oracle's distributed database architecture suggests that all databases that are members of the architecture be integrated as a single logical distributed database. Although each database is autonomous regarding maintenance and administration, they gain the benefit of being able to access and share data with the other member databases.

The following sections discuss issues and topics regarding the distributed database.

Distributed Database Administrators

Each database that is a member of a distributed database must have its own database administrator. This person is responsible for local issues such as security. The administrator is also responsible for coordinating with the other distributed database administrators on issues relating to all database members. These issues might include database designs and backup and recovery.

Network and Communications

The database administrator and network administrator must guarantee that networks connect all the machines referenced in distributed transactions. This includes installing and administering SQL*Net.

SQL*Net is Oracle's network interface that enables Oracle tools running on a network to communicate with each other. Through SQL*Net, applications can access, modify, and store data on any of the nodes of a distributed network.

Global Names

In a distributed database architecture, all object names at each of the distributed sites must be globally unique. This is necessary so that you can access any object directly. A database's global database name is composed of two parts: name component and network domain component.

When creating a new database in a distributed database, choose a database name that is unique among the network of databases. Consider the following points when naming a database:

- The name component of a global database reflects the contents of the database. For example, if the database contains personnel information, you might want to name it employee or personnel.

- The name component should not imply a location. This is a good practice to ensure location transparency.

- You should have some level of administrative control over the network domain that contains the database.

- Put related databases in the same network domain. This improves organization within network domains.

- The network domain name should follow standard Internet conventions.

Specify the new database's name in the db_name and the db_domain parameters before you actually create the database. The db_name parameter determines the name component of a database global object name and the local database object name. The db_domain parameter indicates the location of the database within the network.

A SQL statement can access a remote object by referencing its global object name. To resolve the name in a distributed environment, Oracle searches for database links that match the specified database. Then Oracle searches for the specified object in the remote database.

When searching the database links to find a reference to the global name, Oracle searches the private database links first, then the public database links, and finally the network database links, until the match is found.

If a match on the global name is not found, Oracle returns an error, and the SQL statement cannot execute.

Transparency

The distributed database system must be designed in such a manner that physical locations of a distributed database are transparent to the end users, developers, and administrators. Location transparency exists if a user can refer to the same table in the same way regardless of the node to which the user connects.

Location transparency provides the following benefits:

- Accessing remote data is simplified because the users do not need to know the location of the objects
- Objects can be moved around without any impact on developers and users

Location transparency is not automatic. It can be provided by using several different methods, including the following:

- A locally defined view can be created to mask the remote nature of the tables in its definition
- A local synonym can hide the database link used to access a remote table or view
- Although users can call a procedure, remote calls can be made internally to the procedure without end users knowing it

Database Links

A database link is created to facilitate connections to remote databases when a global name is used. This link defines the path to the remote database.

The database administrator is responsible for creating and maintaining public and network database links. A public database link is defined so that the following two items are true:

- All users of the local database can access data in remote databases of the system, as long as they have the necessary authorizations in the remote databases
- Users who create matching private database links do not have to be concerned with specifying complicated database strings

Data Location

The application developers and the database administrators must work together to decide the best location for the data. Following is a list of issues that must be considered when deciding data location:

- The amount of data used by each node
- The performance and integrity of the network
- The speed of the nodes and the capacity of their disks
- The number of transactions at each location
- The magnitude of impact if the network fails

Failure and the Distributed Database

Oracle has built safeguards into the distributed database architecture to protect against network or hardware failures. If a network or system fails during a commit of a distributed transaction, the transaction is globally resolved by Oracle when the network or system is restored. Globally resolved refers to the rolling back or committing of the transaction at all nodes of the distributed network.

Oracle has an internal background process, named reco, that is responsible for recovering pending or in-doubt distributed transactions. These are transactions that are not committed or rolled back when a network or system failure occurs. When the failure is resolved, the reco process of the involved database servers automatically resolves the outcome of any pending distributed transaction.

Distributed Database Limits

In a distributed database, you can establish several constraints to help performance, including the following:

- You should limit the number of distributed transactions per node. The parameter distributed_transactions controls the number of possible distributed transactions in which a given instance can concurrently participate. This value should be monitored to ensure all distributed transactions are being processed and not turned down due to a low parameter value. Also, if all the nodes have a value that is too high, an overload of the network could occur, which could bring about a network failure.

- Establish a commit point strength for each instance. This is necessary to ensure that the most critical server can be "non-blocking" in the event of a failure during a two-phase commit. This commit point strength should relate to the estimated number of collisions that can result from data locking by in-doubt transactions. To establish the proper strength, all database administrators that have membership in the distributed architecture need to communicate with each other and mutually come to an agreed-upon value.

Two-Phase Commits

Oracle automatically watches over the global database and controls the global commits and rollbacks of the distributed transaction. The two-phase commit is Oracle's way of controlling and managing distributed commits and rollbacks. The two-phase commit is completely transparent to the user community, and no programming is required by an application developer.

Commits and rollbacks over a distributed database must be coordinated through the network so that all members of the global database either all commit or rollback the distributed transaction. You don't want one node to commit a portion of a transaction and another node to roll back their part of the same transaction. This simultaneous commit or rollback must even be coordinated when a network failure occurs. The two-phase commit mechanism guarantees that all nodes in the global database work together in unison to commit or roll back the transaction, thus maintaining data integrity.

The two-phase commit is used only for DML statements or a remote procedure call that references a remote object using its global object name. If the DML statement does not perform any updates, Oracle recognizes the read-only status of the transaction and does not apply the use of the two-phase commit. All implicit DML statements performed by integrity constraints, remote procedure calls, and triggers are protected by the two-phase commit.

The two-phase commit has, as its name implies, two phases to its operation. These phases are as follows:

- Prepare phase
- Commit phase

The prepare phase consists of the following steps:

1. The transaction issues a `commit` command.
2. The local database asks all nodes in the global database that are referenced in the transaction to prepare to commit. No commit is performed at this time. The reference nodes record enough information so that they can either commit or roll back the transaction. Once the referenced nodes record their information, they send a message back to the host node with one of the following three messages:
   - Prepared—The node has been successfully prepared.
   - Read-only—Preparation is not necessary because the transaction is read-only on the referenced node.
   - Abort—The node cannot successfully prepare.

   If an abort message is issued by any of the nodes participating in the distributed transaction, the nodes release the resources currently held by the transaction and roll back the local portion of the transaction.

The commit phase begins when all nodes referenced by the transaction are prepared. Once prepared, the `commit` command is issued to all participating nodes, and the transaction is committed.

Distributed Processes

A distributed process is the use of more than one processor to divide the processing for an individual task. A good example of this is the client-server configuration. The client can initiate the process and perform some preprocessing activities such as data formatting and then pass the task to the server for final processing.

Many benefits are gained by using distributed processes, especially with a client-server configuration. The following points highlight some of these benefits:

- Data processing is the responsibility of the server system. Clients do not have to worry about data processing. This enables the client application to capitalize on the power of the client and use this power for GUI interfaces.
- Client applications can be designed without having to worry about data locations. If a database were to move, usually no client code change is required to keep working.
- The application can take advantage of Oracle's multitasking and shared-memory facilities.
- Low-cost networks can be utilized to connect the client to the server.

Distributed Applications

The following sections review several topics that must be taken into consideration when developing a distributed application.

Sequences

A remote sequence can be referenced if both the following items are true:

- All sequences, updated tables, select for update tables, long columns, and locked tables referenced in the statement are located in the same node
- At least one referenced table is at the same node as the sequence

For example, the following statement is permitted because it satisfies the preceding prerequisites:

```
insert into mst_parts@inventory_01
select sq_1.nextal@inventory_01, part_id, part_name, part_price
from routings@inventory_01;
```

Referential Integrity

Oracle does not allow referential integrity to be declared across nodes of a distributed database. You cannot have a referential integrity constraint on one table specifying a foreign key that references a primary or unique key on a remote table. However, parent/child relationships are permitted across distributed databases. This relationship can be maintained only through the use of triggers.

Distributed Queries

You can use a trigger or stored procedure to create a distributed query. On the local node, Oracle decomposes the query into corresponding remote queries sent to the remote node for execution. The remote node processes the query and responds to the local database with the query results. The local node then performs the necessary post process and returns a response to the initiating application.

If an error occurs during this remote processing, Oracle returns an error message and the subsequent statements return error messages until a rollback is completed.

Snapshots

Oracle permits the replication of a master table on other nodes by an unlimited number of snapshots. A snapshot is a static picture of the table that is read-only. Refer to Chapter 9, "Snapshots," for additional information on snapshots. Snapshots are ideal for tables that change values infrequently but are accessed heavily from remote nodes. Snapshots also enable data to continue to be available to users at other nodes, even if the master table becomes unavailable.

One of the main reasons an application should take advantage of a snapshot is to reduce the load on the network. Also, response time improves because you reference the snapshot locally.

In a distributed database, Oracle performs the following actions when creating a snapshot:

- On the snapshot node, a base table is created to store the rows as defined by the snapshot's query.
- On the snapshot node, a read-only view is created on this base table.
- Locally, Oracle creates a view on the remote master table. This view is used to refresh the snapshot.

Essential Summary

A distributed database is a database that logically appears to be a single database but is physically composed of several independent components. These components include remote standalone databases, remote and local servers, and clients. A distributed database is one that is tied together by its network. **What**

Distributed databases and processes offer today's user flexibility and security that is not available with a single database. For example, the distributed database offers data security in situations where the host node fails. In this scenario, your local database continues to function normally and is unaffected by the failure of the host node. **Why**

Establishing a distributed database starts with planning. Defining the participants of the global database is important, as well as understanding how each member interacts with the database. **How**

The Optimizer

What Is the Optimizer?

What The optimizer is the portion of the Oracle server that determines the most efficient way to execute any Data Manipulation Language statement. The optimizer considers several factors to make a choice between multiple alternatives. This choice is usually the best or most efficient of all the options. However, the application developer knows more about the applications data than the optimizer does. Therefore, sometimes the application developer is able to make a better execution plan than the optimizer.

The optimizer uses two different techniques to formulate the most efficient path to execute the statements. These options are the rule-based approach and the cost-based approach.

Why Use the Optimizer?

Why For every SQL statement, the Oracle optimizer generates an execution plan, which is a series of steps that Oracle takes to execute the statement. Because you know more about the application data than the optimizer does, you can suggest to Oracle the way to optimize a SQL statement. These suggestions, called hints, let you force the optimizer to choose your execution plan.

Hints are not directives; they merely impose your execution desires on the optimizer. Some hints limit the scope of information used to optimize a SQL statement, whereas others suggest overall strategies. You can use hints to specify the following:

- Access path for each referenced table
- Join order for a join
- Method used to join tables
- Goal of the cost-based approach for a SQL statement
- Optimization approach for a SQL statement

Additional information on hints is included in Chapter 37, "Tuning SQL Statements."

How to Use the Optimizer

This chapter reviews the various approaches Oracle can take to optimize the execution of statements.

The Execution Plan

The execution plan is created by Oracle and defines the steps Oracle takes to process statements. Each step of the execution plan returns data that is either used by another step or returned to the issuing statement.

You can examine the execution plan of a statement by using the `explain plan` command. This command creates the execution plan in a table that can be examined. The following is an example of the output from the `explain plan` command:

```
OPERATION OPTION OBJECT_NAME
---------------------------------------------
select statement
table access by rowid dept
index range scan dpt_indx
```

The following section describes the explain plan process in more detail.

explain plan

The first step in using the `explain plan` command is to create a table to hold the output from the command. You can either use the Oracle `utxplan.sql` script to create the table in your schema or manually create the table.

Once the output table is created, you can execute the `explain plan` command. Let's perform an `explain plan` command on the following statement:

```
select part_name, part_nbr, part_id, part_cost
from mst_part, inventory
```

```
where mst_part.part_nbr = inventory.part_nbr
and not exists
(select * from obsolete_parts
where part_code > min_cost);
```

To perform an evaluation of the execution plan that the Oracle optimizer creates, use the explain plan command as shown in the following example:

```
explain plan
set statement_id = 'part_cost'
select part_name, part_nbr, part_id, part_cost
from mst_part, inventory
where mst_part.part_nbr = inventory.part_nbr
and not exists
(select * from obs_parts
where part_code > min_cost);
```

Once the preceding statement is executed, you can evaluate the execution plan output or results that Oracle has created by evaluating the output table shown in the following statement:

```
OPERATION OPTIONS OBJ_NAME ID PARENT_ID POS.
- - - - - - - - - - - - - - - - - - - - - - - - - - - - - - - - - - - - - - - - - - - - -
SELECT STMT 0 5
FILTER 1 0 0
NESTED LOOP 2 1 1
TABLE ACCESS FULL MST_PART 3 2 1
TABLE ACCESS FULL INVENTORY 4 2 2
TABLE ACCESS FULL OBS_PARTS 5 1 3
```

In this example, the optimizer performs three full table scans to generate the results set. You want to design your code to maximize efficiency according to the concepts presented in the remainder of this chapter. One example of improving efficiency is to minimize full table scans on tables with many rows.

Two Approaches to Optimization

Oracle chooses one of the following optimization approaches when creating an execution plan:

■ Rule-based—Oracle chooses an execution plan based on the access paths available and assigns a rank to these paths. Oracle always chooses the path with the lower rank over one with a higher rank. See the section titled "Access Path Selection" later in this chapter for a further explanation of the ranking of paths.

■ Cost-based—Oracle considers available access paths and determines which execution plan is most efficient based on statistics in the data dictionary for the tables accessed by the statements and their associated clusters and indexes. Cost-based optimization generally takes these three steps:

1. Several alternative execution plans are generated based on available paths and hints.

2. The optimizer estimates the cost of each execution plan.

3. The optimizer selects the execution plan with the smallest cost.

SQL Optimization

The following sections explain how Oracle optimizes SQL statements.

Evaluation of Expressions and Conditions

Expressions and conditions are the first items evaluated by the optimizer. Syntactic constructs are translated into equivalent constructs to boost performance. In the following example, the first condition would be translated into the second condition by the optimizer:

```
dozens = 12000/12
dozens = 1000
```

When designing conditions, constants should be compared to columns whenever possible, rather than having conditions with expressions compared to columns, such as in this example:

```
price > cost*1.25;
```

The following example illustrates some of the other conversions that the optimizer performs on conditions and expressions:

```
month in ('JAN','MAR','MAY')
is converted to:
month = 'JAN' or month = 'MAR' or month = 'MAY'
part_nbr > (:new_part, :old_part)
is converted to:
part_nbr > any (:new_part, :old_part);
```

Statement Transformation

The optimizer often transforms one statement into a different statement that achieves the same goal. The following transformations are made by the optimizer to boost performance:

- Queries containing OR are transformed into statements containing union all unless one of the conditions requires a full table scan. A full table scan is indicative of a column without an index.
- Complex statements are transformed into join statements.

Complex statements are transformed into equivalent join statements when possible. For example, the following complex statement

```
select chemical_name
from master_chemical
where chemical_id in
(select chemical_id from chemical_archive)
```

is transformed by the optimizer into this:

```
select chemical_name
from master_chemical
where master_chemical.chemical_id =
chemical_archive.chemical_id;
```

View Merging

When optimizing statements that contain views, the optimizer chooses one of the following:

- Transform the statement into an equivalent statement
- Issue the view query and then process the results with the original statements as though it were a table

For example, consider the following view and view query:

```
create view parts
as select part_nbr, part_name
from mst_parts
where mfg_pt = '45J';
select part_name
from parts
where part_nbr like '95-%';
```

The Oracle optimizer transforms the view query into this:

```
select part_name
from mst_parts
where part_nbr like '95-%'
and mfg_pt = '45J';
```

Optimization Approach Decisions

When selecting an optimization approach, the optimizer considers the following:

- Value of the `optimizer_mode` initialization parameter
- The `optimizer_goal` parameter on the `alter session` command
- Statistics in the data dictionary
- Hints in the statement

The `optimizer_mode` parameter can have one of the following values:

- `cost`—This parameter value forces the optimizer to choose either the cost-based or the rule-based approach as the most efficient approach. If the data dictionary contains statistics for one of the columns in the table, the optimizer selects the cost-based approach. If there are no statistics in the data dictionary, the rule-based approach is selected.
- `rule`—This forces the optimizer to use the rule-based parameter.

The `optimization_goal` parameter can equate to one of the following:

- `choose`—This forces the optimizer to select between cost-based and rule-based approaches
- `all_rows`—This forces the cost-based approach with the goal being throughput
- `first_row`—This forces the cost-based approach with the best response time
- `rule`—This forces the optimizer to select the rule-based approach

Access Path Selection

One of the most important tasks the optimizer does happens during the creation of the execution plan. The optimizer must decide on the best approach to retrieve data from the database.

Following are the various methods to access data and tables:

- Full table scan—Every row in the table is read to determine whether it satisfies the statement
- Table access by rowid—Locating a row by its rowid is the fastest way Oracle can retrieve data
- Cluster scans—The rows with the same cluster key are retrieved
- Hash scans—All the rows with the same hash value are retrieved
- Indexed scans—Data is retrieved from an index based on the value of one or more columns of the index

The optimizer ranks each access path according to the following information. The path with the lowest value is selected as the preferred access path. The numeric values in the following list represent the rank of each path:

1	Single row by rowid
2	Single row by cluster join
3	Single row by hash cluster key by unique name or primary key
4	Single row by unique name or primary key
5	Cluster join
6	Hash cluster key
7	Indexed cluster key
8	Composite index
9	Single column index
10	Bounded range search on indexed columns
11	Unbounded range search on indexed columns
12	Sort-merge join
13	Max and min of indexed columns
14	Order by on indexed columns
15	Full table scan

Choice of Join Orders

The following reviews the two approaches to handling joins.

The optimizer follows these steps to define an execution for join statements while using the rule-based approach:

1. The optimizer creates a series of joins using a different table as the first table. To fill in the order of tables after the first table, the optimizer chooses the combination of tables that produces the best access path according to the ranking system defined in the previous section. Once the order of tables is decided, the access method for each table to access the table previous to it is decided.

2. The possible execution plans are evaluated and one is selected. The goal of the optimizer in this selection process is to find an execution plan that maximizes the number of nested loop join operations in which the inner table is accessed using an index scan.

With the cost-based approach, the optimizer generates an execution plan by the following steps:

1. A series of possible execution plans is generated based on the possible join orders, join operations, and available access paths.

2. The optimizer then calculates a cost for each possible execution plan. These costs are based on the following:

   - Cost of nested loops is based on the cost of reading each selected row of the outer join and each of its matching rows of the inner table into memory.

   - Cost of sort-merge joins is largely based on the cost of reading each source into memory and sorting them.

   - Factors such as sort size, indexing, multiple block reads, and sequential reads all factor into the cost calculations.

In the cost-based approach, the order of the join execution can be defined by the user with the ordered hint.

Choice of Join Operations

To join two row sources, Oracle must perform one of the following operations:

- Nested loop
- Sort-merge
- Cluster

Oracle follows these steps when performing a nested loop join:

1. One table is selected as the driving or primary table, and the other table is called the inner table.

2. For each row in the primary table, all rows in the inner table are found that satisfy the join condition.

3. Data from each pair of rows that satisfy the join condition is combined and returns the resulting rows.

For sort-merge joins, Oracle performs the following steps:

1. Each row to be joined is sorted on the column used in the join.

2. The two sources are merged so that each row on one source is combined with each row of the other source containing matching values for the joining columns. The resulting rows are then returned.

Oracle can perform a cluster join only for an equi-join statement that equates the cluster key columns of two tables that are stored in the same cluster. Oracle accesses only the clustered key values that are stored in the same block. A cluster join is simply a nested loop join involving two tables that are stored together in a cluster.

Types of SQL Statements

Oracle optimizes the following types of SQL statements:

- Simple statements like `insert` or `update`—Involve a single table
- Simple queries—Involve a single table
- Joins—Select data from more than one table
- Equi-joins—Join conditions containing an equality operator
- Non-equi-joins—Join conditions containing something other than an equality operator
- Outer joins—Join conditions that use the `outer join` operator
- Cartesian products—Joins with no join condition
- Complex statements—`insert`, `update`, `delete`, or `select` statements that contain a form of a `select` statement
- Compound queries—Statements that use set operators such as `union`, `minus`, and `intersection` to combine two or more simple or complex statements
- Distributed statements—Statements that access data on one or more remote databases

Compound Queries

A compound query is broken down into components by the optimizer. Each component is then given an execution plan, and the results of each component are combined using `union`, `intersection`, and `minus` operations.

For the `union all` operator, full table scans are performed on each table and the results are combined to create the resulting selection set.

The `union` operator is similar to `union all` in that full table scans are performed and results are combined. But a `sort-unique` operation is executed on the combined results to create the resulting selection set.

The intersection operator performs full table scans on each table and performs a sort-unique operation on each individual full table scan. The results of the sort-unique operation are combined so that only the rows that appear in both sort-unique result sets are combined into the final selection set.

Distributed Statements

To choose an execution plan for SQL statements that access data on remote databases, Oracle chooses a execution plan in a similar method as it does for accessing a local database. The optimizer considers the following:

- If the tables for the SQL statement reside on a single remote database, the remote instance generates the execution plan and resulting output set according to the rules described so far in this chapter. In essence, it acts as a local database would.

- If the tables for the SQL statement are distributed over multiple remote nodes, Oracle decomposes the statement into individual fragments that access a single database. These fragments are sent to the remote database for execution. The remote databases generate an execution plan as described earlier in this chapter and return a resulting selection set to the calling database. The local calling database can then perform additional processing if needed.

Optimization Hints

The discussion so far in this chapter is how the Oracle optimizer works. You may also impose your execution wishes on the optimizer by utilizing hints. Hints are your suggestions to the optimizer that can specify any of the following:

- The optimization approach for a SQL statement
- The goal of the cost-based approach for a SQL statement
- The join order for a join statement
- A join operation in a join statement

Refer to chapters 37 and 38, "Tuning Applications," for additional information on using hints and other related tuning topics.

Essential Summary

Optimization is the process that Oracle goes through to determine the most efficient execution path for a statement.

What

Optimization is critical to keep the Oracle database performance optimized. Optimization also enables you to inject your ideas on the best optimization approach based on your understanding of the application and its data.

Why

Oracle automatically optimizes every line of SQL code. You can, however, instruct Oracle to accept your recommendations for a particular execution path.

How

Appendixes

Oracle Products

This appendix reviews many of the Oracle products available.

Oracle7 Release 7.2 RDBMS

Oracle7 release 7.2 is a maintenance release of the Oracle7 server. Included in this release are new improvements to many of their tools, which greatly improve scalability, developer productivity, application readability, and performance.

Included in release 7.2 are the following product components:

Server:

- Oracle7 Server release 7.2
- Oracle Server Manager Version 2.1

PL/SQL and Programmatic Interfaces:

- PL/SQL release 2.2
- Oracle Call Interface (OCI) release 7.2
- Pro*C release 2.1
- Oracle Precompilers release 1.7
- SQL*Module release 1.1

Networking:

- SQL*Net version 2.2
- Oracle Network Manager version 3.0
- Secure Network Services version 2.0

Trusted Oracle7

Trusted Oracle7 provides the high security required by applications that process sensitive, proprietary, or classified information, while providing functionality, performance, portability, and interoperability. These make Oracle the leading DBMS worldwide.

SQL*Net

SQL*Net Version 2.0 eliminates many of the barriers that existied previously for client/server applications. With SQL*Net Version 2.0, any client can access any server without regard to the network protocols available. SQL*Net Version 2.0 permits connectivity between client applications and database servers independently of connectivity between the computers they run on.

Developer/2000

Oracle Developer/2000 enhancements are geared towards rapid application development and productivity. These applications range from the individual workstation to the corporate distributed databases. The three main components of Developer/2000 are Oracle Forms, Oracle Reports, and Oracle Graphics.

Oracle Forms

Using Oracle Forms, you can create advanced forms-based applications with sophisticated graphical user interfaces. Your applications can incorporate push buttons, radio groups, list boxes, icons, images, menus, and alerts for accessing and manipulating data. These graphical features ensure that your applications are intuitive and easy to learn and use. By including boilerplate text and graphics, such as lines, arcs, ellipses, and polygons, you can create applications that are visually appealing as well.

Oracle Forms is designed to use the powerful capabilities of the Oracle Cooperative Server Database, but it also provides unlimited access to all data in your organization, regardless of where that data is stored. Using Oracle Open Gateway products, your Oracle Forms applications can transparently access and modify data stored in non-Oracle data sources including IBM's DB2 and SQL/DS. Oracle Forms also provides the transactional trigger set, a fully published interface that enables you to write third-generation language (3GL) code to access data stored in any data source.

Oracle Reports

With Oracle Reports, you can create reports with a wide variety of formats, such as tabular, master-detail, multicolumn mailing label, and matrix reports. You can also combine different formats within a single report. Oracle Reports leverages the full power of SQL. It supports an unlimited number of database queries and can access both textual and image data. Using these capabilities, you can create any report to suit your business needs.

Oracle Reports also enables you to deliver highly graphical reports. You can enhance your reports with a variety of fonts, colors, patterns, boilerplate graphics, and images. Reports can contain artwork created within Oracle Reports or imported from other graphics products. You can dynamically change the graphical attributes of both data and boilerplate objects at run time to convey information visually. Oracle Reports' graphical capabilities enable you to create more attractive and more informative reports.

Oracle Graphics

Using Oracle Graphics, you can create data visualization applications that turn your data into information. Your applications can combine text, chart, drawing, and multimedia objects to represent data relationships in a meaningful graphical format. Oracle Graphics' multimedia capabilities enable you to incorporate images dynamically and to record and play back sounds. You can define application objects with visual attributes that change in response to changing data, making Oracle Graphics an ideal tool for creating data monitoring applications. With capabilities such as graphical buttons, multiple active windows, and drill-down from summary to detail information, Oracle Graphics enables you to develop powerful graphical front-ends, executive information systems, and interactive decision support systems.

Designer/2000

Designer/2000 supports the modeling of a system with built-in utilities for business process reengineering, analysis, and design. This suite of tools empowers your organization to work together with corporate business partners.

Designer/2000 has five components:

- Process Modeller—Captures the essential steps of a business process and how they are integrated.
- Systems Modeller—Captures traditional system analysis requirements.
- System Designer—Produces data definitions, business rule and procedure definitions, transaction definitions, data usage definitions, and workflow definitions.
- Generators—Generates client-side and server-side code with layout, most validation, referential, and other integrity rules.
- Repository Administrator—Management tools for team environments to share definitions and reuse components.

Oracle Workgroup/2000

Oracle Workgroup/2000 includes five fully integrated tools:

- Personal Oracle7—Oracle7's RDBMS designed for the single user. This database will run on a Windows-based personal computer.
- Oracle7 Workgroup Server—Oracle7's RDBMS designed as a server for several users but is still based on the personal computer platform.
- Oracle Power Objects—Oracle Power Objects delivers the first truly usable object model for building client/server applications. You create objects and add them to your applications by simply dragging and dropping them. Each object can then be modified as needed, and full inheritance ensures that changes to the master object are reflected consistently across every application.
- Oracle Objects for OLE—Provides OLE 2.0-based connectivity for building windows-based client-server applications.

Oracle Data Browser

Oracle Data Browser is a graphical data access client that enables nonprogrammers to easily locate, query, and display information stored in networked, distributed databases. As part of Oracle's Cooperative Development Environment, Browser provides decision makers with ad hoc access to mission-critical information systems.

Oracle Procedure Builder

Oracle Procedure Builder is a GUI-based tool for developing, debugging, and maintaining your PL/SQL code. This tool provides a complete GUI editing environment, a dynamic code browser, rapid prototyping and iterative development environment, and an integrated source-level debugging tool.

Oracle Book

With Oracle Book you can create and view sophisticated on-line documents. Your documents can include text, hypertext links, images, digital sounds, and digital video clips. Oracle Book is ideal for on-line distribution of application documentation, manuals, catalogs, and other documents.

Oracle Precompilers

By enabling you to embed SQL in programs written in Ada, C, COBOL, FORTRAN, Pascal, and PL/I, the Oracle Precompilers supply the best of both worlds: procedural host language capabilities, and the flexibility and ease of use of SQL. With the Oracle Precompilers, you retain your investment in host language training and applications while writing powerful programs that interface with the Oracle Cooperative Server Database and other SQL-based database systems. In addition, the Oracle Precompilers are part of Oracle's Cooperative development environment, an integrated life-cycle development environment for creating mission-critical client/server applications.

Oracle Call Interface

The Oracle Call Interface is an application programming interface that enables third-generation languages (3GLs), such as Ada, C, COBOL, and FORTRAN, to manipulate data and schema in an Oracle cooperative server database. The Oracle Call Interface gives you precise control over SQL statement execution, while still using powerful language-specific editors and debuggers to develop your application. In addition, the Oracle Call Interface is a component of the Oracle Cooperative development environment, so all of your organization's information systems developers can share or enhance applications developed with the Oracle Call Interface.

Oracle Glue

Your organization has invested in a new generation of clients, servers, and networks, but you still haven't been able to build a new generation of applications. You have data in databases, in mail systems, and on file servers. You have networks connecting all these servers to PCs and workstations, and you have your favorite development tools on various platforms. But you still don't have a consistent, high-level way to get your data to the desktop. Oracle Glue is the adaptable, portable, integrated application programming interface (API) that gives you a consistent, high-level way to use your favorite tools with any data on any server. In an era of exploding diversity, Oracle Glue is the ultimate software unifier.

Oracle Mail

Oracle Mail is a portable client/server electronic mail system that enables users to exchange messages across any operating system, hardware platform, or network. Oracle Mail offers a full complement of e-mail functions and powerful administrative tools in the native look and feel of popular graphical user interfaces (GUIs), including MS Windows and Macintosh, in addition to character mode.

Oracle Protocol Adapters

Today's network environments are collections of multivendor solutions built up from different machines joined by different protocols. Developing network applications is made more difficult by the evolution of different application programming interfaces (APIs). Oracle's Transparent Network Substrate (TNS) defines a consistent set of application-to-application service functions that operate across all popular network protocols. The Oracle Protocol Adapters are the interfaces that enable any two TNS-based applications to communicate across any network.

Oracle SQL Reserved Words

The following list contains Oracle SQL reserved words:

ACCESS—Makes a database object available to users.

ADD—Used in SQL statements to add a column or integrity constraint.

ALL—Specifies a comparison operator or causes a group function to consider all values in a specified selection set.

ALTER—Used in numerous statements to redefine current values for the statement.

AND—A logical operator.

ANY—A logical operator.

AS—A clause that is used in conjunction with the create command to insert the rows returned by the subquery into the table upon creation.

ASC—To create an ascending list; for example, used with indexes.

AUDIT—Enables the auditing of specified statements or objects.

BETWEEN—A comparison operator.

CHAR—A datatype of CHARACTER that is a fixed length.

CHECK—A constraint which explicitly defines a condition.

CLUSTER—A means of storing database data together from multiple tables, when the data in those rows contains common information that is typically accessed concurrently.

COLUMN—A subdivision of a table that contains a name and a specific datatype.

COMMENT—Command to insert a comment phrase in the data dictionary about a table or column.

CONNECT—Commits pending changes, logs you off of Oracle, and logs on to Oracle as a specific user.

CREATE—Used to create a specific database object.

CURRENT—Used in conjunction with cursors to specify the recently fetched row.

DATE—A datatype of DATE that is fixed length data and time data.

DECIMAL—A datatype of DECIMAL which only specifics fixed point numbers.

DEFAULT—A clause or option value that is used if no alternative is specified.

DELETE—Command to remove rows from a table or from a view's base table.

DESC—To create a descending list. A typical application of this reserved word would be with indexes.

DISTINCT—Part of a statement indicating uniqueness.

DROP—To completely remove or delete an object from the database.

ELSE—A statement which evaluates two conditions which may evaluate to TRUE.

EXCLUSIVE—Used to mount the database in exclusive mode. This means the database will be mounted one instance at a time.

EXISTS—An operator that returns True in a WHERE clause if the subquery that follows it returns at least one row.

FILE—A storage area used to store all database data.

FLOAT—A datatype of FLOAT.

FOR—Used in iterative logic to limit the number of times a statement is executed.

GRANT—Used to apply permission to users and roles.

HAVING—Restricts the groups of rows returned to those groups for which the specified condition is TRUE.

IMMEDIATE—Used in the `alter tablespace` command which does not ensure that tablespace files are available and does not perform a checkpoint.

IN—A logical operator used in the `WHERE` clause.

INCREMENT—Used in creating sequences to indicate intervals between sequential numbers.

IDENTIFIED—Used while altering a user; indicates how Oracle permits user access.

INDEX—A database object used to improve access speeds.

INITIAL—Specifies the beginning storage space requirements.

INSERT—Used to add rows to a table or to a view's base tables.

INTEGER—A datatype of `INTEGER`.

INTERSECT—A set operator that returns the common rows between two different sets of rows.

INTO—Specifies the table or object in which it is the recipient of an action.

IS—Used with the `NULL` logical operator to test for the presence of a value.

LEVEL—This is a pseudocolumn which equates to 1 for the root node, 2 for the child node, and 3 for the child of a child node.

LIKE—Used to perform character string comparisons with pattern-matching.

LOCK—Oracle mechanisms used to restrict access of users for a particular object.

LONG—A datatype of `LONG` that is variable length character data with a maximum length of 2 gigabytes.

MAXEXTENTS—Specifies the total number of extents that may be allocated for a particular object.

MINUS—A set operator that returns all distinct rows that are in the first query, but not in the second query.

MODE—Establishes the process as either single-mode or multi-processor mode.

MODIFY—Modifies the definition of an existing table column.

NOAUDIT—Stops the auditing activities for a particular statement or object.

NOT—Precedes and reverses the effects of logical operators.

NOWAIT—Directs Oracle to return control back to you when the object is already locked by another user.

NULL—Indicates the absence of a value.

NUMBER—A datatype of `NUMBER` that is variable in length and may have a precision.

OF—Precedes a list of items that are to be evaluated.

OFFLINE—Takes a particular object offline and prevents further access to it.

ON—Identifies the object on which the statement will act.

ONLINE—Takes a particular object online and makes access available to users.

OPTION—Provides the user a list of choices to make for the statement.

OR—An operator that combines expressions with a result being TRUE or FALSE.

ORDER—Guarantees that a list of numbers will be created in the order of the request.

PCTFREE—Specifies the percentage of space in each object reserved for future updates to the object.

PRIOR—An operator that evaluates a specified expression for the parent row of the current row in a hierarchy.

PRIVILEGE—The permission granted to a user to perform some action.

PUBLIC—A database group in which all users of the database have access. Or it may mean a database item, such as a synonym, that is available to all users.

RAW—A datatype of RAW. This is binary in format and should not be directly interpreted.

RENAME—Changes the name of an object to a new name.

RESOURCE—This is a generic word for a database object or a physical device.

REVOKE—Takes privileges away from users and roles.

ROW—A collection of information from table columns that corresponds to a single record.

ROWID—This is a pseudocolumn that represents the logical address in the table for a row.

ROWLABEL—A column automatically created by Trusted Oracle in every table.

ROWNUM—This is a pseudocolumn that contains a number indicating the order in which Oracle selects the row from a table of a set of joined rows.

ROWS—One or more rows of data from a table.

SELECT—A SQL command to retrieve data from one or more database objects.

SESSION—A specific connection by a user to the database instance.

SET—Used to enable a specified item.

SHARE—Allows sharing of an object or resource.

SIZE—Specifies the size of the resource in bytes.

SMALLINT—A compatible datatype from DB2 for Oracle's datatype number (38).

START—Used to initiate an action such as starting a database.

SYNONYM—An alias for a table or view that may be used to refer to the table or view.

SYSDATE—The system date and time.

TABLE—The basic unit of storage in an Oracle database. It is comprised of rows and columns.

THEN—Associates the preceding condition with the statements that follow.

TO—Identifies the item to which some action will occur.

TRIGGER—A stored procedure associated with a table that is automatically executed on a specified event.

UID—A pseudocolumn that contains a unique number assigned to each user.

UNION—A SQL function that combines the results of two queries.

UNIQUE—Specifies that an item is to have uniqueness against other similar items.

UPDATE—Command to change the values in a table or a view's base tables.

USER—A pseudocolumn that contains the user's login username.

VALUES—Assigns a list of values to corresponding columns.

VARCHAR—A datatype of VARCHAR that is variable in length and can have a maximum length of 200 bytes.

VARCHAR2—A datatype of VARCHAR that is variable in length and can have a maximum length of 200 bytes. With the current release of Oracle, this datatype is synonymous with VARCHAR.

VIEW—A database object that is a logical representation of one or more tables.

WHENEVER—Used in conjunction with the audit command to make auditing contingent on the success of a statement.

WHERE—Used in statements to specify which rows are affected by the command.

WITH—Provides a supplemental item to include in the statement.

SQL*Loader Reserved Words

The following terms are reserved words used by SQL*Loader. SQL*Loader, like other Oracle utilities, must follow the standard naming conventions for naming database objects. Reserved words cannot be used to name tables and columns unless they are enclosed in double quotes.

AND—Specifies a trailing enclosure delimiter, which may be different from the initial enclosure delimiter.

APPEND—If data already exists in a table, SQL*Loader appends the new rows to it; if the doesn't already exist, the new rows are inserted.

BADDN—Specifies the name of the file that contains bad records.

BADFILE—This is the same as BADDN. Specifies the name of the file that contains bad records.

BEGINDATA—Used in conjunction with the insert keyword and is placed in the control file between the control file specifications and the input data.

BLANKS—Keyword makes it possible to easily determine if a field of unknown length is blank.

CHAR—Defines the datatype of the field as character.

CONCATENATE—Directs field1 to be concatenated to field2.

CONSTANT—Data that is interpreted by SQL* Loader as character data.

CONTINUE_LOAD—Used after a direct load failure and with the SKIP keyword.

CONTINUEIF—Used to form a logical record from multiple physical records.

COUNT—This specifies that the sequence will start with the number or rows already in the table, plus the increment.

DATA—Defines the data filename.

DATE—Defines a datatype of DATE.

DECIMAL—Defines a datatype as packed DECIMAL format.

DEFAULTIF—Defines a default column value if a specified condition is true.

DISCARDDN—Defines the record discard file.

DISCARDFILE—Defines the file where discarded records are placed.

DISCARDMAX—The maximum number of discards allowed.

DISCARDS—Defines the discard filename.

DOUBLE—A datatype of DOUBLE.

ENCLOSED—Defines that a data value is found between two delimiters.

EXTERNAL—Used with numeric datatypes to stored this type of data in human readable form and not binary form.

FIELDS—Used in the control file to specify the default delimiters.

FLOAT—A datatype that holds a single-precision floating point binary number.

FORMAT—Used to load DB2-generated data.

GRAPHIC—A datatype that is a string of double-byte characters.

INDDN—A control file keyword that specifies the input datafile name.

INDEXES—A flag to indicate whether to load indexes.

INFILE—A control file keyword that specifies the input datafile name.

INSERT—Instructs SQL*Loader to insert data into the table. This requires that the table be empty prior to using this keyword.

INTEGER—A datatype that contains a full word binary integer.

INTO—Defines the table in which the data is to be loaded.

LAST—Used with the continueif keyword to determine if the last physical record is to be concatenated to the current record.

LOAD—Specifies the number of records to be loaded.

LOG—Defines the name of the log file.

MAX—Establishes the maximum value that a sequence may grow to.

NEXT— Used with the continueif keyword to determine if the next physical record is to be concatenated to the current record.

NULLCOLS—Used with the trailing keyword to treat any fields that are missing at the end of a record as null.

NULLIF—Sets the field to null if a certain condition exists.

OPTIONALLY—Provides an alternative way to delimit input data.

OPTIONS—Enables you to specify runtime arguments.

PART—Used to load a DB2-partitioned table.

PIECED—Allows the last columns of the input data record to be loaded in pieces.

POSITION—Used to define the column position for input data as the logical record.

PRESERVE—Used to retain any leading whitespace.

RAW—A datatype of RAW that contains *raw* binary data.

RECNUM—Represents the number of the logical record that has been loaded.

REPLACE—During loading, all pre-existing rows are deleted and then the data is loaded.

RESUME—Used with the DB2 syntax to load data into tables that are not empty.

SEQUENCE—Creates a unique sequential number during data loading.

SKIP—Defines the number of logical records to skip.

SMALLINT—A datatype of SMALLINT that contains a halfword binary integer.

SORTDEVT—Used in DB2 and specifies the type of temporary datasets required for sorting.

SORTNUM—Used in DB2 and specifies the type of temporary datasets required for sorting.

SORTED—Defines whether indexes will be sorted or not.

SQL/DS—A DB2 file format statement.

SYSDATE—Established by the system date and time.

TABLE—A database object that is the target for data loading.

TERMINATED—Defines what the individual fields are terminated by.

THIS—Used with the `continueif` keyword to determine if the next physical record is to be concatenated to the current record.

TRAILING—Directs SQL*Loader to treat any relatively positioned columns that are not present in a particular manner.

VARCHAR—A datatype of VARCHAR that contains variable length character strings.

VARGRAPHIC—A datatype that contains varying length double-byte character strings.

WHEN—Specifies the condition to be met before the next statements are executed.

WHITESPACE—Tabs and blanks in the data.

WORKDDN—For DB2-compatible files that define a temporary working file for sorting.

ZONED—This data is in zoned decimal format—which is a string of decimal digits, one per byte, with the sign included in the last byte.

APPENDIX
D

SQL*DBA Reserved Words

Like other Oracle reserved words, SQL*DBA reserved words can not be used to name a database object unless they are enclosed in double quotes. The following is a list of the SQL*DBA reserved words.

ABORT—Used to shut down a running Oracle instance. Proceeds with the fastest possible shutdown.

ACCESSES—Defines which privileges are granted to the user.

ALL—Used in conjunction with the show command to display all settings except for errors and parameters.

ALTER—Command to change an existing setting or parameter.

ARCHIVE—Used to create an archived backup copy of the instance, data file, or logs.

ARRAYSIZE—The number of rows fetched at a time from the database.

AUTORECOVERY—Causes the recovery command to automatically apply the default filenames of archived redo log files needed during recovery.

BEGIN—Used to identify the beginning of a block structure.

BINARY—A datatype format that is native to the computer's memory.

BODY—Used to recompile the body of a package.

CACHE—Specifies the number of values specified for object in memory.

CHAR—Specifies the char datatype.

CHARWIDTH—Establishes the column display width for char data.

CLOSE—Used to close a cursor.

COMMIT—Used to permanently store the changes made to the database.

COMPATIBILITY—Sets the compatibility mode for either Oracle version 6 or version 7.

CONNECT—Command to connect to the database.

CREATE—Used to create database objects such as tables and segments.

CYCLE—Establishes the cycle time for a monitor session.

DATABASE—Identifies specific database operations such as opening or mounting.

DATAFILE—Identifies the data file associated with the database.

DATEWIDTH—Displays the column's display width for date data.

DBA—Initials for Database Administrator.

DECLARE—Used to declare a cursor or a block structure.

DEFAULT—Establishes the value a parameter will assume if no explicit value is provided.

DESCRIBE—Describes a table, stored procedure, or function.

DISCONNECT—Command to disconnect from the Oracle server.

DISMOUNT—Command to dismount the database.

ECHO—Used to toggle on and off the echoing of commands entered for the command files.

END—Used to identify the end of a block structure.

ENQUEUE—Used to identify the current locks on a given resource.

ERRORS—Used to display the errors generated from the last compilation of a procedure, package, or function.

EXCLUSIVE—Signifies that the database can only be mounted and opened by the current instance.

EXECUTE—Executes a single PL/SQL command.

EXIT—Exits the SQL*DBA session.

FETCHROWS—Defines the limit on the number of records returned by a select command.

FILE—Name of the SQL*DBA file menu.

FORCE—Used to shut down the current Oracle instance.

FUNCTION—Names the stored function object.

HELP—Name of a SQL*DBA menu.

HISTORY—Determines the size of SQL*DBA's command history buffer.

HOST—Used to execute an operating system command without exiting SQL*DBA.

IMMEDIATE—Used to shut down the running instance without waiting for current calls to complete.

INFINITE—Specifies that there is an unlimited number of retries permitted.

INSTANCE—Identifies the connect string for the current instance.

INTERNAL—A special username that is only available through SQL*DBA.

IO—Used during monitoring of I/O statistics.

LABEL—A Trusted Oracle parameter.

LABWIDTH—A Trusted Oracle parameter.

LATCH—Displays a screen summarizing the current latches.

LINES—Specifies the number of lines of output that can be stored in SQL*DBA's output window.

LIST—Requests a display that shows the range of redo log files to be archived.

LOCAL—Specifies that the command is to apply only to your instance.

LOCK—Used to monitor database locks.

LOG—The file specification for the spooled file.

LOGIN—Command to login to current database.

LOGSOURCE—Specifies the location from which archive logs are retrieved during recovery.

LONG—Specifies the datatype LONG.

LONGWIDTH—Sets the column display width for long data.

MAXDATA—Defines the maximum data size.

MODE—Used to specify if server is a single- or multiple- process server.

MON—Shortened version of the monitor command.

MONITOR—Displays real-time information about locks, enqueues, processes, and other database utilities.

MOUNT—Mounts the specified database but does not open it.

NEXT—Used in conjunction with the `continueif` command.

NOMOUNT—Causes the database not to be mounted upon instance startup.

NOPAGE—Specifies that there is no page limit for the output.

NORMAL—Used during shutdown of database instance which waits for all calls to complete normally before termination occurs.

NUMBER—The datatype of `number`.

NUMWIDTH—Defines the display width for number data.

OFF—Disables the specified parameters or option.

ON—Enables the specified parameters or option.

OPEN—Opens the current Oracle database.

OR—A logical operator.

OUTPUT—Defines the output filename.

PACKAGE—Specifies the PL/SQL package name and components.

PAGE—Specifies that only one page of output is to be displayed at a time.

PARALLEL—Must be specified if the database is to be mounted by multiple instances.

PARAMETER—Used to identify the specific parameters.

PFILE—Defines the name of the startup parameter file.

PRINT—Prints the value of a variable defined with the `variable` command.

PROCEDURE—Used to identify the specific procedure.

PROCESS—Used to monitor the current Oracle processes.

RECOVER—Performs media recovery on one or more tablespaces, database files, or the entire database.

REDO—Defines the redo log filename.

RESTRICT—Allows only Oracle users with the restricted session system privilege to connect to the database.

RETRIES—Specifies the number of retries that will be attempted when restarting an instance in parallel mode.

RETRY—Specifies that opening the database should be attempted every five seconds if the instance is busy.

ROLLBACK—Monitors the rollback segments.

SET—Used to establish or change characteristics of the current SQL*DBA session.

SGA—Used to display information about the current instance's System Global Area.

SHARED—This is a synonym for `parallel`.

SHOW—Displays current settings that are in effect.

SHUTDOWN—Used to shut down the currently running Oracle instance.

SPOOL—Used to identify the spool filename.

START—Used to start instance processes such as redo logs.

STARTUP—Used to start up an Oracle instance.

STATISTICS—Used to monitor different instance statistics.

STOP—Used to stop instance processes such as redo logs.

STOPONERROR—Stop current task when an error is detected.

TABLE—Identifies the Oracle database object table.

TABLESPACE—Identifies the name of the tablespace.

TERM—Defines terminal specific characteristics.

TERMOUT—Specifies if terminal output is provided.

TIMING—Specifies if timing information is provided.

TRIGGER—The name of the database object.

UNTIL—Performs specific action until condition is met.

USER—Specifies the user ID for which requested action occurs.

V6—Represents Oracle Version 6.*x*.

V7—Represents Oracle Version 7.*x*.

VAR—Defines the names and datatypes of one `bind` variable.

VARCHAR2—Defines a datatype of VARCHAR2.

VARIABLE—Declares a `bind` variable for use in the current session.

VIEW—Used to specify the name of the view.

PL/SQL Reserved Words

The following is a list of the PL/SQL reserved words:

ABORT—Used to shut down a running Oracle instance. Proceeds with the fastest possible shutdown.

ACCEPT—Command to receive input from the user's terminal input.

ACCESS—Identifies the privileges that are currently granted to the user.

ADD—Used in SQL statements to add a column or integrity constraint.

ALL—Used in conjunction with the show command to display all settings except for errors and parameters.

ALTER—Command to change an existing setting or parameter.

AND—Logical operator used with two expressions.

ANY—Compares a value to each value in a list or returned by a subquery and evaluates to true if all of the individual comparisons yield a true result.

ARRAY—Allows the program to execute a single statement many times with only a single call to Oracle.

ARRAYLEN—Defines the size of an ARRAY to be processed.

AS—A clause that is used in conjunction with the create command to insert the rows returned by the subquery into the table upon creation.

ASC—A command used to define the sorting sequence for an index of a list.

ASSIGN—Sets the current value of a variable, formal parameter, or field in a record.

AT—Identifies the database or database object to which an action will occur.

AUTHORIZATION—The permission to grant a system privilege or role.

AVG—A group function to determine the average of a specified set of numbers.

BASE_TABLE—The table or tables from which views derive their data.

BEGIN—Used to identify the beginning of a block structure.

BETWEEN—Used with logical operators for comparisons between two expressions.

BINARY_INTEGER—A datatype to store signed binary numbers.

BODY—The main portion of a PL/SQL package.

BOOLEAN—A literal or variable that may evaluate to either true or false.

BY—Forces PL/SQL to act according to the statement following the reserved word.

CHAR—Specifies the characters datatype.

CHECK—A constraint which explicitly defines a condition.

CLOSE—Allows resources held by an opened cursor to be reused.

CLUSTER—An alternative way to store data that have tables with common columns stored together.

COLAUTH—Authorization that is granted on specific columns.

COLUMN—A subdivision of a table that contains a name and a specific data type.

COMMIT—Explicitly makes permanent any changes made to the database during the current transaction.

CONNECT—The command used to log a specific user onto Oracle. If the user is already connected, then the current session is disconnected before the new connection is attempted.

CONSTANT—A declared variable that is initialized when created.

COUNT—Group functions that return the number of rows in a table.

CREATE—Used to create a specific database object.

CURRENT—Used in conjunction with cursors to specify the recently fetched row.

CURRVAL—The current value of a sequence.

CURSOR—A portion of memory used to manage queries that return more than one row. This command enables you to process each of the returned rows individually.

DATABASE—Identifies specific database operations such as opening or mounting.

DATE—Datatype of date to store fixed length date values.

DBA—Initials for database administrator.

DEBUGOFF—Disables debugging.

DEBUGON—Enables debugging.

DECIMAL—A datatype of decimal which only specifies fixed point numbers.

DECLARE—Identifies to the program the variables, constants, other objects that will be used.

DEFAULT—Establishes the value a parameter will assume if no explicit value is provided.

DELETE—Removes entire rows of data from a specified table or view, as long as the view deals with one table.

DESC—To create a descending list. For example, used with indexes.

DIGITS—A number from 0 to 9.

DISTINCT—A row operator that eliminates duplicate rows from the result of query.

DROP—To completely remove or delete an object from the database.

ELSE—A statement that evaluates two conditions which may evaluate to true.

ELSIF—Used to assist in the selection of mutually exclusive options.

END—Used to signify the end of a PL/SQL block.

EXCEPTION—An exception declaration names a user-defined exception.

EXCEPTION_INIT—Associates an exception name with an Oracle error number.

EXISTS—A comparison operator that returns true if a subquery returns at least one row.

EXIT—Used to exit a loop.

FETCH—Retrieves the next row of data from the active set.

FLOAT—A datatype of float.

FOR—Used in the loop iterative process for a specified number of loops.

FROM—Used in statements to identify the object that the action is to act on.

FUNCTION—A schema object that returns a value.

GOTO—Branches to a labeled statement of PL/SQL block unconditionally.

GRANT—Extends more system privileges to a user or role.

GROUP—Causes an action to be performed on a collection of rows.

HAVING—Restricts the groups of rows returned to those groups for which the specified condition is true.

IDENTIFIED—Used to determine or display the password for the current session. Indicates how Oracle permits user access.

IF—Statement that lets you execute a sequence of statements conditionally.

IN—A logical operator used in the where clause.

INDEX—A database object used to improves access speeds.

INDICATOR—An integer variable that indicates the value or condition of a host variable.

INSERT—Adds a row of data to a specified database table or view, as long as the view deals with just one table.

INTEGER—A datatype of integer.

INTERSECT—A set operator that returns the common rows between two different sets of rows.

INTO—Specifies the table or object in which it is the recipient of an action.

IS—Used with the null logical operator to test for the presence of a value.

LEVEL—This is a pseudo-column which equates to 1 for the root node, 2 for the child node, and 3 for the child of a child node.

LIKE—Used to perform character string comparisons with pattern matching.

LOOP—Executes a sequence of statements multiple times.

MAX—A group function that returns the maximum value in the specified list.

MIN—A group function that returns the minimum value in the specified list.

MINUS—A set operator that returns all distinct rows that are in the first set but not in the second set.

MLSLABEL—A datatype used in Trusted Oracle to store binary data.

MOD—Divides a value by a divisor and gives the remainder.

NATURAL—Used to produce the natural logarithm of a value.

NEW—Used in statements to return a new value.

NEXTVAL—Returns the next sequential number from the specified sequence generator.

NOT—Precedes and reverses the effects of logical operators.

NULL—A statement that explicitly specifies inaction, it does nothing more than pass control to the next statement.

NUMBER—A datatype of number that is variable in length.

OF—Precedes a list of items that are to be evaluated.

OPEN—Executes the query associated with an explicitly declared cursor.

OPTION—Provides the user a list of choices to make for the statement.

OR—An operator that combines expressions with the results being true or false.

ORDER—Guarantees that a list of numbers will be created in the order of the request.

OUT—A parameter that lets you return values to the caller of the subprogram.

PACKAGE—A database object that groups logically related PL/SQL blocks, types, and sub-programs.

PCTFREE—Specifies the percentage of space in each object reserved for future updates to the object.

POSITIVE—A number beginning with 1 and ascending in value.

PRAGMA—A compiler directive which is executed at compile time and not execution time.

PRIOR—A row operator that refers to the parent row of the current row returned by a tree-structured query.

PRIVATE—Referring to objects within a package that are not accessible to anything outside the package.

PROCEDURE—A named PL/SQL block which can take parameters and be invoked.

PUBLIC—A database group in which all users of the database have access to. Or it may mean a database item, such as a synonym, that is available to all users.

RAISE—A statement that stops normal execution of a PL/SQL block or subprogram.

REAL—A datatype of real.

RECORD—Objects of type record. These have uniquely named fields that can store data values of different types.

RELEASE—Releases allocated storage space for a cursor.

REM—Indicates that the current line is a remark.

RENAME—To change the name of a database object.

RESOURCE—A general term for a logical database object or physical structure.

RETURN—Immediately completes the execution of a subprogram and returns control to the caller.

REVOKE—Takes privileges away from users and roles.

ROLLBACK—The inverse of commit statements. This undoes some or all database changes made during the current transaction.

ROWID—A pseudo-column that represents the logical address in the table for a row.

ROWLABEL—A column automatically created by Trusted Oracle in every table.

ROWNUM—A pseudo-column that contains a number indicating the order in which Oracle selects the row from a table in a set of joined rows.

ROWTYPE—An attribute that provides a record that represents a row in a table or view.

RUN—Executes the specified file or script.

SAVEPOINT—A command to name and mark the current point in the processing of a transaction.

SCHEMA—A collection of logical structures of data or other schema objects like tables, synonyms, and clusters.

SELECT—A SQL command to retrieve data from one or more database objects.

SET—Used to enable a specified item.

SIZE—Specifies the size of the resource in bytes.

SMALLINT—A compatible datatype from DB2 for Oracle's datatype number (38).

SQL—Initials for Structured Query Language.

SQLCODE—A function that returns the number code associated with the most recently raised exception.

SQLERRM—A function that returns the error message associated with its error-number or the equivalent of the SQLCODE.

START—Used to initiate an action such as starting a database.

STATEMENT—A SQL instruction to Oracle.

STDDEV—A group function that calculates the standard deviation.

SUBTYPE—Specifies the type of data and length of data.

SUM—A group function that calculates the sum of numbers.

TABLE—The basic unit of storage in an Oracle database. It is comprised of rows and columns.

TERMINATE—Represents the ending of a statement.

THEN—Associates the preceding condition with the statements that follow.

TRUE—A predefined Boolean value.

UNION—A SQL function that combines the results of two queries.

UNIQUE—Specifies that an item is to have uniqueness against other similar items.

UPDATE—Command to change the values in a table or a views base table.

USE—Specifies the objector file to be used in the statement.

VALUES—Assigns a list of values to corresponding columns.

VARCHAR—A datatype of VARCHAR that is variable in length and can have a maximum length of 2,000 bytes.

VARCHAR2—A datatype of VARCHAR that is variable in length and can have a maximum length of 2,000 bytes. With the current release of Oracle, this datatype is synonymous with varchar.

VARIANCE—A function that determines a value's variance.

VIEW—A database object that is a logical representation of one or more tables.

WHEN—Specifies the condition to be met before the next statements are executed.

WHERE—Used in statements to specify rows that are affected by the command.

WITH—Provides supplemental items to include in the statement.

WORK—An option keyword to be used with commit or rollback.

SQL*Plus Reserved Words

The following terms are reserved words used by SQL*Plus. SQL*Plus, like other Oracle utilities and tools, must follow the standard naming conventions for naming database objects. Reserved words cannot be used to name tables and columns unless they are enclosed in double quotes.

@—Runs the specified command file.

@@—Runs a nested command file.

ACCEPT—Reads a line of input from the input screen and stores it in a given user variable.

APPEND—Adds specified text to the end of the current line in the buffer.

BREAK—Specifies where and how formatting will change in a report, or lists the current break definition.

BTITLE—Places and formats a specified title at the bottom of each report page.

CHANGE—Changes text on the current line in the buffer.

CLEAR—Resets or erases the current value or setting for the specified option, such as breaks or columns.

COLUMN—Specifies display attributes for a given column. Or, lists the current display attributes for a single column or for all columns.

COMPUTE—Calculates and prints summary lines, using various standard computations, on subsets of selected rows.

CONNECT—Connects a given username to Oracle.

COPY—Copies data from a query to a table in a local or remote database.

DEFINE—Specifies a user variable and assigns it a char value. Or, lists the value and variable type of a single variable or all variables.

DEL—Deletes the current line of the buffer.

DESCRIBE—Lists the column definitions for the specified table, view, or synonym.

DISCONNECT—Commits pending changes to the database and logs the current username off ORACLE, but does not exit SQL*Plus.

EDIT—Invokes a host operating system text editor on the contents of the specified file or on the contents of the buffer.

EXECUTE—Executes a single PL/SQL statement.

EXIT—Commits all pending database changes, terminates SQL*Plus, and returns control to the operating system.

GET—Loads a host operating system file into the buffer.

HELP—Accesses the SQL*Plus help system.

HOST—Executes a host operating system command without leaving SQL*Plus.

INPUT—Adds one or more new lines after the current line in the buffer.

LIST—Lists one or more lines of the buffer.

PAUSE—Displays an empty line followed by a line containing text, then waits for the user to press the return key. This reserved word may alternately display two empty lines and wait for the user's response.

PRINT—Lists the current value of a bind variable.

PROMPT—Sends the specified message or a blank line to the user's screen.

REMARK—Begins a comment in a command file.

RUN—Lists and executes the SQL command or PL/SQL block currently stored in the SQL buffer.

RUNFORM—Invokes a SQL*Forms application from within SQL*Plus.

SAVE—Saves the contents of the buffer in a host operating system file (a command file).

SET—Establishes an aspect of the SQL*Plus environment for your current session.

SHOW—Lists the value of a SQL*Plus system variable.

SPOOL—Stores query results in a host operating system file and, optionally, sends the file to a default printer. This reserved word also lists the current spooling status.

SQL*Plus—Starts SQL*Plus from the operating system prompt.

START—Executes the contents of the specified command file.

TIMING—Records timing data for an elapsed period of time, lists the current timing area's title and timing data, or lists the number of active timing areas.

TTITLE—Places and formats a specified title at the top of each report page, or lists the current ttitle definition.

UNDEFINE—Deletes a given user variable that you defined either explicitly (with the define command) or implicitly (with an argument to the start command).

VARIABLE—Declares a bind variable which can be referenced in PL/SQL.

WHENEVER OSERROR—Exits SQL*Plus if an OS command generates an error.

WHENEVER SQLERROR—Exits SQL*Plus if a SQL command or PL/SQL block generates an error.

Index

SYMBOLS

PLUG YOURSELF INTO...

MACMILLAN INFORMATION SUPERLIBRARY™

que · SAMS PUBLISHING · Hayden Books · que COLLEGE · NRP · alpha books · Brady · ADOBE PRESS

THE MACMILLAN INFORMATION SUPERLIBRARY™

Free information and vast computer resources from the world's leading computer book publisher—online!

FIND THE BOOKS THAT ARE RIGHT FOR YOU!

A complete online catalog, plus sample chapters and tables of contents give you an in-depth look at *all* of our books, including hard-to-find titles. It's the best way to find the books you need!

- **STAY INFORMED** with the latest computer industry news through our online newsletter, press releases, and customized Information SuperLibrary Reports.

- **GET FAST ANSWERS** to your questions about MCP books and software.

- **VISIT** our online bookstore for the latest information and editions!

- **COMMUNICATE** with our expert authors through e-mail and conferences.

- **DOWNLOAD SOFTWARE** from the immense MCP library:
    - Source code and files from MCP books
    - The best shareware, freeware, and demos

- **DISCOVER HOT SPOTS** on other parts of the Internet.

- **WIN BOOKS** in ongoing contests and giveaways!

TO PLUG INTO MCP: →

GOPHER: gopher.mcp.com
FTP: ftp.mcp.com

WORLD WIDE WEB: http://www.mcp.com

Home Page · What's New · Bookstore · Reference Desk · Software Library · Macmillan Overview · Talk to Us

Add to Your Sams Library Today with the Best Books for Programming, Operating Systems, and New Technologies

The easiest way to order is to pick up the phone and call

1-800-428-5331

between 9:00 a.m. and 5:00 p.m. EST.
For faster service, please have your credit card available.

ISBN	Quantity	Description of Item	Unit Cost	Total Cost
0-672-30757-X		Developing Personal Oracle7 Applications	$45.00	
0-672-30855-X		Teach Yourself SQL in 14 Days	$29.99	
0-672-30474-0		Windows 95 Unleashed (Book/CD-ROM)	$35.00	
0-672-30602-6		Programming Windows 95 Unleashed (Book/CD-ROM)	$49.99	
0-672-30717-0		Tricks of the DOOM Programming Gurus (Book/CD-ROM)	$39.99	
0-672-30714-6		Internet Unleashed, 2E (Book/3 CD-ROMs)	$35.00	
0-672-30737-5		World Wide Web Unleashed (Book/CD-ROM)	$39.99	
0-672-30669-7		Plug-n-Play Internet (Book/Disk)	$35.00	
0-672-30537-2		TWG UNIX Communications and the Internet	$35.00	
0-672-30676-X		Teach Yourself PowerBuilder in 14 Days	$25.00	
0-672-30695-6		Developing PowerBuilder Applications, 3E (Book/CD-ROM)	$45.00	
0-672-30685-9		Windows NT Unleashed, 2E	$39.99	
0-672-30561-5		C Progamming: Just the FAQs	$25.00	
0-672-30705-7		Linux Unleashed (Book/CD-ROM)	$49.99	
❏ 3 ½" Disk		Shipping and Handling: See information below.		
❏ 5 ¼" Disk		TOTAL		

Shipping and Handling: $4.00 for the first book, and $1.75 for each additional book. Floppy disk: add $1.75 for shipping and handling. If you need to have it NOW, we can ship product to you in 24 hours for an additional charge of approximately $18.00, and you will receive your item overnight or in two days. Overseas shipping and handling adds $2.00 per book and $8.00 for up to three disks. Prices subject to change. Call for availability and pricing information on latest editions.

201 W. 103rd Street, Indianapolis, Indiana 46290

1-800-428-5331 — Orders   1-800-835-3202 — FAX   1-800-858-7674 — Customer Service

Book ISBN 0-672-30873-8